South Asian
Bond Markets

South Asian Bond Markets

Developing Long-Term Finance for Growth

Kiatchai Sophastienphong

Yibin Mu

Carlotta Saporito

THE WORLD BANK

Washington, D.C.

ISBN-13: 978-0-8213-7601-0
eISBN: 978-0-8213-7602-7
DOI: 10.1596/978-0-8213-7601-0

Library of Congress Cataloging-in-Publication Data

Sophastienphong, Kiatchai.
   South Asian bond markets : developing long-term finance for growth / Kiatchai Sophastienphong, Yibin Mu, and Carlotta Saporito.
      p. cm.
   Includes bibliographical references and index.
   ISBN 978-0-8213-7601-0 — ISBN 978-0-8213-7602-7 (electronic)
   1. Bond market—South Asia. 2. Finance—South Asia. I. Mu, Yibin, 1968–
II. Saporito, Carlotta, 1981– III. World Bank. IV. Title.
   HG5720.8.A3S67 2008
   332.63'230954—dc22

                                                              2008031703

Cover design by Drew Fasick

Contents

Boxes

Figures

Tables

Foreword

There has been much interest in South Asia in developing domestic debt securities markets. In recent years countries in the region have sought to develop both government and corporate bond markets. However, these remain at an early stage of development relative to both the domestic banking sectors and to bond markets in other emerging market economies at a similar level of economic development.

The Poverty Reduction, Economic Management, Finance and Private Sector Development Unit of the World Bank's South Asia Region undertook a comprehensive study of the bond markets in five South Asian countries—Bangladesh, India, Nepal, Pakistan, and Sri Lanka—to support the region's efforts to promote financial sector development. The study, carried out in collaboration with local partners and the Bank's Financial and Private Sector Development Network, was aimed at identifying key impediments to the development of bond markets and proposing ways to overcome them. It was also intended to bring the Bank's technical expertise and global experience to a debate under way among the region's policy makers on strategies for financial sector development and regional financial integration.

The study was timely. As South Asian economies continue their rapid growth, they face an increasing need for diverse and sophisticated financial services and risk management products, including financing for infrastructure. And as they become increasingly integrated with global financial markets, deeper domestic bond markets can help reduce volatility associated with capital flows.

Moreover, the region's banking systems, though they dominate local financial markets, remain fragile, posing a risk of growing financial sector vulnerability. At the same time they remain unable to fully meet the needs of commerce and industry. A well-developed domestic bond market, as part of a diversified financial system, reduces risks in the financial sector while allowing companies to access long-term financing.

The study has added to the Bank's knowledge base on the financial sector in the region and will contribute to regional and country assistance strategies in ways that will have a visible impact in reducing rural and urban poverty. It will also help deepen the Bank's involvement in regional forums focusing on regional financial integration, helping to shape the debate and strategic vision on the policy and institutional development agenda.

Ernesto May
Director
Poverty Reduction, Economic Management, Finance
and Private Sector Development
South Asia Region

About the Authors

Kiatchai Sophastienphong is Senior Financial Sector Specialist, Poverty Reduction, Economic Management, Finance and Private Sector Development at the World Bank South Asia Region. His recent activities include leading the Financial Sector Assessment Program (FSAP) update mission to Sri Lanka. Mr. Sophastienphong has also helped to design and implement restructuring and bank privatization programs in Bangladesh, Nepal, and Pakistan, and has led the dialogue on financial sector issues in several client countries at both the policy and technical level. He has designed the overall financial sector strategies for these countries in addition to developing a program to implement these strategies. Prior to joining the Bank, he held senior executive positions at the Bank of Thailand (the central bank) and two private commercial banks in Thailand. He also worked at the Asian Development Bank as the Senior Financial Economist, in the Regional and Sustainable Development Department. Among his publications, he recently co-authored the book *Getting Finance in South Asia 2009: Indicators and Analysis of the Commercial Banking System* (World Bank publication). His research interests include bank restructuring and privatization, corporate debt restructuring, and bond market developments. He received his Bachelor of Arts (BA) and Master of Arts (MA) in Economics from the University of Cambridge, United Kingdom.

Dr. Yibin Mu is a Senior Financial Economist/Senior Capital Markets Specialist at the World Bank /International Finance Corporation joint Global Capital Markets Development Department. Over the past eight years, he has provided policy and technical advice on the financial sector development issues to about 30 World Bank client countries around the world. Prior to joining the World Bank, he worked at the Hong Kong Monetary Authority and China's Central Bank for another eight years, where he was mainly responsible for supervising foreign financial institutions in China and Chinese financial institutions overseas. His research interests include capital markets development, cash/debt management, access to finance, and prudential supervision and regulation. Dr. Mu has an MPA degree from Harvard University, as well as a Ph.D degree in Finance and an MA degree in Economics. He is also a CFA charter holder.

Carlotta Saporito is a Junior Professional Associate at the World Bank/ International Finance Corporation. Over the past two years, she has worked with the Financial Sector Operations & Policy Department and with the Foreign Investment Advisory Service. She recently participated in the Financial Sector Assessment Program (FSAP) update mission to Sri Lanka, and she led a survey of the credit market and lending practices in Ghana. She obtained her MA in International Relations from Johns Hopkins University/Paul H. Nitze School of Advanced International Studies (SAIS) and her BA in International Relations and Arabic from the University of St. Andrews in the UK. Her research interests include bond market development and securitization.

Acknowledgments

The authors wish to acknowledge the invaluable contributions of many individuals. Members of the World Bank's field-based teams facilitated research and operational visits in the five countries studied: A. K. M. Abdullah and Sadruddin Muhammad Salman in Dhaka; Varsha Marathe in Delhi; Sabin Raj Shrestha in Kathmandu; Shamsuddin Ahmad and Isfandyar Zaman Khan in Islamabad; and Sriyani Hulugalle and Lohita Karunasekera in Colombo. In addition, valuable comments were received from Joong Kyung Choi, Simon Bell, Alison Harwood, Priya Basu, JaeHoon Yoo, and Kyoo-Won Oh. Last but not least, Marinela Dado provided substantive, well-organized, and extensive drafting contributions to the executive summary and chapter 1.

The draft output of the study was presented at the South Asian Domestic Debt Markets Study Workshop, December 3–5, 2007 in Seoul and benefited from the discussions in the workshop. The authors offer special thanks to Ismail Dalla and K. R. Ramamoorthy, Consultants, and to the representatives of supervisory authorities who participated in the workshop in each country. In Bangladesh, Salahuddin Ahmed Khan, Chief Executive Officer, Dhaka Stock Exchange; Mohammad Abdul Hannan Zoarder, Executive Director, Securities and Exchange Commission; and Syed Monjurul Islam, Joint Secretary, Resource and Debt Management Wing, Ministry of Finance. In India, Madhu Sudan Sahoo, Director, Capital Markets, Ministry of Finance; Golaka C. Nath, Vice President, Economic Research and Surveillance, Clearing Corporation of India Limited; Radhakrishnan Nair, Executive Director, Securities and Exchange Board of India. In Nepal, Chiranjivi Nepal, Chairman, Securities Board of Nepal; Sita Ram Regmi, Under Secretary, Ministry of Finance; and Rewat Bahadur Karki, General Manager, Nepal Stock Exchange. In Pakistan, Rashid Piracha, Director (Securities Market), Securities and Exchange Commission of Pakistan. And in Sri Lanka, Chandra Premaratne, Superintendent and Registrar of Public Debt; Vajira Peter Weerakkody Wijegunawaardene, Director (Capital Market Development), Securities and Exchange Commission of Sri Lanka; and Sembukutti Arachchige Hyacinth Lalith Rukman de Silva, Director General, Department of Treasury Operations, Ministry of Finance and Planning.

The authors also wish to express their gratitude to the Korean Securities Research Institute for cohosting the previously mentioned workshop. The authors especially thank Hyoung-Tae Kim and Seiwoon Hwang, who made the workshop successful. The presentations by experts from the Korean Securities Research Institute, the Korea Securities Depository, and the Korea Stock Exchange were excellent. The arrangements were outstanding, and the management of the program made for a highly productive visit by high-ranking government officials from South Asian countries. Participants in the workshop gained tremendous knowledge and were impressed with the hospitality and efficiency of the Korean authorities and organizers. In addition, the authors would like to thank Daewoo Securities and the Korea Securities Depository for their warm hospitality.

The authors are also indebted to the peer reviewers for different parts of the study: Anita George (International Monetary Fund), Anjali Kumar, Latifah Merican, and Ijaz Nabi Vinaya Swaroop (overview); A. K. M. Abdullah and Michel Noel (Bangladesh chapter); Priya Basu, Juan Costain and Varsha Marathe (India chapter); Sabin Raj Shrestha and JaeHoon Yoo (Nepal chapter); Juan Costain, Isfandyar Zaman Khan (Pakistan chapter); Sriyani Hulugalle, Lohita Karunasekera, and Michel Noel (Sri Lanka chapter); Eriko Togo (public debt management discussions); Pipat Luengnaruemitchai (money market discussions); and Nagavalli Annamalai and Richard Symonds (legal and regulatory framework discussions). Last but not least, yet importantly, we express our thanks to Anoma Kulathunga (consultant), Vivi Zhang (consultant) and Maria Marjorie Espiritu (program assistant), who provided invaluable research and technical support.

Acronyms and Abbreviations

ADB	Asian Development Bank
BB	Bangladesh Bank
BFS	Board for Financial Supervision
BIS	Bank for International Settlements
BNM	Bank Negara Malaysia
BSE	Bombay Stock Exchange
CB	Commercial Bank
CBLO	Collateralised Borrowing and Lending Obligation
CBSL	Central Bank of Sri Lanka
CCIL	Clearing Corporation of India Ltd
CDNS	Central Directorate of National Savings
CFS	Continuous Financing System
CIBIL	Credit Information Bureau (India) Ltd
CIT	Citizen Investment Trust
CLSE	Colombo Stock Exchange
CRO	Company Registrar's Office
CRIB	Credit Information Bureau
CRAB	Credit Rating Agency of Bangladesh
CRISIL	Credit Rating Information Services of India Ltd
CRISL	Credit Rating Information and Services Limited
CRR	Cash reserve requirement
CSE	Colombo Stock Exchange
DCA	Department of Company Affairs
DEA	Department of Economic Affairs
DEX	Debt Securities Trading System
DFIs	Development Finance Institutions
DPCO	Debt Policy Coordination Office
DSE	Dhaka Stock Exchange
DVP	Delivery-versus-Payments

EAD	Economic Affairs Division
EIU	Economist Intelligence Unit
EPF	Employees' Provident Fund
FCBs	Foreign commercial banks
FI	Financial Institution
FII	Foreign Institutional Investors
FIMMDA	Fixed Income Money Market Dealers Association of India
FY	Fiscal year
G-8	Group of Eight
GDP	Gross Domestic Product
GII	Government Investment Issue
GoB	Government of Bangladesh
GoI	Government of India
ICASL	Institute of Chartered Accountants of Sri Lanka
ICB	Investment Corporation of Bangladesh
IFC	International Finance Corporation
IFS	International Financial Statistics
IMF	International Monetary Fund
IPO	Initial Public Offerings
ISCAP	Institutional Securities Custodian Program
KIBOR	Karachi interbank offered rate
KSE	Karachi Stock Exchange
LCB	Licensed Commercial Bank
MBS	Mortgage backed securities
MGS	Malaysian Government Securities
MFIs	Microfinance institutions
MITBs	Malaysian Islamic Treasury Bills
MLA	Monetary Law Act
MoC	Ministry of Commerce
MOF	Ministry of Finance
NBFI	Non-bank financial institution
NCBs	Nationalized commercial banks
NDS	Negotiated Dealing System
NDS-OM	Negotiated dealing system–order matching
NEPSE	Nepal Stock Exchange
NGO	Nongovernmental organization
NIBs	National Investment Bonds
Nrs	Nepalese rupees
NRB	Nepal Rastra Bank
NSC	National Savings Certificate

NSE	National Stock Exchange
NSS	National Savings Scheme
OCCI	Office of the Chief Controller of Insurance
OECD	Organization for Economic Co-operation and Development
OIS	Overnight Interest Swap
OTC	Over the Counter
PACRA	Pakistan Credit Rating Agency
PCBs	Private Commercial Banks
PD	Primary Dealers
PDD	Public Debt Department
PDAI	Primary Dealers Association of India
PDMD	Public Debt Management Department
PDS	Primary Dealer System
PFRDA	Pension Fund Regulatory and Development Authority
PIB	Pakistan Investment Bond
PPF	Private Provident Funds
PRs	Pakistan rupees
PSU	Public Sector Undertaking
RBI	Reserve Bank of India
Repo	Repurchase Agreement
Rs	Indian rupees
SBP	State Bank of Pakistan
SBs	Specialized banks
SEBI	Securities and Exchange Board of India
SEBON	Securities Board of Nepal
SEC	Securities and Exchange Commission
SECP	Securities and Exchange Commission of Pakistan
SLF	Standing Liquidity Facility
SLR	Statutory Liquidity Reserves
SLRs	Sri Lanka rupees
SRO	Self-regulatory Organization
SSSS	Scripless Securities Settlement System
T-Bills	Treasury Bills
T-Bonds	Treasury Bonds
TFC	Term Finance Certificate
Tk	Bangladesh taka
VPS	Voluntary Pension System
VAR	Value at risk
WDI	World Development Indicators

Notes on Data

Data on financial markets in this study come from different sources and may reflect differences in definitions, coverage, time periods, and reliability of reporting. Measures of market size and other indicators may not be comparable because data compilation may be different in each source. For the methodology used in data compilation, see the original source.

Debt securities markets are measured on the basis of debt securities outstanding as of a particular date, usually the last day of the fiscal year. The terms *bond market, debt securities market,* and *fixed-income market* are used largely interchangeably.

Much of the data is reported on a fiscal year basis. The fiscal year for each of the countries studied is as follows:

Bangladesh   July 1–June 30
India   April 1–March 31
Nepal   July 16–July 15
Pakistan   July 1–June 30
Sri Lanka   January 1–December 31

Official exchange rates to the U.S. dollar for the currencies of the five countries are as follows (as of May 31, 2007):

Bangladesh taka (Tk)   68.7
Indian rupees (Rs)   40.6
Nepalese rupees (Nrs)   67.9
Pakistan rupees (PRs)   60.9
Sri Lanka rupees (SL Rs)   107.7

Executive Summary

Developing deep, well-functioning domestic bond markets can help countries generate the long-term financing needed for sustainable economic growth. In South Asian bond markets still fall short of their potential—in most countries, far short. India has the region's most developed market. Its experience, along with those of East Asian economies, suggests that much potential remains for developing South Asian bond markets and expanding their contribution to growth and development.

Why Do Bond Markets Matter?

Bond markets play an important part in diversified financial systems by linking borrowers that have financing needs with investors that are willing to place funds in interest-bearing securities. They help avoid excessive dependence on banks and diversify corporate risks beyond the banking system.

Deep, well-functioning domestic bond markets are extremely important for a country's economic development, as they facilitate long-term financing for areas such as infrastructure, housing, and private sector development. They also provide long-term investment instruments for institutional investors, such as pension funds and insurance companies. Finally, bond markets help diversify a country's financial sector and reduce foreign currency risk which arises when local investments are financed with foreign currency denominated loans.

But developing deep, diversified bond markets is not easy. It can require overcoming a range of constraints. For East Asian bond markets the biggest constraint to development is the limited liquidity in the secondary market, which undermines market efficiency. Many policy makers and practitioners, in East Asia and elsewhere, have viewed regional integration as a way around this constraint, and the region has undertaken a number of integration initiatives. Integrating bond markets can provide investors with a broader range of investment instruments and firms with a broader investor base. It can also enhance market liquidity, increase competition among markets and intermediaries, lower transaction costs, and strengthen incentives for innovation.

How Do South Asian Bond Markets Compare?

The development of domestic debt securities markets varies substantially among the five South Asian countries studied. India's is the most advanced, and Nepal's the least. But even in India the market is still small relative to GDP, suggesting that long-term debt financing remains at an early stage in the region. Most South Asian bond markets remain negligible in size compared both with the size of the economy and with markets in East Asia.

Equity markets and banks still dominate the region's financial systems. The equity market accounts for 45 percent of South Asian financial assets. The banking sector follows with 35 percent, and the bond market with 20 percent. South Asian financial markets amounted to about $2 trillion in 2006, about 14 percent of the size of East Asia's. India accounted for 89 percent of the total.

But while India dominates all three markets in South Asia, it is Sri Lanka that has the region's largest outstanding bond market size relative to the size of the economy. In Sri Lanka outstanding debt securities amount to almost 51 percent of GDP. Following are the markets in India (36 percent of GDP), Pakistan (26 percent), Nepal (15 percent), and Bangladesh (12 percent). Among eight major East Asian economies, the Republic of Korea has the largest bond market size relative to the size of the economy, at 114 percent of GDP. In the five South Asian countries as a group, outstanding bonds amount to only 34 percent of GDP; in the eight East Asian economies, to 57 percent.

In all five South Asian countries government debt securities dominate the market for fixed-income securities—accounting for 94 percent in India, for example. Corporate bond markets remain negligible in size by any standard. Banks still serve as the main source of funds for the corporate sector. India's corporate bond market, at a mere 2.3 percent of GDP, lags far behind the government debt securities market. In the East Asian economies outstanding corporate bonds amount to about 9 percent of GDP.

Where Are the Constraints?

South Asia's bond markets, though still relatively small, can nevertheless be expected to grow at a very fast pace. The strong GDP growth in the region is likely to continue—leading to a growing number of firms seeking financing and an immense pool of savings needing new investment opportunities. Retail investors will add fixed-income securities to their portfolios to achieve better balance and diversification. Households will seek to finance the purchase of homes with long-term, fixed-interest mortgages—and banks will seek to supply those mortgages by securitizing them and passing them on to investors through the bond markets. And foreign investors will participate more actively in local currency bond markets as these markets become larger, more liquid, and more transparent.

But realizing the full potential of the region's bond markets, and ensuring sound, well-functioning markets, will require putting into place essential elements—or addressing remaining constraints—in supply, demand, market infrastructure, and the legal and regulatory framework.

Supply Side

How a government issues debt is critical to the development of bond markets. Through regular issuance of standard, high-quality debt securities of a few concentrated maturities, governments build their credibility as a debt issuer and establish liquid benchmark securities and yield curves that provide essential guidance on the pricing of other debt securities. In South Asia only India meets this standard—and it has a government debt securities market that is liquid, deep, and comparable to developed markets. The Indian market also has a sovereign yield curve that extends across the full spectrum of maturities to 30 years.

A big factor standing in the way of bond market development is the absence of price mechanisms in the allocation of funds. Several South Asian governments have been reluctant to assume the role of a price taker. Pakistan's, for example, sets the cutoff yield in auctions for medium- and long-term bonds. Sri Lanka's places a large share of its medium- and long-term debt privately with state-owned institutions. In addition, some governments issue nonmarketable debt instruments, often with more attractive terms than marketable bonds. Such practices impede the development of government benchmark securities, which depends on active trading.

Excessive fragmentation of public debt issues, as in Bangladesh and Sri Lanka, also impedes active trading. Consolidating issues in fewer, larger ones can help boost trading activity, making it easier to construct a yield curve that more accurately reflects the underlying factors determining interest rates.

A sound debt management strategy is also key in building a government's credibility as an issuer. This is in part because it establishes predictability. For that, governments need a coherent cash management strategy, to guide deliberate decisions on the volume and maturity of each issuance of government debt securities. Among the five South Asian countries, all but India need to initiate reforms that lead to proper governance and internal processes in debt management and to adequate resources and staff capacity for developing a medium-term debt management strategy.

In the corporate bond market important constraints on supply side include the transaction costs of public issuance. Corporate bond markets in South Asia remain small in part because corporate borrowers find it easier and more convenient to obtain credit from banks than to comply with the rigorous governance standards and issuance guidelines required to tap the bond market. The direct cost of issuing bonds also matters. Because public issuance involves considerably higher costs, companies often resort to private placement instead.

Demand Side

A large and diversified investor base helps ensure strong and stable demand for bonds under a wide range of market conditions. The investor base ideally should include domestic and foreign investors and a broad range of institutions, as well as individual investors. Institutional investors such as insurance companies and pension and provident funds, all with long-term liabilities, can provide long-term funding to the economy.

South Asia's institutional investor base remains too small to support the region's economic potential. Only two countries have made notable progress in developing collective investment schemes such as mutual funds. India has been the most successful in developing an institutional investor base. But while the volume of assets under the management of institutional investors is growing, these holdings remain too restricted and homogeneous, in part because of regulatory and investment restrictions.

The region's retail investor base also remains small. One reason is that most market intermediaries for government bonds are commercial banks, and they naturally have more incentive to market their own products. Another is general lack of awareness of the range of investment opportunities for individual investors. A factor in Bangladesh and Pakistan is the presence of national savings instruments offering above-market interest rates, which divert demand from market-based debt instruments.

Foreign investors play a limited role in South Asian bond markets. India and Sri Lanka have allowed foreign investors, but they also impose regulatory or investment guidelines that limit their participation—and Sri Lanka has not yet opened its corporate bond market to foreign investors. India's ceiling on investment by foreign institutional investors remains low relative to the size of the domestic debt securities market and the level of foreign exchange reserves. Raising it would speed development of the market.

Market Infrastructure

India has a market infrastructure for government debt securities comparable to that in developed countries, with a primary dealer system, electronic trading platforms, state-of-the-art clearing and settlement systems, credit rating agencies, and so on. Built over time, this infrastructure has improved efficiency and lowered costs in the market for public bonds. Not surprisingly, India also has the most liquid secondary market in government debt securities in South Asia.

The other four countries lag behind in developing a sound, efficient market infrastructure. All lack an active and liquid secondary market. Developing one is difficult, requiring a sufficient number of market intermediaries and institutional investors, appropriate types of instruments and transactions, and well-established trading mechanisms.

Besides India, only Sri Lanka has a modern clearing and settlement system based on delivery versus payment—critical for the smooth flow of transactions in the primary and secondary markets and for investor confidence. Pakistan has yet to introduce a fully electronic system of trading, settlement, and clearing, though it plans to implement a real-time gross settlement system soon. Nepal's system falls far short of what is needed to support a well-functioning bond market.

Most South Asian countries have credit rating agencies, essential for providing investors with tools to make informed investment decisions and achieve price discovery. Bangladesh's two credit rating agencies are still at an early stage of development, however. Nepal has no credit rating agency. Nor is one likely to be established as long as sound disclosure requirements, corporate governance guidelines, and accounting and auditing standards are lacking.

Market efficiency also depends on investors' having access to high-quality information about the government's debt structure, funding needs, and debt management strategy. India has a well-developed system for disseminating information, including an issuance calendar for dated government securities. Sri Lanka too publishes a range of data that market participants need, including the government borrowing calendar. Other South Asian governments also publish issuance calendars. But they do not always follow them or specify the volume of issues sufficiently in advance, making it difficult for investors to plan their investments.

Risk transfer mechanisms remain at an early stage of development in South Asia, even in India. That country has a growing securitization market, but transactions are still carried out through private placement. Moreover, despite the growth, the investor base remains limited because of policies restricting the use of below-investment-grade debt instruments as collateral. India's market for debt derivatives is also at an early stage, depriving investors of tools to hedge their risks that could lead to further deepening of the bond market.

Legal and Regulatory Framework

How a bond market functions and develops depends in great part on its legal and regulatory framework. That framework should have three complementary objectives: maintaining a fair, efficient, and transparent market; reducing systemic risk; and protecting investors.

To achieve these objectives, regulators need clear authority, autonomy, and adequate resources. In India, where a complex market means a complex regulatory structure, a high-level committee provides coordination among regulators. Concerns remain, however, about adequate delineation of their regulatory and supervisory roles. In Pakistan the Securities and Exchange Commission has clear responsibilities, an array of powers, and apparent autonomy—though its resources appear to be inadequate. Nepal's apex regulator for the capital market, the Securities Board of Nepal, also appears to lack adequate resources, and its independence remains open to question.

Most South Asian countries have ample scope for improving corporate governance arrangements, for market regulators as well as for market participants. While most have introduced corporate governance standards for listed companies, the standards remain voluntary and few companies have adopted them. In addition, Nepal lacks accounting and auditing standards and an efficient judiciary system, further undermining confidence in the capital market.

Tax policies also play an important part in the development of financial markets. When poorly designed, they can discourage new financial instruments or deter potential investors. In Pakistan different tax treatment favors some debt instruments—including national savings instruments—over others. India and Nepal too have different tax treatment for different instruments. Removing such tax distortions can help create a level playing field for debt instruments.

Nepal also has different tax rates on interest income for individuals and institutional investors. That rules out cross-trading between these two groups of investors, creating another constraint on secondary market activity.

Moving Forward

Action plans and reform programs for each country will need to reflect the development of its market. In Bangladesh and Nepal, with the least advanced bond markets, attention needs to focus on strengthening the primary market while laying the foundation for a solid secondary market structure. In Pakistan and Sri Lanka, with mixed progress, priorities center on improving market efficiency—though for Sri Lanka the first priority is to stabilize the macroeconomic situation by reducing inflation and the fiscal deficit to sustainable levels. For India, despite its more advanced market, the agenda still encompasses reforms to address remaining constraints in supply, demand, the market infrastructure, and the legal and regulatory framework.

1

Regional Overview

Bond markets play an essential part in economies. As part of a diversified financial system, a well-developed domestic bond market can help provide the long-term financing needed for sustainable growth. It can also produce broad-ranging benefits throughout the economy.

In South Asia the development of domestic debt securities markets lags. The markets remain small compared both with the size of the region's economies and with markets in East Asia. Even in India the market is still small relative to GDP, suggesting that long-term debt financing remains at an early stage in the region. Equity markets and banks still dominate South Asian financial systems.

Measures are needed to enhance both the depth and the breadth of South Asian bond markets, to bring them into line with those in East Asia and, in the long run, with those in OECD countries. This study assesses domestic debt securities markets in South Asia, identifies constraints to their development, and recommends measures for developing deeper, broader, and more efficient markets that can provide a competitive source of finance across a wide range of maturities for different debt issuers. The study covers five countries—Bangladesh, India, Nepal, Pakistan, and Sri Lanka (all references to South Asia relate only to these five countries).

Within the region the development of domestic debt securities markets varies widely. India's is the most developed. Its experience, along with those of East Asian economies, suggests that much potential remains for developing South Asian bond markets and expanding their contribution to growth and development. Greater regional integration of South Asian bond markets could add to the benefits.

The Importance of Bond Markets

Bond markets gained prominence after the 1997 financial crisis in East Asia. The crisis prompted a rethinking of the role of financial markets in economic development (see Eichengreen and Luengnaruemitchai 2004). Several weaknesses of banking systems were exposed, including maturity and currency mismatches and moral hazard problems. When confidence was shaken during the crisis, banks called in their loans, subjecting their borrowers to a painful credit crunch. Governments incurred huge fiscal costs in restructuring banks.

The banking crisis in East Asia created an awareness of the need to supplement bank finance with better diversified debt securities markets and, specifically, medium- to long-term bond markets. Bank and bond finance each have different advantages. Bonds do better at sharing risks, by better matching the liabilities of investors with the assets of borrowers.

Yet bond finance is not inherently superior to bank finance. Countries have benefited and still benefit from well-diversified financial systems with roles for both well-regulated banks and well-functioning bond and equity markets. Diversification helps an economy achieve a better position on the frontier of feasible tradeoffs between risks and returns. It also promotes financial stability and efficient resource allocation in support of medium-term economic growth.

Realizing these benefits, however, requires developing debt securities markets in ways that ensure their soundness. That lesson is apparent in the subprime mortgage crisis that emerged in 2007 in the United States. The paradox of the crisis is its apparent roots in both the successes of financial markets (securitization, globalization, nonbank mortgage lending) and their failures. Financial innovations have tended to obscure rather than expose underlying risks. The problem can lead to a crisis of confidence in the financial system. That has emerged, for example, in banks' increasing unwillingness to lend to one another, as reflected in the rising interbank rates in Europe and the United States.

Reasonable regulation of debt securities markets allows them to function in an efficient and constructive way. What led to the crisis were debt instruments made and sold in the unregulated sector. At every step in the process—from loan origination to the use of exotic, unsuitable mortgages to the sale of securities backed by those mortgages—largely unregulated, uninsured firms have created problems, while regulated, federally insured banks and savings institutions have not.

Economic and Financial Benefits

Bond markets play an important role in diversified financial systems by linking borrowers that have financing needs with investors that are willing to place funds in interest-bearing securities.[1] Equally important, robust, diverse, and inclusive financial systems help reduce poverty by promoting economic growth, broadening the scope for social and economic mobility, and directly improving the lives of poor people through access to financial services. Research by the World Bank and others has shown that deepening finance, including capital markets, has a strong causal effect on economic growth—and that deeper financial systems are associated with growth that is more propoor.[2]

Bond markets are critical to financial development in several ways. They generate market interest rates that reflect the opportunity cost of funds at a wide range of maturities, information essential for decisions by investors and borrowers. They help avoid excessive dependence on banks and diversify corporate risks beyond the banking system. They help guide macroeconomic policy making; because bond markets are sensitive and quick to react to macroeconomic policies and conditions, they send signals allowing early policy adjustments.

Domestic bond markets benefit participants at all levels of the economy. Governments, as bond issuers, have both fiscal and monetary reasons for encouraging the growth of well-functioning domestic bond markets. On the fiscal side, such markets enable governments to gain better control of their costs of borrowing. On the monetary side, a bond market with a well-defined yield curve and appropriate risk management instruments aids the smooth operation of monetary policy by providing effective mechanisms for transmission of policy.

For both national and local governments (states, municipalities, cities), deeper bond markets make it easier to undertake infrastructure projects, whose long maturities are better suited to bond financing than to bank lending. For the private sector, deeper bond markets mean lower funding costs and access to sophisticated instruments that can be tailored to a range of individual needs for structured finance. And for households and consumers, such markets provide access to a wider range of housing finance and savings and investment instruments.

Added Benefits through Regional Integration

The experience of East Asia in developing its bond markets may offer lessons for South Asia. East Asian financial markets are growing rapidly today, far outpacing growth in South Asian markets. Since the 1997 financial crisis East Asia has accumulated international reserves at unprecedented levels, more than $3.9 trillion by the end of 2007. The size of the reserves reflects the buildup of the region's own savings as well as the resumption of capital flows after the resolution of the crisis.

East Asia's bond markets have recorded sizable growth since the 1997 crisis, though the pace of growth has varied substantially among economies. For the eight East Asian economies covered here, outstanding bonds amounted to $2.7 trillion in 2006.[3] But much of the growth in the bond markets—and more than half the growth in 1997–2004 in all these economies except Hong Kong, China and the Republic of Korea—has come from bonds issued by governments, largely to restructure banking systems whose vulnerabilities came to a head during the crisis. Corporate bonds, though they have accounted for a reasonable share of the market growth in many of the region's economies, remain a small part of its total bond market.

The biggest constraint to the development of East Asian bond markets is the limited liquidity in the secondary market, which undermines market efficiency. Of course, bond markets have limited liquidity even in the most advanced economies.

Even so, bond markets in East Asia are on average much less liquid than those of advanced economies. And not surprisingly, liquidity is even lower in the region's corporate bond markets.

One vehicle for deepening and diversifying bond markets, in the eyes of many policy makers and practitioners in East Asia and worldwide, is regional cooperation. The integration of bond markets can provide investors with a broader range of investment instruments and firms with a broader investor base. It can also enhance market liquidity, increase competition among markets and intermediaries, lower transaction costs, and strengthen incentives for innovation. But achieving the benefits of regional integration still requires putting into place the basic elements of bond markets at the national level—supply, demand, market infrastructure, and a sound legal and regulatory framework.

East Asia has undertaken a number of integration initiatives. Among these are two Asian bond funds launched in 2002 and 2005 by the regional association of central bankers—for Australia; China; Hong Kong, China; Japan; Korea; Malaysia; New Zealand; the Philippines; Singapore; and Thailand. The bond funds, created by tapping the international reserves of these economies, are aimed at providing investors with a transparent and cost-effective mechanism for accessing local bond markets.

Such regional initiatives have also received attention from the Group of Eight (G-8), for which promoting the development of domestic debt securities markets in developing and emerging market economies has become a key policy focus. Recognizing the importance of domestic bond markets in financial stability and the savings and financing opportunities they offer for households and firms, the G-8 finance ministers gave the issue a high profile at their Potsdam meeting in May 2007. The meeting led to an action plan that calls for promoting regional initiatives such as the Asian Bond Market Initiative as well as for such measures as strengthening market infrastructure and broadening the investor base for fixed-income securities (G-8 2007).[4]

Profile of Regional Financial Markets

South Asian economies share common characteristics—including high GDP growth, high savings and investment rates, and persistent budget deficits. The structures of their financial markets reveal common patterns. Yet the development of their domestic debt securities markets varies substantially, with India's the most advanced and Nepal's the least.

Macroeconomic Conditions and Market Patterns

Domestic macroeconomic conditions are the building blocks of a stable and efficient financial system, including the domestic debt securities market. Beyond a credible and stable government, specific requirements include sound management of fiscal and monetary policies, aimed at achieving or sustaining a prudent

Table 1.1 GDP Growth, Selected South Asian and East Asian Economies, 2002–07

(percent)

Economy or region	2002	2003	2004	2005	2006	2007[a]
Bangladesh	4.4	5.3	6.3	6.0	6.7	6.5
India	3.8	8.5	7.5	9.0	9.2	8.0
Nepal	−0.4	3.0	3.5	2.3	2.3	2.8
Pakistan	3.1	4.7	7.5	8.6	6.6	6.8
Sri Lanka	4.0	6.0	5.4	6.0	7.2	6.1
South Asia	3.7	7.8	7.4	8.7	8.7	7.7
East Asia[b]	7.5	7.3	8.4	8.3	8.7	8.0

Source: ADB 2007.
a. Estimated.
b. Data are for China; Hong Kong, China; Indonesia; the Republic of Korea; Malaysia; the Philippines; Singapore; and Thailand.

fiscal stance, moderate inflation rates and inflationary expectations, and modest government debt; sound management of the exchange rate regime; and appropriate capital account policies.

South Asia recorded favorable macroeconomic performance in 2002–07, with growth averaging 7.3 percent a year. All countries except Nepal had annual growth of 6 percent or more in most years, rates fairly comparable to those in most East Asian economies (table 1.1). As a region, East Asia had annual growth averaging around 8 percent during the period.

Developments in domestic investment in South Asia also are encouraging. As a share of GDP, domestic investment ranges from a low of 20 percent in Pakistan to a high of 35 percent in India (table 1.2). All South Asian countries saw growth in domestic investment in 2002–06, much of it attributable to the stable global macroeconomic conditions. And all except Pakistan and Sri Lanka had national savings hovering around 30–33 percent of GDP in recent years.

The region is characterized by persistent budget deficits. These range from a low of 1.8 percent of GDP in Nepal to a high of 8.4 percent in Sri Lanka. India has reduced its budget deficit considerably, from 9.6 percent of GDP in 2002 to 6.4 percent in 2006, though there is still room for further improvement.

South Asian financial markets amounted to about $2 trillion at the end of 2006, about 14 percent of the size of East Asia's (table 1.3). India accounted for 89 percent of the total. The equity market accounts for the largest share of South Asian financial assets, 45 percent ($877 billion). The banking sector follows with 35 percent ($685 billion), and the bond market with 20 percent ($381 billion).

This pattern is relatively atypical for emerging market economies, where the banking sector tends to dominate the financial system. The unusual structure can be attributed to the situation in India: while the government substantially

Table 1.2 Selected Macroeconomic Indicators, Selected South Asian Countries, 2002–06

(percentage of GDP)

Indicator and country	2002	2003	2004	2005	2006
Gross domestic investment					
Bangladesh	23.1	23.4	24.0	24.5	25.0
India	25.2	28.0	31.5	33.8	35.0
Nepal	24.2	25.8	26.4	28.9	30.3
Pakistan	16.6	16.8	16.6	18.1	20.0
Sri Lanka	21.2	22.2	25.0	26.5	28.7
Gross national savings					
Bangladesh	29	30	31	30	33
India	27	29	31	33	—
Nepal	33	32	32	33	35
Pakistan	20	23	22	21	17
Sri Lanka	20	22	22	20	21
Fiscal balance of central government					
Bangladesh	−4.6	−3.4	−3.2	−3.4	−3.3
India	−9.6	−8.5	−7.5	−7.4	−6.4
Nepal	−3.9	−1.5	−1.0	−0.8	−1.8
Pakistan	−4.3	−3.7	−2.4	−3.3	−4.2
Sri Lanka	−8.9	−8.0	−8.2	−8.7	−8.4

Sources: For gross domestic investment and fiscal balance, ADB 2007; for gross national savings, World Bank, World Development Indicators database.

— = Not available.

deregulated the securities market starting in November 1992 and opened the market to foreign investment, the nationalized banking sector, though restructured, remains largely state owned.

Relative to GDP, South Asian financial markets also lag behind those in East Asia. Equity market capitalization is about 77 percent of regional GDP, banking assets about 61 percent, and outstanding bonds only 34 percent (see table 1.3). In East Asia the corresponding figures are 126 percent, 118 percent, and 57 percent.

Interestingly, while India dominates all three markets in South Asia, it is Sri Lanka that has the region's largest outstanding bond market size relative to the size of the economy. In Sri Lanka outstanding debt securities amount to almost 51 percent of GDP. Among East Asian economies Korea has the largest bond market size relative to the size of the economy, at 114 percent of GDP, followed by Malaysia (98 percent). But even these markets are much smaller relative to GDP than the largest among the OECD countries, those in Japan (194 percent) and the United States (173 percent).

Table 1.3 Financial Market Profile, Selected Economies, 2006

Economy	Domestic debt securities market US$ billions	As % of GDP	Equity market capitalization US$ billions	As % of GDP	Banking assets US$ billions	As % of GDP
South Asia						
Bangladesh	7.3	11.9	3.6	5.8	32.7	52.8
India	325.7	35.9	818.9	90.4	587.4	64.8
Nepal	1.3	15.1	1.3	16.3	4.3	53.8
Pakistan	33.4	26.3	45.4	35.3	50.7	39.4
Sri Lanka	13.7	50.8	7.8	29.8	10.3	38.2
Total	381.3	33.6	877.0	77.5	685.4	60.6
Selected East Asian economies						
China	1,183.6	44.4	2,426.3	90.9	3,509.9	131.6
Hong Kong, China	51.0	26.9	1,715.0	903.6	297.6	156.8
Indonesia	76.4	21.0	138.9	38.1	128.6	35.3
Korea, Rep. of	1,010.0	113.7	834.4	94.0	984.0	110.8
Malaysia	146.2	98.2	235.6	158.2	199.4	133.9
Philippines	44.9	38.4	67.9	58.0	51.5	44.0
Singapore	79.2	59.9	384.3	290.8	162.9	123.3
Thailand	109.7	53.2	140.2	68.0	228.7	110.9
Total	2,700.9	57.3	5,942.5	126.0	5,562.5	118.0
Selected OECD countries						
Australia	456.7	59.5	1,095.9	142.7	952.3	124.0
Canada	984.7	78.7	1,700.7	135.9	1,732.4	138.4
Germany	2,247.7	77.3	1,637.6	56.3	4,063.7	139.8
Japan	8,406.2	193.7	4,795.8	110.5	8,984.6	207.0
New Zealand	20.4	19.7	44.8	43.2	166.5	160.3
United Kingdom	1,237.6	52.8	3,794.3	161.8	4,423.2	188.6
United States	22,827.6	172.9	19,286.2	146.1	12,260.4	92.9

Sources: For debt securities, BIS 2007 (for Bangladesh, Nepal, and Sri Lanka, central banks); for equity, World Federation of Exchanges, http://www.world-exchanges.org/WFE/home.asp?menu=421&document=4444 (for Bangladesh, India, Nepal, Pakistan, and China, the World Bank's World Development Indicators database); for banking assets, International Monetary Fund, International Financial Statistics database (for Sri Lanka, Economist Intelligence Unit estimate).

Note: Data for domestic debt securities markets and equity market capitalization may differ from those reported elsewhere in this chapter and in country chapters because of differences in conversion rates and GDP measures used. Banking assets are claims of deposit money banks on the central government, state and local governments, nonfinancial public enterprises, and private sector nonbank financial institutions. They do not include assets of development banks, savings banks, and other specialized banks. Nor do they include fixed assets, receivables, interbank transactions, and other assets. Data on banking assets reported in this table may therefore differ from those reported elsewhere in this chapter and in country chapters.

Financial Sector Reforms

All five South Asian countries have pursued reforms aimed at strengthening their financial sector in recent years. Bangladesh has pursued legal, policy, and institutional reforms to improve financial intermediation and promote efficient allocation of resources since the 1990s. India has transformed its financial sector from one dominated by state-owned banks into a vibrant, broad-based system. Nepal's central bank was recently granted stronger supervisory and regulatory powers and is implementing new banking regulations aimed at bringing the country's banking sector up to international standards.

Pakistan introduced financial sector reforms that led to substantial structural changes in the banking industry and big improvements in banks' financial performance. The Central Bank of Sri Lanka has taken a series of actions to strengthen the country's financial system and improve its efficiency, and national policy makers have proposed amendments to banking laws aimed at strengthening financial stability.

Rankings of the five countries' financial markets based on the World Bank's Getting Finance indicators put India's at the top. The rankings are based on scores in four core areas of financial performance and soundness: access to finance, performance and efficiency, stability, and corporate governance (see World Bank 2006c).

Pakistan and Sri Lanka follow in the rankings. Both countries have made some progress in recent years, though fundamental issues remain to be tackled. Bangladesh ranks next, on the basis of both its Getting Finance score and the country's recent economic growth and consistent implementation of its financial reform strategy. Nepal's financial markets rank as the least advanced in South Asia.

Recent Developments in Domestic Debt Securities Markets

India accounted for 86 percent of South Asia's $380 billion in outstanding fixed-income securities at the end of 2006 (table 1.4). Following far behind were Pakistan, Sri Lanka, Bangladesh, and finally Nepal. As noted, however, Sri Lanka appears to have the largest outstanding bond market size relative to the GDP (based on the value of existing bonds as a percentage of GDP), followed by India and Pakistan (table 1.5). Surprisingly, Bangladesh, though much larger than Nepal in population, land area, and other measures, has the region's smallest outstanding market size relative to the GDP (based on existing bonds as a percentage of GDP).

In all five countries government debt dominates the market for fixed-income securities—accounting for 94 percent in India, for example. Government bonds are the cornerstone of most debt markets, in developed and developing countries alike. They provide financing for the government's operations or for public policy purposes, and they also serve as instruments for domestic savings. In the East Asian economies government debt amounted to about 56 percent of outstanding bonds in 2006, and in a group of OECD countries to about 44 percent.[5]

Deficit financing has provided some motivation for government borrowing in South Asia. Yet India, where the fiscal deficit has been declining steadily, has seen

Table 1.4   Domestic Debt Securities Markets, Selected South Asian Countries, 2002–06

(US$ millions except where otherwise specified)

Country	2002	2003	2004	2005	2006	Share of total, 2006 (%)
India	155,800	203,100	249,500	279,100	325,680	85.6
Pakistan	28,403	30,905	31,495	33,964	33,362	8.5
Sri Lanka	9,822	10,574	10,954	12,428	13,712	3.6
Bangladesh	8,773	7,057	7,960	7,870	7,345	1.9
Nepal	940	1,143	1,200	1,183	1,265	0.3
Total	203,738	252,779	301,109	334,545	381,364	100.0

Sources: For India and Pakistan, BIS 2007; for Bangladesh, Nepal, and Sri Lanka, central banks.

Table 1.5   Domestic Debt Securities Markets as a Percentage of GDP, Selected South Asian Countries, 2002–06

Country	2002	2003	2004	2005	2006
India	30.7	33.7	35.9	34.6	35.9
Pakistan	37.8	36.7	33.0	30.9	26.3
Sri Lanka	59.4	58.0	54.6	52.8	50.8
Bangladesh	18.5	13.6	14.0	13.1	11.9
Nepal	17.1	19.5	17.8	16.0	15.1

Sources: For GDP, World Bank, World Development Indicators database; for debt securities, BIS 2007, central banks, and securities and exchange commissions.

the strongest growth in the domestic debt securities market. Initially the government financed its large budget deficits primarily through borrowings at submarket rates—using government debt securities to "capture" banking resources by prescribing high statutory liquidity ratios for commercial banks. But government borrowings have become increasingly market based over time, consistent with the government's policies aimed at developing a liquid and efficient government debt securities market.

Pakistan has achieved rapid economic growth and has steadily implemented reforms since late 1999. Yet its bond market remains small relative to those of comparable emerging market economies in Asia. In 2006 the domestic debt securities market stood at a mere 26 percent of GDP. Pakistan too met its public borrowing needs initially through captive funding. Its bond market consists almost entirely of government debt securities, amounting to 97 percent of the total outstanding in 2006. Pakistan remains relatively underleveraged as an economy compared with regional counterparts at similar income levels.

Government debt also makes up the lion's share of Sri Lanka's fixed-income securities market, accounting for more than 99 percent of outstanding bonds in 2006. In Nepal, where the bond market remains in its infancy, domestic bonds amounted to 15 percent of GDP and government debt securities to more than 98 percent of the total outstanding. While Bangladesh has outstanding bonds amounting to only 12 percent of GDP, the government has taken steps toward improving the functioning of the interbank and treasury bill markets, and its recent financial reforms are encouraging.

Corporate bond markets in all five South Asian countries remain negligible in size by any standard. Banks still serve as the main source of funds for the corporate sector. India's corporate bond market, at a mere 2.3 percent of GDP, lags far behind that for government debt. Pakistan's corporations are insignificant players in the bond market, with outstanding debt amounting to 0.8 percent of GDP. Sri Lanka's corporate bond market is similarly underdeveloped, at 0.6 percent of GDP. And in Bangladesh the bond market has only eight corporate bonds (debentures).

Corporate bond markets amount to vastly larger shares of GDP in more advanced economies: 29 percent of GDP in Korea in 2006, 21 percent in the United States, 16 percent in Japan, 11 percent in the European Union. In the East Asian economies corporate bonds amounted to about 9 percent of GDP, and in the OECD countries to about 16 percent.

Constraints in Domestic Debt Securities Markets

South Asia's bond markets, though still relatively small, can nevertheless be expected to grow at a very fast pace. The strong GDP growth in the region is likely to continue, and that will produce a growing number of firms seeking to finance their operations with debt as well as equity. The economic expansion will also give rise to an immense pool of savings, leading to a search for new investment opportunities. Retail investors will move beyond their traditional concentration in equity and real estate investments and add fixed-income securities to their portfolios to achieve better balance and diversification. Households will seek to finance the purchase of homes with long-term, fixed-interest mortgages—and banks will seek to supply those mortgages by securitizing them and passing them on to investors through the bond market. And foreign investors will participate more actively in local currency bond markets as these markets become larger, more liquid, and more transparent.

But realizing the full potential of the region's bond markets, and ensuring sound, well-functioning markets, will require putting into place essential elements—or addressing remaining constraints—in supply, demand, market infrastructure, and the legal and regulatory framework.[6]

Supply Side

Regular issuance by the government of standard, high-quality debt securities of a few concentrated maturities is critical to the development of bond markets. Regular issuance builds the government's credibility as a debt issuer with investors. And issuance of standard instruments with a range of maturities helps build a long-term sovereign yield curve, providing essential guidance on pricing for both primary and secondary markets. For the corporate bond market, conditions conducive to both bond issuance and investment are essential for building supply.

Government Debt Issuance. In South Asia only India meets the standard in government debt issuance. Its government issues treasury bills in three maturities as well as a range of medium- and long-term securities. Treasury bill auctions are volume driven, with the quantity available announced before each auction. Long-term government securities known as dated government securities amounted to 63 percent of outstanding domestic government debt at the end of March 2007, and treasury bills (of 91, 182, and 364 days' maturity) for just 3 percent. The result is a government debt securities market that is liquid, deep, and comparable to developed markets.

In the region's other countries the government debt securities market has been concentrated in treasury bills (though Bangladesh recently reversed this trend), and mostly in those with the shortest maturities. Pakistan's government, like India's, preannounces debt issuance, but only auctions for treasury bills have been conducted regularly. Issuance of Pakistan Investment Bonds, with maturities ranging from 3 to 20 years, has been erratic in recent years. Sri Lanka has made efforts to lengthen the maturity of government debt instruments, but inflationary expectations, rising interest rates, and large budget deficits have led to a preference among investors for treasury bills.

A big factor standing in the way of bond market development is the absence of price mechanisms in the allocation of funds. Barriers to market pricing include interest rate controls, nonmarket pricing, and "captive market" arrangements in which financial institutions face statutory requirements to hold government debt. In Pakistan, for example, the government sets the cutoff yield for medium- and long-term Pakistan Investment Bonds and has in some instances canceled auctions rather than accepting the price the market was willing to pay.

The Sri Lanka government too has been reluctant to assume the role of a price taker, because of expectations that current inflationary conditions would lead to soaring interest rates if auction prices were determined entirely by demand and supply. The government places 80 percent of its medium- and long-term debt privately with two state-owned institutions, the Employees' Provident Fund and the National Savings Bank, at the latest guided auction prices or at the prevailing guided market rates. The Nepalese government, while it auctions both short- and long-term instruments, also avoids the role of a price taker. Auctions remain driven by yields rather than by announced volumes.

Some governments issue nonmarketable debt instruments. While these may encourage investments by retail investors, they impede the development of liquid and efficient bond markets. In Pakistan national savings instruments, with higher yields and more easily available than Pakistan Investment Bonds, make these market-based bonds less attractive, hindering the establishment of a long-term benchmark. Bangladesh and Nepal have similar savings instruments. Sri Lanka is phasing out its nonmarketable debt instruments, called Rupee Loans.

Benchmark Securities and Yield Curves. Government benchmark securities play a crucial part in the efficient functioning of both primary and secondary bond markets. They serve as a bellwether of prevailing interest rate structures and of market expectations of future interest rate movements, inflation, and associated risk premiums. They serve as hedging vehicles for some underwriting and trading risks. Finally, they enable investors in fixed-income securities to identify what share of issuance yields relates to credit and default risk and thus to accurately price those securities.

However, development of a sovereign benchmark depends on a sufficiently developed bond market—and on government bond issues sufficiently concentrated in standard, popular maturities—to support active trading.

In South Asia, India is the only country to have succeeded in building a risk-free sovereign yield curve that can provide guidance to market players across the broad spectrum of maturities. The central bank, the Reserve Bank of India, has followed a consistent policy of passive consolidation—largely reopening existing securities rather than launching new ones—and a lengthening of the maturity profile of government securities. These efforts have extended the sovereign yield curve to 30 years.

Other countries face a range of obstacles to developing a market-based sovereign yield curve. In Pakistan, because of the supply constraints resulting from the government's price-setting role and the negligible trading activity, long-term yields do not reflect true market conditions. In Nepal several factors, including the limited availability of debt instruments, have worked against the establishment of a liquid benchmark security.

In Sri Lanka, as noted, the government finds it difficult to act as a price taker. In addition, despite efforts to lengthen the maturity of public debt securities, investor preferences have continued to move toward the shorter end of the market because of inflationary expectations. And in Bangladesh as well as Sri Lanka the excessive fragmentation of public debt issues results in limited trading in any one issue, impeding the development of benchmark instruments.

Creating a small number of large benchmark securities to replace a multiplicity of issues can benefit the financial system. Trading is more active where there are a small number of large benchmark issues, and that makes it easier to construct a yield curve that more accurately reflects the underlying factors determining interest rates, such as the supply of and demand for money and predicted future interest and inflation rates. One way to create large benchmark issues is to restrict the securities issued to certain prespecified maturities and coupons and offer an exchange program allowing investors to swap existing securities for the new benchmark issues.

Both Bangladesh and Sri Lanka have begun moving toward fewer issues. The Bangladesh government has started issuing benchmark treasury bonds with maturities of 5, 10, 15, and 25 years on a regular schedule. In addition, it is concentrating on the issuance of benchmark 5- and 10-year bonds by reopening the existing securities. The Central Bank of Sri Lanka reduced the number of bond series by more than half between 2003 and 2007 and intends to reduce it further.

Public Debt Management. A sound debt management strategy is key in building a government's credibility as a borrower, in part by establishing predictability. Establishing sound debt management requires a coherent public cash management strategy, to guide deliberate decisions on the volume and maturity of each issuance of government debt securities. It also requires a strong organization capable of attracting and retaining a professional staff. And it requires ensuring that the staff have access to the analytical and information tools needed for efficiency in day-to-day debt management operations.

All five countries except India need to initiate reforms that lead to proper governance and internal processes in debt management and to adequate resources and staff capacity for developing a medium-term debt management strategy. The strategy, which would need to be updated yearly, should be based on a sound analysis of cost and risk, taking into account macroeconomic and market constraints. Execution of the strategy must be efficient as well as prudent in managing operational risk.

Bangladesh has taken steps to strengthen debt management operations by separating the government's cash management needs from its debt financing operations. But it lacks the capacity to carry out cash projections, constraining its ability to honor its newly published issuance calendar. Nepal also publishes an issuance calendar, developed at the beginning of each fiscal year on the basis of the planned budget deficit. But immediate financing needs drive decisions on maturities and volumes throughout the year. This erratic issuance undermines the government's credibility as a borrower and deprives the market of a sufficient volume of liquid debt instruments, impeding the development of a sovereign benchmark.

In Pakistan a priority is to develop a risk management system with a view to minimizing interest costs while avoiding maturity bunching and potential rollover problems. Sri Lanka will need to reduce the fiscal deficit and contain inflation before much progress can be made in lowering the risks in the domestic debt portfolio. The country's sizable external debt means that management of foreign currency borrowings is also important.

Corporate Bond Market. A well-developed corporate bond market allows financial diversification for both issuers and investors and helps companies (AAA-rated as well as subinvestment-grade ones) obtain the long-term financing needed for growth. But corporate debt markets in South Asia remain small in part because corporate borrowers find it easier and more convenient to obtain credit from banks than to comply with the rigorous governance standards required to raise funds through the bond market.

In India elaborate guidelines for corporate bond issuance have prompted most bond issuers to turn to private placements or overseas borrowings, which provide quick access to funds at fairly competitive rates. But recent measures have inhibited smaller, lower-rated corporate entities from accessing the bond market through private placement. Regulators have imposed disclosure requirements to improve transparency in the private placement market. They have also required that privately placed securities be listed on the exchanges to be considered eligible investments for institutional investors.

In Bangladesh and Nepal the corporate bond market suffers from lack of investors as well as issuers. In addition, past defaults by bond issuers have undermined investor confidence. In Pakistan and Sri Lanka both market capitalization and new issues have remained minimal. In Pakistan corporate bonds (known as term finance certificates) face stiff competition from national savings instruments. But Tier 2 capital requirements for financial institutions led to an increase in the issuance of corporate bonds in 2007.

The cost of issuing bonds has a direct impact on the development of corporate bond markets. Because public issuance involves considerably higher costs, companies often resort to private placement instead. Private placement requires no prospectus, reducing expenses for printing, attorneys' fees, and brokerage. (The actual costs of bond issuance depend, of course, on the issuer's ability to negotiate favorable fees for the services involved.)

Today the cost of bond issuance in South Asian countries ranges from 0.233 percent of the value of the issue in India to 7.439 percent in Pakistan (table 1.6). The differing stages of market development mean that these costs are not comparable, however. As bond markets grow, more intermediaries participate in trading, thereby promoting more competitive pricing.

Demand Side

A large and diversified investor base helps ensure strong and stable demand for bonds. The investor base ideally should include domestic and foreign investors and a broad range of institutions—such as commercial banks, insurance companies, pension funds, and mutual funds—as well as individual investors.

The structure and composition of a bond market's investor base are closely linked to the development and sophistication of the country's financial system. What role state-owned institutions play, whether foreign banks and insurance companies are present, how strong contractual savings institutions are, and how much financial wealth is held by the household sector all matter for how well the debt securities market functions. Promoting a diversified investor base with varying time horizons, risk preferences, and trading motives is vital to stimulate active trading and increase liquidity. A varied investor base also enables a government to meet its funding needs under a wide range of market conditions.

Table 1.6 Cost of Bond Issuance, Selected South Asian Countries, 2007
(percentage of issue size)

Item	Bangladesh	India	Nepal	Pakistan	Sri Lanka
Securities and exchange commission registration	0.155	0.004	0.225	—	0.211
Publication of prospectus	0.100	. .	0.013	1.021	—
Printing of prospectus and applications	0.150	. .	0.001	—	0.145
Printing of certificates; postissue expenses; postage	0.500	. .	0.003	—	0.728
Listing fee	0.400	0.004	0.075	0.070	0.025
Annual stock exchange fee	—	—	0.025	0.500	—
Issue manager or underwriter	0.150	0.120	0.100	3.800	0.750
Trustee fee	0.050	0.01–0.05	0.025	—	0.100
Credit rating; bankers; legal and audit	0.200	0.05–0.10	0.040	0.750	0.550
Central depository fees	0.242	0.002	—	0.299	—
Broker commission	—	0.01–0.15	0.200	1.000	0.250
Registrar and share transfer fee	—	—	—	—	—
Underwriting fee	—	—	—	—	—
Total cost	1.947	0.233	0.707	7.439	2.744

Source: Country authorities and market information.
Note: The size of the bond issue is assumed to be 200 million units in the local currency. Fees for different services may be negotiable.
. . = Negligible. — = Not available.

Institutional Investors. East Asian economies have developed strong institutional investors such as pension funds, provident funds, and insurance companies. Because of their long-term liabilities, they can provide long-term funding to the economy. In South Asia, by contrast, only two countries have made notable progress in developing collective investment funds such as mutual funds. The institutional investor base thus remains too small to support the economic potential of the region.

India has been the most successful in developing mutual funds. Its pension and provident fund industry also has shown notable growth. Reforms in the insurance sector have encouraged private companies to enter the industry, and these are beginning to invest in the bond market. But while the volume of assets under the management of institutional investors is growing, these holdings remain too restricted and homogeneous.

Pakistan has one of the smallest institutional investor bases among emerging markets. The contractual savings industry—insurance, pension, and other collective schemes—plays a minor role in bond markets despite the large financing requirements for housing, infrastructure, and consumer durables.

The government practice of relying on captive sources of funding—requiring financial institutions to purchase and hold government debt securities, often at below-market interest rates—while lessening in many countries, persists to some extent in South Asia. In Bangladesh commercial banks, life insurance companies, and pension and provident funds are all captive investors in government debt securities, driven by the need to comply with statutory reserve requirements. Nonbank investors play only a marginal role in the government debt securities market. While Sri Lanka has an institutional investor base, it is dominated by a few state institutions, such as the Employees' Provident Fund, that in effect serve as captive sources of funding for the government.

Retail Investors. The retail investor base in South Asia remains small, for three main reasons. First, most market intermediaries for government bonds are commercial banks, and they naturally have more incentive to market their own products than to market government debt securities. Depending on banks to mobilize savings to fund the purchase of government bonds can be costly for both governments and investors.

Second, the public is generally unaware of the range of investment opportunities available to individual investors. The Central Bank of Sri Lanka, in an attempt to build the retail investor base for government debt securities, is establishing new retail sales outlets throughout the country.

Third, in Bangladesh and Pakistan national savings instruments offering above-market interest rates divert demand from market-based debt instruments.

Foreign Investors. Foreign investors also play a limited role in South Asian bond markets. In many countries, not just those in South Asia, capital account policies inhibiting the participation of foreign investors can constrain the growth of bond markets. For example, restrictions on capital account receipts and payments may hamper the sale, purchase, or transfer of securities between residents and nonresidents. Requirements that nonresidents obtain authorization to trade in primary and secondary bond markets, to invest in domestic collective investment funds, and to repatriate investment proceeds also impede foreign investment.

By contrast, a liberalized capital account facilitates the development of domestic bond markets. Indeed, countries that have received the largest external portfolio inflows have had the greatest growth in securities market capitalization. Even so, capital account policies need to be coordinated with other macroeconomic policies mitigating the risks of contagion from external crises or of margin erosions brought about by foreign investors or excessive reliance on short-term external finance.

India and Sri Lanka have allowed foreign investors, but these countries also impose regulatory or investment guidelines that limit their participation. India, for example, has set a ceiling of $3.2 billion on total investment in government debt securities by foreign institutional investors—low relative to the size of the domestic debt securities market and the level of foreign exchange reserves. Raising that ceiling would speed development of the bond market.

Sri Lanka has opened its government debt securities market to foreign investors, also with an investment ceiling, but has not yet opened its corporate bond market to foreign investors. Nepal permits foreign investors to participate in its financial system only through a joint venture with a Nepalese entity.

Market Infrastructure

A third set of elements essential for developing bond markets relates to market infrastructure—market intermediaries, trading mechanisms, the issuance process, dissemination of information, risk transfer mechanisms, and a credit rating industry.

Operations in the primary market should be transparent and predictable, and they should maximize competition among investors to produce the best possible results for issuers. That means ensuring that the primary market is open to and accessible for the largest possible number of participants and disseminating, in advance, relevant and timely information on the issuer's finances and funding operations. For government debt securities a network of primary dealers—financial intermediaries selected by the government—typically promotes investment and activity in the market.

Developing a market in government debt securities also requires transparent, market-based issuing techniques—public subscription, auction, and syndication. More advanced operations, such as the reopening of existing issues, buyback programs, and switch transactions, could be used when markets become more sophisticated. An issuing strategy should weigh the preferences of investors against the government's own cost and risk targets and should, to the extent possible, promote benchmark issues in key maturities that facilitate the growth of the secondary market. Effective coordination between fiscal and monetary authorities is essential for avoiding the failure of auctions.

Establishing a competitive market structure can heighten trading activity and liquidity. Competition is beneficial not only among dealers but also sometimes among trading platforms—when activity is consolidated in a small number of liquid instruments, transaction costs (including transaction taxes) are minimized, the market infrastructure is sound and robust, and market participants have varying transaction needs and investment horizons. Primary dealers (that comply with their market-making obligations) and interdealer brokers (that facilitate trading among dealers) contribute to greater market liquidity.

India has a market infrastructure for government debt securities comparable to that in developed countries, with a primary dealer system, electronic trading platforms, state-of-the-art clearing and settlement systems, rating agencies, and so on. Built over time, this infrastructure has improved efficiency and lowered costs in the market for public bonds.

Primary Markets. A primary dealer system with well-defined privileges and obligations can increase efficiency in the government debt securities market when there are a large number of investors, especially institutional investors, as long as the risk of collusion can be minimized. India's primary dealer system has done much to help deepen and widen the country's government debt securities market. Primary dealers serve as market makers, providing two-way (buy and sell) quotes in the secondary market and thus supporting development of the retail market.

In Pakistan and Sri Lanka government debt securities are also distributed through a network of primary dealers. These dealers (and, in Sri Lanka, the Employees' Provident Fund) have exclusive access to the primary auctions. Participation in Bangladesh's primary market is in principle more open: all financial institutions that maintain an account at the central bank can participate directly in the primary market auctions of government debt securities. But clear rules on the rights and obligations of the primary dealers are not yet in place.

Sri Lanka shows what can happen when the obligations of primary dealers are incompatible with market conditions. Primary dealers are required to act as market makers. But because of a range of factors, trading in the secondary market is limited, and primary dealers are unable to provide two-way quotes for all lines of government debt securities.

Secondary Markets. Well-functioning secondary markets promote efficient price discovery, facilitate liquidity and risk management, and bolster the development of the primary market. They do so by providing a cost-efficient environment in which market participants can trade bonds through fair and transparent transactions. Active secondary markets improve the valuation and pricing of bonds, especially medium- and long-term bonds that are by definition issued less frequently than short-term bills. They provide an exit mechanism for investors in medium- and long-term securities while permitting governments to issue longer-term debt to better manage their exposure to interest rate and rollover risk.

But active and liquid secondary markets are difficult to develop. They require a sufficient number of market intermediaries and institutional investors with incentives to trade, appropriate types of instruments and transactions, and well-established trading mechanisms. Such mechanisms include not only the technical infrastructure for trading, clearing, and settlement facilities but also prudential and business conduct rules, effective market surveillance, and investor protection. Malaysia's experience points to some of the mechanisms that can help improve liquidity (box 1.1).

Of the five countries, India has the most liquid secondary market in government debt securities. Secondary trading in dated securities with maturities of up to 15 years is particularly active. Primary dealers are the main intermediaries for secondary market transactions and account for most of the trading in government debt securities.

In Sri Lanka secondary market trading in treasury bonds dropped significantly in recent years. In Pakistan the secondary market for government debt securities is

---

Box 1.1   *How Malaysia Enhanced Liquidity in Its Domestic Bond Market*

Malaysia, though at the forefront in developing domestic bond markets, had to contend with limited liquidity in the secondary market for some time. To address the issue, the country's central bank, Bank Negara Malaysia, introduced several changes in January 2005, all of which are viewed as having helped develop a more liquid market with better price discovery:

- Active use of repurchase agreements (repos) as a monetary policy instrument
- A program for the borrowing and lending of securities
- A securities lending facility for principal dealers

Repurchase Agreements as a Monetary Policy Instrument
Bank Negara Malaysia started using repurchase agreements—transactions combining a sale of securities with an agreement to reverse the transaction in the near future—as a monetary policy instrument to manage liquidity in the banking system. Its repo operations are aimed at encouraging market participants to actively use repos as an alternative funding instrument, making it easier for market participants to use these securities in managing settlement risks and trading strategies, and further strengthening risk management in the banking industry by encouraging banks to move toward collateralized interbank transactions.

Securities Borrowing and Lending
Bank Negara Malaysia developed the Web-based Institutional Securities Custodian Pro-gram to encourage institutional investors to participate in securities lending activities. Through this program the central bank borrows securities, mainly Malaysian government securities, from major institutional investors for use in its repo operations. The program, by "freeing" captive holdings of Malaysian government securities for trading operations, is aimed at increasing overall liquidity in the bond market.

Securities Lending Facility for Principal Dealers
The securities lending facility, introduced for the 10 principal dealers, is designed to support market-making activities and competitive pricing. The facility, by lending Malaysian government securities to principal dealers, improves their ability to quote continuous prices for the securities, further enhancing price discovery and liquidity in the secondary market. The securities come from the Institutional Securities Custodian Program or from Bank Negara Malaysia's own holdings. Because sufficient supply is critical, the central bank may also purchase Malaysian government securities from the primary and secondary markets at market prices. To ensure that these purchases do not influence or distort market prices, those in primary auctions are to be based on the weighted average price of the auction and limited to no more than 10 percent of the issue size, while those in the secondary market are to be limited to 10 percent of the outstanding amount of the issue.

Source: Bank Negara Malaysia press release, January 7, 2005.

---

dormant. And in Bangladesh and Nepal secondary market activity is practically nonexistent.

Clearing and Settlement Systems. Efficient infrastructure for securities settlement is essential for the sound development of bond markets. It facilitates the smooth flow of transactions in the primary and secondary markets, strengthens investor confidence, stimulates market growth, and limits exposure to systemic risk. To operate effectively, securities settlement systems need internal rules and procedures that are enforceable with a high degree of certainty. Also essential is a clear and sound legal framework that includes property and insolvency laws and laws specific to the operation of securities settlement systems. These specific laws should ensure that transactions are enforceable and client assets protected. They should provide for storage of securities in a depository (immobilization) or their issuance in securities accounts rather than in paper form (dematerialization). The laws should specify arrangements for ensuring that securities are delivered only if cash payment occurs (delivery versus payment). And they should provide for netting arrangements, securities lending, default rules, and liquidation of collateral and pledged assets.

The five South Asian countries have greatly varying clearing and settlement systems in their domestic debt securities markets. Both India and Sri Lanka have a modern framework based on delivery versus payment, though in Sri Lanka the delivery-versus-payment framework works only for government debt securities. The two countries also both have in place real-time gross settlement, an electronic fund transfer and settlement system.

Pakistan has yet to introduce a fully electronic means of trading, settlement, and clearing. Its planned implementation of a real-time gross settlement system in the second half of 2008 is a welcome development.

Nepal's system falls far short of what is needed to support a well-functioning bond market. All debt instruments are issued in paper form, which not only adds to the time and cost of transactions but also increases the risk of theft, forgery, and destruction. Introducing a scripless securities settlement system would be a critical step toward efficient clearing and settlement of traded securities and recording of information.

Bangladesh has a manual payment system for securities transactions, which prevents settlement on a delivery-versus-payment basis.

Risk Transfer Mechanisms. Financial innovations that transfer risks from parties seeking to mitigate their risk exposure to those willing to take on more risk are at an early stage of development in South Asia. Even in India the securitization market is still in its early phases, with all transactions carried out through private placement. Although securitization initiatives started in 1991 in India, growth picked up only in 2002, when the applicable law came into force. Transactions then grew rapidly for the next three years as a result of the strong growth in the Indian economy and in consumer lending. The investor base remains limited, however, because institutional investors face regulatory restrictions on investing in below-investment-grade debt instruments.

India's market for debt derivatives is also at an early stage. A vibrant derivatives market can help investors hedge their risks. It can also help foster the development of risk management products, which in turn would further deepen the Indian bond market.

Tools for Risk Assessment and Dissemination of Information. Credit rating agencies are an essential part of an efficient bond market infrastructure, providing investors with tools to make informed investment decisions and achieve price discovery. In Malaysia the government made credit rating of certain instruments and corporations mandatory, a move that had a major impact in developing domestic rating agencies and the bond market, especially the corporate bond market.

Nepal has no credit rating agency, and none is likely to be established in the present environment, which lacks sound disclosure requirements, corporate governance guidelines, and accounting and auditing standards. At the other end of the spectrum, India has been very successful in integrating credit rating structures into the local bond market. All major international credit rating agencies (Fitch Ratings, Moody's, Standard & Poor's) are represented in India, and the country's major rating agency, CRISIL, was recently acquired by Standard & Poor's.

Pakistan and Sri Lanka each have two credit rating agencies. In Sri Lanka the Central Bank advised all banking institutions to obtain and publish credit ratings to improve investor confidence in the financial system. Bangladesh also has two credit rating agencies, both at an early stage of development.

Governments can enhance transparency and increase participation in their debt securities market by ensuring that market participants and the general public have access to high-quality information about the government's debt structure, funding needs, and debt management strategy. India has a well-developed system for disseminating information. In the primary market an issuance calendar for dated securities has been published since 2002, enabling institutional and retail investors to better plan their investments and improving market efficiency. The central bank announces the results of auctions soon after they are completed and posts information on its Web site on all transactions on the day of settlement.

Sri Lanka has improved the dissemination of information. It publishes a range of data that market participants need, including the government borrowing calendar, auction information and results, bond market data, fiscal developments, money market information, and key macroeconomic indicators. It has also developed and published a bond index useful to both issuers and investors.

Legal and Regulatory Framework

A country's legal and regulatory framework shapes the structure of its bond market and affects how the market functions and develops. The regulatory framework for the bond market, like that for any securities market, should have three distinct but complementary objectives:

- Maintaining a fair, efficient, and transparent market
- Reducing systemic risk
- Protecting investors

Legislation should allow the government to borrow and to set ceilings on public debt. Legislation should also clarify the authority of different government entities to act in the market and should appoint the central bank or another institution to act as the agent for the government. An appropriate set of rules and regulations for intermediaries and investors, rules commensurate with the level of development of local markets, should govern the organization of the primary and secondary bond markets. Such rules should also influence the roles of the different market participants.

Authorities should aim to ensure equitable treatment of all types of investors and should regulate financial institutions to ensure their solvency and sound operation. Asset allocation limits and valuation rules, which have broad effects on the investment policies of institutional investors, need to be designed carefully and adapted to the changing circumstances of the regulated institutions.

Regulatory Structures. In South Asia there are two basic regulatory models for securities markets: merit based and disclosure based. India and Sri Lanka have disclosure-based regulatory systems, while Bangladesh, Nepal, and Pakistan have adopted merit-based ones.

In India the country's large size and large market, with intermediaries operating at both national and state levels, have led to a complex regulatory structure requiring close coordination among the different regulators. A high-level committee provides this coordination, though concerns remain about adequate delineation of regulatory and supervisory roles. Issues of overlapping jurisdiction tend to increase as financial markets become more open and complex, adding to the challenge of regulating and supervising the markets.

Regulatory and investment guidelines imposed on institutional investors in India discourage them from holding lower-rated, relatively illiquid bonds, allowing them less flexibility in managing their portfolios than their counterparts in more mature fixed-income securities markets. Similarly, foreign institutional investors, which have the risk appetite to invest in bonds across the credit spectrum, face caps on their debt investments in the country.

In Pakistan the central bank has overall responsibility for supervising financial markets and acts as the government's agent in issuing debt securities. The Securities and Exchange Commission of Pakistan is responsible for regulating securities, insurance, and companies. The commission has clear responsibilities, appears able to operate free of external influences, and enjoys an array of powers. But concerns remain about the adequacy of its resources.

Sri Lanka has made much progress in developing its regulatory framework for the capital market. The Securities and Exchange Commission of Sri Lanka, responsible for regulating all aspects of the capital market except government debt, was recently granted expanded jurisdiction and greater powers, enhancing its effectiveness as a regulator.

The Securities Board of Nepal is the apex regulator for that country's capital market, working in coordination with other regulators and the stock exchange. But while the board has ultimate oversight over the capital market, its independence is open to question and its resources apparently inadequate to support its enforcement powers. Corporate governance guidelines exist, but their enforcement has been lax. In addition, the lack of accounting and auditing standards and an efficient judiciary system undermines confidence in the capital market.

In Bangladesh, where several government authorities and regulators play correspondent roles in regulating the bond market, the central bank and the Securities and Exchange Commission have signed a memorandum of understanding aimed at improving coordination.

Most South Asian countries have ample scope for improvement in corporate governance arrangements, both those for the market regulator and those for market participants. While most have introduced corporate governance standards for listed companies, the standards remain voluntary and few companies have adopted them.

Tax Regime. Taxation has important implications for the development of capital markets. The tax rules relating to income from debt securities and capital gains affect consumption, saving, and investment decisions and thus influence the general level of savings, the demand for financial assets, and the size and type of investments. Poorly designed tax policies can impede the development of financial markets by discouraging new financial instruments or deterring potential investors.

In India the tax treatment of income from debt instruments varies depending on the type of instrument. In Pakistan different tax treatment also favors some debt instruments over others, including national savings instruments. Removing these tax distortions would help create a level playing field for debt instruments.

Tax treatment also varies by debt instrument in Nepal. In addition, interest income from corporate bonds and from taxable government bonds is taxed at one rate if owned by an individual and at a higher rate if owned by an institutional investor. That rules out cross-trading between the retail public and institutional investors, further reducing the possibility of secondary market activity.

Sri Lanka has taken some positive steps to ensure equal tax treatment for investors across different instruments and asset classes. Bangladesh has recently removed the withholding tax on interest income from government bonds.

A Varied Agenda

Unleashing the full potential of domestic debt securities markets in South Asia will require concerted efforts by policy makers across the region. Action plans and reform programs for each country will need to reflect the development level and technical progress of its market.

In Bangladesh and Nepal, the least advanced bond markets in the region, attention needs to focus on strengthening the primary market while laying the foundation for a solid secondary market structure. Priorities for Bangladesh are strengthening the government debt securities market, developing market infrastructure, and aligning returns on national savings certificates with market rates. In addition, promoting corporate bonds could help diversify the market. And encouraging foreign as well as domestic investment could help enlarge the investor base.

Priorities for Nepal center on developing a reliable issuance calendar, establishing a primary dealer system, and strengthening the market infrastructure.

Pakistan and Sri Lanka, with mixed progress in market development, face a different set of priorities. For Pakistan priorities include following a regular calendar (with targets) for auctions of Pakistan Investment Bonds, promoting secondary market trading by limiting the number of maturities in these bonds, and making national savings instruments more market based. For Sri Lanka the first priority is to stabilize the macroeconomic situation by reducing inflation and the fiscal deficit to sustainable levels. The second is to develop a benchmark yield curve by consolidating the fragmented debt stock—through buyback or conversion and a reduction in the number of bond series—and introducing a benchmark bond series.

For India, despite its more advanced debt securities market, the agenda still encompasses reforms to broaden the range of issuers, to expand the investor base, and to promote the corporate bond market by developing a central database on corporate bond issues. But India's longer experience in developing its market allows the country to be more strategic in the timing of reforms.

Endnotes

1. Much of the discussion in this section draws on World Bank and IMF (2001).

2. See, for example, Harwood, Pomerleano, and Litan (1999); Adams, Pomerleano, and Litan (2000); Litan, Masson, and Pomerleano (2001); and Pomerleano, Litan, and Sundararajan (2003).

3. The eight economies are China; Hong Kong, China; Indonesia; the Republic of Korea; Malaysia; the Philippines; Singapore; and Thailand.

4. The Asian Bond Market Initiative encompasses the members of the Association of Southeast Asian Nations (Brunei Darussalam, Cambodia, Indonesia, the Lao People's Democratic Republic, Malaysia, Myanmar, the Philippines, Singapore, Thailand, and Vietnam) as well as China, Japan, and the Republic of Korea.

5. The group of OECD countries are Australia, Canada, Germany, Japan, New Zealand, the United Kingdom, and the United States.

6. Much of the discussion in the following sections draws on World Bank and IMF (2001).

References

Adams, Charles, Michael Pomerleano, and Robert E. Litan, eds. 2000. *Managing Financial and Corporate Distress: Lessons from Asia.* Washington, DC: Brookings Institution Press.

ADB (Asian Development Bank). 2005. *Bond Market Settlement and Emerging Linkages.* Manila: ADB.

———. 2007. *Asian Development Outlook 2007: Growth Amid Change.* Manila: ADB.

Arnone, Marco, and George Iden. 2003. "Primary Dealers in Government Securities: Policy Issues and Selected Countries' Experience." IMF Working Paper WP/03/45, International Monetary Fund, Washington, DC.

Balalle, N. B. S. B. 2006. "Reform of the National Savings Scheme in Bangladesh." Study report sponsored by the International Development Association of the World Bank Group, Washington, DC.

Bambang Kusmiarso. 2005. "The Development of Domestic Bond Market and Its Implication to Central Banks: Country Experiences." South East Asian Central Banks (SEACEN) Research and Training Centre, Kuala Lumpur.

BIS (Bank for International Settlements). 2006. *Quarterly Review.* September. Basel.

———. 2007. *Quarterly Review.* September. Basel.

BIS (Bank for International Settlements), Committee on the Global Financial System. 2007. *Financial Stability and Local Currency Bond Markets.* CGFS Papers, No. 28. Basel: BIS.

CBSL (Central Bank of Sri Lanka). 2004. *Public Debt Management and Debt Profile of Sri Lanka.* Colombo.

———. 2006. *Financial System Stability Review.* Colombo.

———. 2007. *Public Debt Management in Sri Lanka: Performance in 2006 and First Half 2007; Strategies for 2007 and Beyond.* Colombo.

Colombo Stock Exchange. 2007. "Debt Security Trading System." Colombo.

Crimson Capital. 2006. "Bangladesh: Study on the Development of the Bond Market for Mortgage Backed Securities (MBS)." Study report prepared for the International Finance Corporation of the World Bank Group, Washington, DC.

Dalla, Ismail. 2003. *Harmonization of Bond Market Rules and Regulations.* Manila: Asian Development Bank.

———. 2005. "Deepening Capital Markets in East Asia." Background paper for East Asian Financial Markets Study, East Asia and Pacific Region, World Bank, Washington, DC.

Deutsche Bank. 2004. "Asian Bond Market Insights." Singapore.

Eichengreen, Barry, and Pipat Luengnaruemitchai. 2004. *Why Doesn't Asia Have Bigger Bond Markets?* NBER Working Paper 10576. Cambridge, MA: National Bureau of Economic Research.

Faulkner, Mark. 2004. *An Introduction to Securities Lending.* International Securities Lending Association.

Fitch Ratings. 2006. "Indian Securitisation Market Q & A." New York.

G-8 (Group of Eight). 2007. "G-8 Action Plan for Developing Local Bond Markets in Emerging Market Economies and Developing Countries." G-8 2007 Finance Ministers Meeting, Potsdam, May 19.

Harwood, Alison, Michael Pomerleano, and Robert E. Litan, eds. 1999. *Financial Markets and Development: The Crisis in Emerging Markets.* Washington, DC: Brookings Institution Press.

HSBC. 2005. "Back into the Fold: Asia Invests in Itself." Background paper for East Asian Financial Markets Study, East Asia and Pacific Region, World Bank, Washington, DC.

IMF (International Monetary Fund). 2004. *Emerging Local Securities and Derivatives Markets: Recent Developments and Policy Issues.* World Economic and Financial Surveys Series. Washington, DC: IMF.

———. 2006. "Bangladesh: Fifth Review under the Three-Year Arrangement under the Poverty Reduction and Growth Facility and Request for Waiver of Performance Criteria, Extension of the Arrangement, and Rephrasing—Staff Report." Washington, DC.

Karachi Stock Exchange. 2007. *Annual Report 2006.* Karachi.

Karunasena, A. G. 2005. "Development of Government Bond Market with Special Reference to Developing a Yield Curve: Experience of Sri Lanka." Staff Study, Central Bank of Sri Lanka, Colombo.

Lanka Rating Agency. 2005. "Debt Market Review." Colombo.

Litan, Robert E., Paul Masson, and Michael Pomerleano, eds. 2001. *Open Doors: Foreign Participation in Financial Systems in Developing Countries.* Washington, DC: Brookings Institution Press.

NSE (National Stock Exchange of India). 2006. *Indian Securities Market: A Review.* Vol. 9. Mumbai: NSE.

OECD (Organisation for Economic Co-operation and Development). 2002. *Debt Management and Government Securities Markets in the 21st Century.* Paris: OECD.

Patil Committee. 2005. *Report of the High Level Expert Committee on Corporate Bonds and Securitization.* New Delhi: Ministry of Finance.

Pomerleano, Michael, Robert E. Litan, and V. Sundararajan, eds. 2003. *The Future of Domestic Capital Markets in Developing Countries.* Washington, DC: Brookings Institution Press.

RBI (Reserve Bank of India). Various years. *Annual Report.* New Delhi.

Securities and Exchange Commission of Sri Lanka. 2005. *Annual Report.* Colombo.

Trilegal. 2007. "The Indian Corporate Debt Market: Legal and Regulatory Issues." Draft. Mumbai.

World Bank. 2006a. "Developing India's Corporate Bond Market." Finance and Private Sector Unit, South Asia Region, Washington, DC.

———. 2006b. *East Asian Finance: The Road to Robust Markets.* Washington, DC: World Bank.

———. 2006c. "Getting Finance in South Asia: An Analysis of the Commercial Banking Sector." Report 37295, South Asia Region, Washington, DC.

———. 2006d. *Global Development Finance 2006: The Development Potential of Surging Capital Flows.* Washington, DC: World Bank.

———. 2007. *Developing Markets for Long-Term Finance.* Washington, DC.

World Bank and IMF (International Monetary Fund). 2001. *Developing Government Bond Markets: A Handbook.* Washington, DC: World Bank and IMF.

World Federation of Exchanges. 2006. *Annual Report and Statistics 2005.* Paris.

2

Bangladesh

The Bangladesh bond market, the smallest in South Asia relative to GDP, has thus far played only a limited role in the economy. But the country has been taking positive steps toward developing the market. The government has started issuing benchmark bonds at scheduled intervals. The authorities have taken important measures toward developing an active secondary market for government securities—and that in turn will help establish benchmark yields and promote the development of a corporate bond market.

Introduction

The Bangladesh economy is poised to grow by 6 percent in fiscal 2008, following the sustained growth of more than 6 percent in the previous four years. Manufacturing and services sectors have recorded robust growth despite the high and volatile oil prices in the international market. The government has taken measures to limit average annual inflation to around 7 percent.

An environment of macroeconomic stability, along with liberalization and regulatory reforms, has helped strengthen the country's financial sector since the mid-1990s. The banking sector has improved its performance on a range of indicators. The equity market reached new highs in market capitalization. By contrast, the debt securities market has remained stagnant. Commercial banks dominate, accounting for nearly 75 percent of financial assets in the economy (table 2.1).

Banking Sector Reforms

The banking sector consists of commercial banks—30 domestic private banks, 9 foreign ones, and 4 nationalized commercial banks—and 5 government-owned special development banks. One of the four nationalized commercial banks, Rupali Bank, is being divested to a foreign investor; the other three have been

Table 2.1   Structure of Financial System, Bangladesh, 2004–06

Segment	2004		2005		2006	
	US$ millions	Share of total (%)	US$ millions	Share of total (%)	US$ millions	Share of total (%)
Capital market	11,277.38	28.50	10,905.60	26.82	10,954.76	24.98
Domestic debt securities	7,960.40	20.12	7,870.20	19.36	7,344.50	16.74
Equity	3,316.98	8.38	3,035.40	7.47	3,610.26	8.23
Banking assets	28,180.72	71.22	29,602.37	72.81	32,738.39	74.64
Insurance	109.22	0.28	129.03	0.32	147.43	0.34
Mutual funds	—	—	18.00	0.04	21.50	0.05
Total	39,567.32	100.00	40,655.00	100.00	43,862.08	100.00

Sources: For domestic debt securities, Bangladesh Bank; for equity, World Bank, World Development Indicators database; for banking assets, International Monetary Fund, International Financial Statistics database; for insurance and mutual funds, Bangladesh Bank 2006.
— = Not available.

transformed into public limited companies. Private banks have gained in market share, in part because of the ongoing restructuring of the nationalized commercial banks and in part because the private banks offer higher interest rates on deposits. Beyond the traditional banking sector is the microfinance industry, where Bangladesh has been a leader.

Over the past decade and a half, beginning with a financial sector reform program in the 1990s, Bangladesh has pursued a series of legal, policy, and institutional reforms to improve the financial intermediation process and facilitate efficient allocation of financial resources (see annex 2.1). This in turn is expected to improve the competitiveness of the private sector and promote investment and growth in the real sector. The country's central bank, Bangladesh Bank, plans to implement the Basel II Capital Accord beginning in January 2009 to bring domestic banks closer to international standards.

Measures to liberalize the financial sector led to clear benefits. The asset quality and capital base of domestic banks improved. Nonperforming loans, though still high by international standards, declined from about 35 percent in 2000 to about 14 percent in 2006. Most banks maintained a capital adequacy ratio of 9 percent; the exceptions were the nationalized commercial banks. Competition was encouraged, and 8 new foreign banks and 10 private domestic banks entered the market. The large spread between average lending and deposit rates remains a concern, however.

Although traditional banking products still dominate, the commercial banks increasingly are adopting innovative, technology-driven products and services. A few are now focusing on card-based payments using debit, credit, and automated teller machine (ATM) cards. Bangladesh Bank has taken the legal, regulatory, and other measures necessary to speed the transaction and payment process.

Microfinance institutions, though accounting for assets of less than 2 percent of GDP, reach more than 60 percent of households. And while their financial activities are restricted by law to a narrow range, they are continually adding to the quality and coverage of the financial system. Indeed, the country's first microcredit securitization, by BRAC, provided a model of financial innovation for the entire financial sector.

Recent Developments in the Capital Market

The equity market posted an impressive performance in 2007. In June 2007 the market capitalization of the Dhaka Stock Exchange rose to an all-time high of $10 billion, 14 percent of GDP. The Chittagong Stock Exchange also posted better performance.

Still, the Bangladesh equity market remains thin compared with such peers as the Pakistani market. The Bangladesh market remains shallow, and vulnerable to overheating and price shocks. The market surge was mostly demand driven, and there is concern about a risk of collapse unless backed by quality shares with strong fundamentals. Partial divestiture of the two state-owned oil companies and entry by major telecommunications companies are expected to help improve the supply of quality shares.

The government is working to improve the reliability and efficiency of the stock exchanges as an investment market. To protect investors' interests, the Securities and Exchange Commission is initiating appropriate regulatory and supervisory measures aimed at establishing fairness and transparency in capital market operations.

The debt securities market in Bangladesh is very small, accounting for about 17 percent of financial system assets in 2006. Government debt securities overwhelmingly dominate the market, the primary ones being treasury bills and treasury bonds. But nonmarketable instruments known as national savings certificates account for an even larger share (more than three-fifths) of the 28 percent of domestic savings that are invested in debt instruments.

The corporate bond market remains largely undeveloped. Lack of varied corporate debt supply is a major impediment to its development. As in other South Asian countries, corporate borrowers generally prefer to rely for funds on commercial banks rather than the bond market, thereby avoiding the need to comply with disclosure and governance norms.

Supply Side: Debt Instruments and Issuers

The slow growth of the Bangladesh debt securities market can be attributed in part to several important constraints on the supply side, including a lack of benchmark bonds, market distortions caused by the national savings scheme, and a lack of interest from private companies in launching new debt products as a result of the high costs.

Money Market

Bangladesh has yet to develop an active money market. Its money market consists mainly of a thin interbank market with sporadic trading in treasury bills. Trading of treasury bills in the secondary market is limited because these instruments, along with treasury bonds, make up the statutory liquidity reserve and are therefore generally held until maturity by commercial banks and other financial institutions.

Trading is also thin in repurchase agreements (commitments by the seller to the buyer to repurchase the instrument when the buyer intends to sell, or repos), for two main reasons. First, commercial banks have a weak treasury function, and most do not actively manage liquidity.[1] Second, there is no standard master repurchase agreement, a gap that should be addressed to support orderly development of the repo market.

Call Money Market. Commercial banks and nonbank financial institutions access the call money market to bridge overnight funding gaps or park surplus liquidity. A liquidity gap may arise because of a need to meet the regulatory 5 percent cash reserve requirement or because of a sudden outflow of funds to meet liabilities. The call money rates are negotiated and tend to be seasonally volatile. Volatility tends to be especially high during Eid, the Muslim holiday marking the end of Ramadan, when there is a surge in deposit withdrawals and banks face immediate liquidity pressure.

There is a direct and positive relationship between treasury bill rates and call money rates. When there is a seasonal cash shortage, banks rush to the call money market, and the rate peaks. Investors in treasury bills are naturally unlikely to make those instruments available unless offered higher yield rates. Bangladesh Bank monitors the day-to-day liquidity position and eases any substantial volatility in the call money market.

Repo and Reverse Repo Markets. Before 2003 Bangladesh Bank offered investors in treasury bills a premature encashment (redemption) facility, a procedure in which the central bank would buy back the security, paying the amount and accrued interest, when the investor needed cash. This procedure is also called discounting the treasury bills. Today, rather than this discount window, Bangladesh Bank offers a repo facility, allowing investors to borrow against treasury bills for up to 90 percent of their value. In addition, a repo auction is held alongside the treasury bill auction. The yield rate of repos is determined through bid offer and acceptance and is usually higher than the yield of treasury bills.

Which banks and financial institutions are allowed to access the repo facility depends on the liquidity in the market. Repo auctions are available for 28-day treasury bills. The term is usually overnight or one week. Repo auctions are held every working day, with Bangladesh Bank having the discretion to accept or reject bids in part or in full.

Repo rates (for a tenor of one to two days) remained unchanged at 8.50 percent during July–December 2007. During that period there were only four transactions, on three days in December, amounting to Tk 6.08 billion.

In reverse repo transactions a bank or financial institution that has excess liquidity can deposit it with Bangladesh Bank. Reverse repo transactions were on the increase during July–December 2007, and the rates (for a tenor of one to two days) remained unchanged at 6.50 percent.

The interbank repo market, introduced in July 2003, has not been active, though there were 30–40 transactions in July–December 2007. The interest rate ranged from 7.10 percent in July 2007 to 8.00 percent in December 2007.

Monetary Policy Operations. Bangladesh Bank has maintained its restrained monetary policy stance since the second half of fiscal 2005 with a view to curbing excess demand and inflationary expectations.[2] In October 2005, to slow domestic credit growth, it raised the cash reserve requirement for commercial banks to 5.0 percent of time and demand liabilities, and the statutory liquidity requirement to 12.5 percent of these liabilities. Repo and reverse repo interest rates and treasury bill and bond yield rates have sustained an upward trend (table 2.2; figure 2.1). This trend helped reduce private sector credit growth from 25 percent in February 2005 to 15.6 percent in May 2007 and eased the pressure on the foreign exchange market.

Bangladesh Bank has also used the repo and reverse repo facilities to enhance daily monetary operations. But despite its efforts to gradually tighten monetary policy, excess demand from inflationary expectations remains. The inflationary expectations are reflected in the wide gap between the short-term rates of treasury bills and those of the 5- and 10-year treasury bonds. Bangladesh Bank (2007c) has indicated that it would be prudent to narrow the gap by raising the short-term interest rates and developing a secondary market for government securities, leading to a lowering of the yield on treasury bonds.

Government Debt Issuance

The Bangladesh government raises funding through treasury bills (364 days), treasury bonds, National Investment Bonds, and national savings certificates. The largest share, about two-thirds, comes from national savings certificates (table 2.3).

Treasury Bills and Bonds. Bangladesh has been improving the transparency of the primary market in government debt securities in recent years. Since September 2006 the Ministry of Finance, the issuer of treasury bills and bonds, has been publishing an annual calendar of the auctions for these instruments. The calendar announces the dates, types of instruments, and volume for each auction. Bangladesh Bank, which runs the auctions as an agent for the government, promptly publishes the auction results on its Web site. All financial institutions that maintain accounts with Bangladesh Bank can participate directly in the auctions.

Table 2.2 Selected Interest Rates, Bangladesh, September 2005–June 2007
Weighted average rates (%)

Month	Treasury bills				BB bills		Treasury bonds		Repos	Reverse repos	Call rate	Lending rate	Deposit rate
	28 day	91 day	182 day	364 day	30 day	91 day	5 year	10 year	1–2 day	1–2 day			
FY06													
Sept.	6.72	6.85	6.98	7.13	—	—	—	—	—	5.02	6.09	11.15	5.90
Dec.	6.96	7.02	7.20	7.45	—	—	10.50	11.65	—	5.50	8.40	11.25	5.90
Mar.	7.05	7.25	7.49	7.85	—	—	—	—	—	5.60	17.15	11.60	6.26
June	7.10	7.43	7.75	8.30	—	—	10.65	12.10	—	6.04	1.84	12.06	6.68
FY07													
July	7.15	7.45	7.82	8.35	—	—	—	—	—	6.22	7.56	—	—
Sept.	7.24	7.55	7.83	8.38	—	—	10.86	12.49	—	6.49	7.36	12.41	6.98
Dec.	7.33	7.52	7.84	8.45	7.37	—	10.89	12.49	—	6.50	7.16	12.60	6.99
Mar.	7.32	7.58	7.86	8.45	7.38	7.58	—	12.50	9.00	6.50	6.99	12.71	7.02
May	7.33	7.59	7.88	8.46	7.38	7.60	—	12.34	9.00	6.50	7.61	—	—
June	7.32	7.60	7.89	8.48	7.39	7.60	—	12.14	9.25	6.50	7.67	—	—

Source: Bangladesh Bank.
Note: BB bills are Bangladesh Bank bills.
— = Not available (no activity and therefore no published rates).

Figure 2.1   Trends in Selected Interest Rates, Bangladesh, March 2006 – December 2007

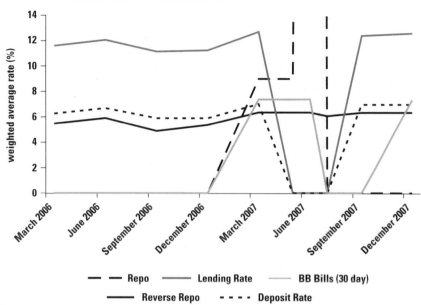

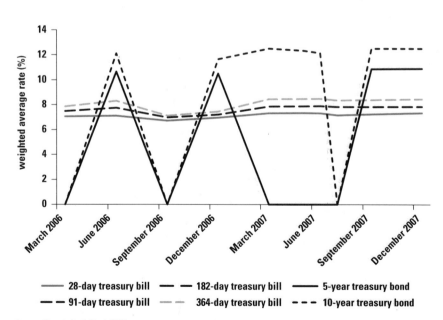

Source: Bangladesh Bank 2007c.
Note: BB bills = Bangladesh Bank bills.

Table 2.3   Composition of Domestic Government Debt, Bangladesh, Fiscal 2000–07

(Tk billions)

Fiscal year	National savings certificates	Treasury bills	Treasury bonds and NIBs	Total
2000	169.32	152.18	39.95	361.45
2001	211.71	179.07	42.09	432.87
2002	258.72	207.34	42.20	508.26
2003	258.87	200.78	43.34	502.99
2004	362.21	123.20	47.17	532.58
2005	366.20	167.52	14.21	547.93
2006	395.89	149.84	26.57	572.30
2007 (Feb.)	421.50	162.16	77.41	661.07

Source: Bangladesh Bank.
Note: Data are for the end of the fiscal year, June 30, except for 2007.
NIBs = National Investment Bonds.

All auctions of treasury bills and bonds are conducted according to the preannounced calendar (table 2.4). The 28- and 91-day treasury bills are auctioned weekly, while the 182- and 364-day treasury bills are auctioned in alternating weeks. The issuance of treasury bills exceeding 364 days was halted in July 2006. Two- and five-year treasury bills, which were issued until September 2006, have also been discontinued.

The Ministry of Finance has been issuing 5- and 10-year treasury bonds since December 2003, and 15- and 20-year bonds since July 2007. The government introduced the long-term bonds to better meet its borrowing needs as well as the appetite of banks looking for ways to meet their statutory liquidity requirements.

To its credit, the government has reversed the past trend of a concentration in treasury bills by substantially increasing the share of treasury bonds while reducing the volume of treasury bills (table 2.5). The ratio of treasury bonds to treasury bills rose from about 20 to 80 in 2005 to 80 to 20 in 2007. The supply of 5- and 10-year treasury bonds has been the key to the reversal of the trend.

National Investment Bonds. Besides treasury bills and bonds, the Ministry of Finance places National Investment Bonds, with a maturity of three years, at a predetermined rate. The rate of these bonds appears to be lower than market expectations. Life insurance companies, which can use National Investment Bonds to meet their reserve requirements, have become the sole investors in these bonds.

National Savings Certificates. The national savings scheme is aimed at mobilizing the savings of small investors and pensioners at attractive interest rates. Under the National Savings Directorate, formed under Public Debt Act, 1943, national

Table 2.4 Results of Treasury Bill Auctions, Bangladesh, Week Ending December 30, 2007

Auction date	Maturity (days)	Bids offered			Total bids	Bids accepted				
		Total bids	Face value (Cr Tk)	Range of yields (%)		Face value (Cr Tk)	Sale value (Cr Tk)	Range of yields (%)	Weighted average price (Tk)	Weighted average yield (%)
Dec. 30	28	21	587.0000	7.32–7.43	9	207.0000	205.8375	7.32–7.35	99.4384	7.34
		Devolvement on primary dealers			7	293.0000	291.3527	7.35	99.4381	7.35
Dec. 30	91	14	236.0000	7.63–7.79	3	59.0000	57.8956	7.63	98.1282	7.63
		Devolvement on primary dealers			8	141.0000	138.3607	7.63	98.1282	7.63
Dec. 23	182	14	220.0000	7.93–8.12	5	100.0000	96.1780	7.93–7.95	96.1780	7.95
		Devolvement on primary dealers			0	n.a.	n.a.	n.a.	n.a.	n.a.
Dec. 30	364	15	159.1000	8.47–8.65	5	56.1000	51.7193	8.47	92.1914	8.47
		Devolvement on primary dealers			9	43.9000	40.4720	8.47	92.1914	8.47

Source: Bangladesh Bank.
Note: Cr Tk = crore taka (10 million taka).
n.a. = Not applicable.

Table 2.5   Pattern of New Domestic Government Borrowing, Bangladesh, Fiscal 2004–07

(Tk billions except where otherwise specified)

Instrument	2004	2005	2006	2007
Treasury bonds	3.17	11.04	12.35	60.09
5 year	2.43	6.41	4.88	24.61
10 year	0.74	4.63	7.47	35.48
Treasury bills	23.32	46.46	67.41	14.66
Total	26.49	57.50	79.76	74.75
Treasury bonds/total (%)	12	19	15	80
Treasury bills/total (%)	88	81	85	20

Source: Bangladesh Bank.
Note: Data are for the end of the fiscal year, June 30.

Table 2.6   Interest Rate on Savings Products by Source and Maturity, Bangladesh, June 2007

Annual interest rate (%)

Source	3–6 months	6 months to 1 year	3 years and above
Post Office	—	—	11.5
Nationalized commercial banks	6.5–7.5	6.75–7.75	8–8.5
Specialized banks	5.75–7.25	6–7.5	6.75–8
Private banks	7–12.75	7.25–13	8–11.75
Foreign banks	3.75–12.5	4–12.25	4.5–11
National Savings Directorate	n.a.	n.a.	12[a]

Source: Bangladesh Bank.
a. Average.
n.a. = Not applicable.

savings certificates are sold through 9,000 post office branches and 3,300 commercial bank branches functioning as commission agents. Bangladesh Bank collects the sales proceeds and reimburses the seller at the time of encashment (redemption).

National savings certificates amounted to Tk 395.89 billion at the end of fiscal 2006 and Tk 421.50 billion at the end of February 2007. The return on national savings certificates had been following a declining trend, dropping from 14.5 percent in 2000 to 10.5 percent in 2005. But more recently the return rose to 12 percent, comparable to the rates offered by private and foreign commercial banks (table 2.6).

The savings scheme suppresses potential demand for market-traded instruments. While the national savings certificates offer a return consistent with market rates, they also carry the implied sovereign guarantee, shorn of credit risk. As a

---

Box 2.1   Islamic Bonds Offering a New Alternative for Issuers and Investors

Islamic bonds, developed as an alternative to conventional bond products, are designed to achieve compliance with Shari'ah, which prohibits the charging of interest. In Islamic finance, lenders are considered an investment partner of the borrower, sharing in the returns and risks relating to the underlying physical assets.

Islamic bonds are structured financial instruments based on a contract of exchange, such as for the sale and purchase of an asset through deferred payment, leasing of assets, or participation in a joint venture. Issued both internationally and domestically by sovereign or corporate entities, the bonds generally have a medium-term maturity and risk and return characteristics similar to conventional debt securities. They can be structured to provide investors additional protection, through credit or liquidity enhancement schemes, against late payment, prepayment, and poten-

tial write-offs. The structuring of Islamic bonds requires approval from recognized Shari'ah advisers to ensure compliance with Islamic principles.

Islamic bonds have become increasingly popular. For institutional or individual investors with roots in Islam, they provide an avenue for investing in Shari'ah-compliant instruments. The bonds also appeal to conventional investors looking for attractively priced, liquid instruments for income and capital gains. For issuers, the demand from investors has allowed a lower cost of finance. To support efficient price discovery for Islamic securities, the Malaysian government has issued Malaysian Islamic treasury bills and Government Investment Issues. These products have established an Islamic benchmark yield curve.

Source: Institute of Islamic Banking (http://www.islamic-banking.com/).

---

result, they have become the preferred investment choice for savers. Even though the aim of the national savings scheme is to provide savings instruments for small investors and pensioners, small savers (those with deposits of up to Tk 50,000) account for only 20 percent of the funds mobilized, according to a recent study (Balalle 2006).

Islamic Bonds. A new government bond product in Bangladesh is the Islamic bond (box 2.1). Issued by Bangladesh Bank in October 2004, after extensive research and long discussion, the Bangladesh Government Islamic Investment Bond has a maturity of six months, one year, or two years. The bond is designed in large part to provide Islamic banks and financial institutions with a Shari'ah-compliant instrument for meeting statutory liquidity requirements as well as investing or procuring funds. The bond is also open for investment by any private individual or corporation. At the end of June 2007 the total sales of this bond amounted to Tk 14.8 billion, up from Tk 6.4 billion a year earlier (Bangladesh Bank 2007a).

Sovereign Yield Curve

Lack of benchmark bonds has been among the main reasons that the Bangladesh debt securities market has not taken off. Without benchmarks in place, all other fixed-income instruments, including corporate bonds, have lacked a pricing base.

Figure 2.2   Weighted Average Yield of Treasury Bills Based on Auction of December 30, 2007 Bangladesh

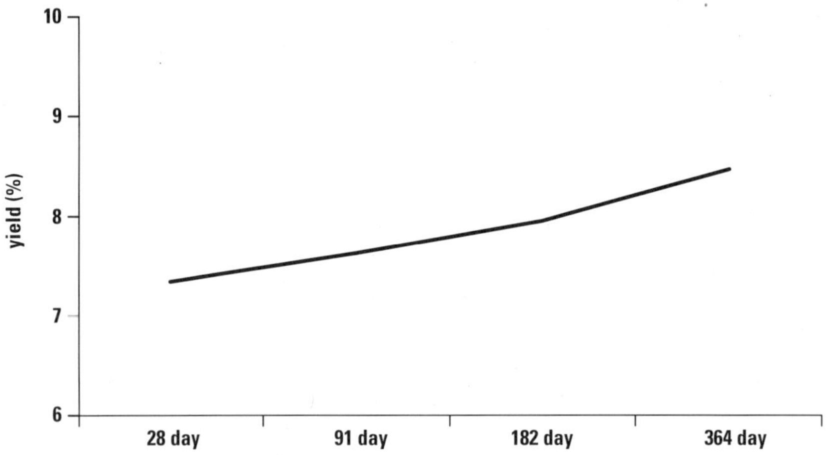

Source: Bangladesh Bank.

The authorities have been working on developing benchmark bonds. The government is now issuing, on a regular schedule, benchmark treasury bonds with maturities of 5, 10, 15, and 25 years. In addition, the government has maximized the issuance of marketable bonds, concentrating on a few benchmark bonds by using reopening. With little trading activity in the secondary market, however, these efforts have not yet led to a liquid benchmark that can serve as a pricing guide. Figure 2.2 shows the yield curve reflecting prices in primary auctions of treasury bills and treasury bonds.

Public Debt Management

The Bangladesh government has a good track record of fiscal discipline, keeping its overall deficit within the target. To strengthen public debt management, the government and the central bank have recently taken several steps to improve its governance and transparency. At the beginning of fiscal 2007 a modified arrangement for the government's bank borrowings was put into place under the supervision of the Cash and Debt Management Committee to strengthen the coordination of borrowing activities. The new arrangement included a higher ways and means advance limit (Tk 10.00 billion, up from Tk 0.65 billion), as well as auctions of treasury bills and bonds according to volumes preannounced in the borrowing calendar.

This new arrangement segregates Bangladesh Bank's role in government debt management from its monetary policy operations, increasing the independence of momentary policy. But it lacks a built-in mechanism to keep government bank borrowings within budgetary limits. Until recently Bangladesh Bank would hold treasury bills and bonds at the cutoff rate i   e market supply of funds fell short of the government's demand as set by the Cash and Debt Management Committee (a process known as devolvement). The Cash and Debt Management Committee has agreed in principle that the devolvement system would be replaced by a system in which the extra amount would be devolved on the primary dealers (Bangladesh Bank 2007b).

Corporate Bond Market

The corporate bond market in Bangladesh remains at a nascent stage, with a shallow debenture market. In 1987–2005 only 17 debentures were issued through public offerings. The eight debentures still outstanding at the end of 2005 had an issue value of only $2 million.[3] The corporate bond market faces important constraints—but also a potential for growth in bank and infrastructure bonds that could spark its development.

Constraints on Market Development. The market suffers from lack of issuers as well as investors. Much of this has to do with excessive dependence on bank credit: corporate borrowers find it easier to access credit from banks than to comply with the governance standards required for raising funds through the bond market or to meet the disclosure requirements for listings on one of the exchanges. For the debentures that are listed on an exchange, liquidity is insignificant because of the small number of investors and their buy-and-hold mentality—but also because of the inferior quality of the instruments.

Market development has also been constrained by high costs. Given the traditionally high interest rates, borrowing on a long-term basis is prohibitively costly for issuers. And while the high interest rates stifle supply, they also reduce demand for long-term securities as a result of investor uncertainty.

On the issuer side the high transaction costs of bond issuance also play a part (table 2.7). In particular, the registration fee, stamp duties, annual trustee fees on outstanding amounts, and ancillary charges have stifled demand. Registration fees for debentures, however, have been significantly reduced in recent years to ease this burden.

On the investor side a big factor is poor confidence in issuers, the market, and the legal and regulatory framework—a result of a failure by issuers to meet contractual payment terms, a failure by trustees to enforce debenture holders' rights, and a failure by market regulators to discipline firms listed on the exchanges for not complying with the contractual terms of the debentures issued (out of fear of the potential impact on individual issuers and overall market capitalization). Some efforts have been made to improve conditions to promote investor confidence and participation, including household (retail) participation. But weaknesses persist, constraining liquidity and demand.

Potential Starting Points. Bank bonds and infrastructure bonds could be potential starting points for promoting the development of the corporate bond market.

Table 2.7   Cost of Bond Issuance, Bangladesh, 2007

Item	Share of issue (%)	Tk
Securities and exchange commission registration	0.155	310,000
Publication of prospectus	0.100	200,000
Printing of prospectus and applications	0.150	300,000
Printing of certificates; postissue expenses; postage	0.500	1,000,000
Listing fee	0.400	800,000
Issue manager or underwriter	0.150	300,000
Trustee fee	0.050	100,000
Credit rating; bankers; legal and audit	0.200	400,000
Central depository fees	0.242	483,500
Total cost	1.947	3,893,500

Source: Country authorities and market information.
Note: The size of the bond issue is assumed to be Tk 200 million.

Bank bonds offer a way for banks and other financial institutions to meet Tier 2 capital requirements. Beginning in January 2008 these entities were required to raise their total capital to 10 percent of risk-weighted assets, or up to Tk 2 billion ($29.11 million)—half from Tier 1 capital sources and the other half from Tier 2 sources (figure 2.3). Among the Tier 2 capital sources, several are limited by the financial institution's lending business and fixed assets transactions—general provision, asset revaluation reserve, and exchange rate equalization account. Of the remaining two, preference shares will be costlier than debt.

That suggests a potential for financial institutions to raise Tier 2 capital by issuing bank bonds. (The regulatory limiting factor is that Bangladesh Bank retains the authority to decide how much of the bond issue should be treated as Tier 2 capi-

Figure 2.3   Components of Bank Capital, Bangladesh

Tier 1
Paid-up capital
General reserve
Statutory reserve
Retained earnings
Noncumulative irredeemable preference
   shares
Dividend equalization account

Tier 2
General provisions (1% of unclassified
   loans)
Asset revaluation reserve
Preference shares (except
   noncumulative irredeemable
   preference shares)
Perpetual subordinated debt
Exchange rate equalization account

Source: Bangladesh Bank.

Table 2.8   Government-Sponsored Infrastructure Investment Projects in the Pipeline, Bangladesh

Sector	Project	Amount (US$ millions)
Power	Small power plants	182
Power	Large power plants	2,430
Port and container terminals	Land port and jetty	27
	Inland container terminal	175
Telecommunications	Telephone and optical-fiber cable network	900
Transport	Elevated expressway, flyover, and national highways	1,440
Civil	Park and civil construction	10
Housing	Flats for low and middle-income people	1,230
Total		6,394

Source: Infrastructure Investment Facilitation Center.
Note: Excludes planned investments in telecommunications infrastructure by private sector telephone companies. Data are as of the end of 2007.

tal.) One commercial bank has already done so. In 2007 Islami Bank Bangladesh issued a Tk 3 billion perpetual bond. This first-ever perpetual bond issue in Bangladesh was well received by investors, as shown by the huge oversubscription of the initial public offering. Another commercial bank, Dhaka Bank, is expected to issue a $30 million–equivalent subordinated convertible bond in the second half of 2008.

Infrastructure bonds could play a key part in raising funds for private investors in infrastructure. Governments in low-income countries, faced with enormous investment requirements in infrastructure, are encouraging private sector financing. Best practice worldwide has been private investment under two methods: build, own, and transfer, and build, own, operate, and transfer. Bangladesh, with among the world's lowest infrastructure performance indicators, lags in promoting these two methods of infrastructure financing.

While there has been no infrastructure bond financing in Bangladesh so far, one transaction is in the pipeline. The Industrial and Infrastructure Development Finance Company, a Bangladesh development finance institution, plans to launch the country's first-ever infrastructure bond to arrange finance for four small power plants, to be constructed under the government's small-power-plant program. The $56.47 million issue is expected to go mainly to private commercial banks through syndication. Encouragingly, the prospective private investments in infrastructure projects are sizable (table 2.8).

One potential source for financing these infrastructure projects through bond issues is the remittances from nonresident Bangladeshis working abroad. In fiscal 2006 such remittances amounted to about $4.6 billion. In 2007 the remittances grew by a record 23 percent. A recent study found that almost 80 percent of remittances to Bangladesh go to nonproductive expenditures (INAFI 2006). Through savings instruments that the government offers for nonresident Bangladeshis (such as nonresident foreign currency deposits, U.S. Dollar Premium Bonds, and Wage Earners Development Bonds), some of these funds could be pooled and used instead to issue infrastructure bonds.

Demand Side: The Investor Base

In Bangladesh commercial banks and institutional investors—life insurance companies, pension and provident funds—are captive investors in government securities, a result of their need to comply with mandatory reserve requirements or investment restrictions. Public pension schemes dominate the pension fund industry, while the government-owned Investment Corporation of Bangladesh dominates the mutual fund industry. The Investment Corporation of Bangladesh, brought under the supervision of the Securities and Exchange Commission, also holds a large part of the shares on the Dhaka Stock Exchange. With few private institutional investors, the investor base remains undiversified, adversely affecting the development of the Bangladesh debt securities market.

Commercial Banks

The statutory liquidity requirements for commercial banks are the biggest driver of demand for government securities. Banks must maintain liquidity reserves of 18 percent: 12.5 percent in eligible assets such as government securities and 5.5 percent in cash.

Not surprisingly, commercial banks, along with Bangladesh Bank, dominate the holdings of marketable government securities (table 2.9). By contrast, nonbank investors play only a marginal role in the market for treasury bills and bonds.

Table 2.9   Holdings of Treasury Bills and Bonds by Investor Category, Bangladesh, 2002–06

(Tk billions)

Instrument and investor category	2002	2003	2004	2005	2006
Treasury bills					
Bangladesh Bank	112.8	67.0	113.0	150.6	195.5
Commercial banks	132.2	172.3	150.9	169.0	155.2
Nonbank investors	0.3	5.2	10.0	11.8	11.5
Total	245.3	244.5	273.9	331.4	362.2
Treasury bonds					
Bangladesh Bank	0	0	0	0	0
Commercial banks	1	0.3	0.5	0.3	0.3
Nonbank investors	0	0	0	0	0
Total	1	0.3	0.5	0.3	0.3

Source: IMF 2006 (table A3).

Insurance Industry

The insurance industry is a growing and potentially important institutional investor segment for government securities, with a strong appetite for longer-tenor bonds. The strongest potential source of demand is life insurance companies, which are required to maintain statutory reserves of 30 percent in cash, treasury bills, treasury bonds, and National Investment Bonds. While the general insurance sector appears to be stagnant, life insurance penetration has been increasing. Per capita premium income for the overall insurance industry has also been increasing gradually, though it remains considerably lower than that in India and Sri Lanka. In 2005 gross premium income reached Tk 9.4 billion, about 0.23 percent of GDP.

The industry, liberalized in 1984, includes 62 insurance companies. Of these, 18 operate in life insurance, including the state-owned Jiban Bima Corporation and the foreign-owned American Life Insurance Company (ALICO). The other 44 operate in general insurance, including the state-owned Sadharan Bima Corporation, the most active in that segment. Thirty-two insurance companies, 9 of them in the life insurance segment, are listed on a stock exchange.

Both public and private insurance companies have been facing growing competition in underwriting new businesses. Public insurance companies (both life and general) have been losing businesses to private ones, mainly because of a business-as-usual approach and an apparent lack of incentive to compete. As the economic significance of the industry continues to grow, orderly development of this market will become increasingly important.

Pension and Provident Funds

In Bangladesh only 5–10 percent of workers, primarily civil servants, are covered by formal retirement plans. Civil servants participate in two types of retirement plans. The first is a noncontributory, defined-benefit scheme. The second is a contributory provident scheme, the General Provident Fund, which de facto operates as an unfunded system: contributions deducted from workers' salaries are used to pay benefits, while the surplus is allocated to the budget. These schemes are required to invest 75 percent of their assets in government securities.

State-owned enterprises and nationalized commercial banks also offer retirement plans, though no consolidated data are available on these plans. Pension plans offered by financial institutions are negligible, but large private firms have established pension schemes for their employees. Companies offer both defined-benefit and provident fund plans. These funds have traditionally invested in national savings certificates.

Mutual Funds

The mutual fund industry in Bangladesh remains poorly developed, perhaps because the capital market is still small and lacks an adequate number of good-quality securities. But the industry, aided by tax benefits, is beginning to be a preferred investment option for savers. More private mutual funds, and active participation by those funds, are needed to promote development of the debt securities market.

The first private mutual fund in Bangladesh started operating in May 2000. By May 2007 there were 14 mutual funds, with a total market capitalization of Tk 29.7 billion. Of these, eight are managed by the government-owned Investment Corporation of Bangladesh, three by the ICB Asset Management Company (a subsidiary of the Investment Corporation of Bangladesh), one by Bangladesh Shilpa Rin Sangstha, and the other two by the privately owned Asset and Investment Management Services (AIMS) of Bangladesh. The Investment Corporation of Bangladesh has played a key role in developing mutual funds and has a long history of successfully managing closed-end mutual funds.

Mutual funds in Bangladesh invest mainly in equities and corporate debentures. Recently neither mutual funds nor foreign investors have shown much interest in investing in government securities. The yields of government securities appear to be relatively low compared with market expectations. Indeed, the long end of the yield curve is falling steeply despite current high inflationary trends, reflecting investor demand and expectation of long-term stable inflation.

Market Infrastructure

The government and the central bank have taken several steps to improve the infrastructure of the debt securities market and promote the development of the secondary market. One such step has been the introduction of repo and reverse repo auctions. Others include developing a primary dealer system and an auction calendar, important steps that will help establish benchmark yields and promote the development of a corporate bond market. A central depository system has been created for all securities. And to encourage securitization, the stamp duty on transfer of assets has been eliminated.

Primary Dealers

Eight banks and one nonbank financial institution serve as primary dealers and participate in the auctions for treasury bills and bonds. Bangladesh Bank, which regulates the primary dealers, recently took steps aimed at improving the viability of their business. In June 2007, by amending the guidelines applicable to primary dealers, Bangladesh Bank made them eligible for commission and liquidity support. The amended guidelines require each primary dealer to underwrite a minimum share of the auction amount (12 percent for bank primary dealers and 4 percent for nonbank ones in fiscal 2008). In return, primary dealers will be paid an underwriting commission at a rate determined by the government. Each primary dealer also is eligible for liquidity support up to the amount of the treasury bills and bonds devolved on that primary dealer in primary auctions, after adjustment for any shortfall in statutory liquidity reserves and minimum stock, for up to a month at a time.

Secondary Market

Most secondary market activity is in repos and reverse repos. Trading in treasury bills and bonds is very limited. Because commercial banks and other financial institutions subscribe to treasury bills and bonds to meet the statutory liquidity requirements, they tend to hold these securities until maturity. Other reasons for the dormant market in treasury bonds include the taxation of interest earnings and, for retail investors, the large denominations. The limited trading in treasury bonds also suggests that there is little market interest in long-term instruments— and that apart from the institutional investors acquiring treasury bonds to meet statutory liquidity requirements, the yields are too low to prompt investors to assume long-term exposures.

Nor is there much appetite for long-term corporate bonds. This may be in part because of the poor past performance of debentures, which has undermined investor confidence in private sector securities.

Government securities are traded in two places, the organized segment at the stock exchanges and the over-the-counter (OTC) segment. That treasury bonds are listed on the stock exchange is commendable, but there has been virtually no trading in these securities. Statistics of the Dhaka Stock Exchange show that of the 34 treasury bond issues listed on the exchange in 2005 and 2006, only one 10-year treasury bond has been traded. The issues listed had an aggregate value of Tk 4.5 billion (with a denomination of Tk 100,000 for each bond).

In the OTC market the primary dealers handle secondary transactions in treasury bills and government bonds. In June 2007 treasury bills accounted for 80 percent of transactions and 67 percent of trading volume. The weighted average yield was 7.31 percent. But the real rate of return for investors was negative. Of the treasury bonds, 49 percent are 5-year bonds and the rest are 10-year bonds. Transactions averaged far less than $1 million (Tk 68.7 million). Yields ranged from 10.79 percent to 12.14 percent.

Clearing and Settlement System

Both stock exchanges in Bangladesh have an automated system for the trading of securities. And, as noted, the country has a securities depository, Central Depository Bangladesh, for all securities. But payments in securities transactions are handled manually, which means that securities cannot be settled on a delivery-versus-payment basis. The clearing and settlement system needs to be improved to enhance the transparency and integrity of the market.

Securitization

Securitization is widely used in developed financial markets to provide long-term funding that financial institutions can regularly tap for on-lending to clients. It is

Table 2.10 Securitization Transactions, Bangladesh, 2004–07

Issuer	Amount (US$ millions)	Year
Industrial Promotion and Development Company of Bangladesh (IPDC)	5.2	2004
Industrial Development Leasing Company (IDLC)	1.9	2005
BRAC	180	2006
United Leasing Company (ULC)	5.8	2007

Source: Issuing companies.

a fairly new concept in Bangladesh: so far only four securitization deals have been done in the financial market, most by nonbank financial institutions (table 2.10). One of these was an innovative microcredit securitization by BRAC (box 2.2). In addition, the government is moving ahead with the securitization of toll revenues from Jamuna Bridge.

All four securitization deals have been asset based. But there is also good potential for developing mortgage-backed securities. The Bangladesh housing market suffers from an acute shortage of supply, exacerbated by population growth and low levels of financing relative to GDP. In Dhaka, the main housing market,

---

Box 2.2   A Pioneering Securitization of Microcredit Receivables in Bangladesh

Bangladesh can boast the world's first AAA-rated, local currency securitization of microcredit receivables. The bond transaction, completed in 2006, is a securitization of receivables arising from microcredit loans extended to low-income borrowers by BRAC, the country's largest NGO, primarily in rural communities not reached by commercial banks. The structure involves a special-purpose trust that purchases the receivables from BRAC and issues to investors certificates representing the beneficial interest in those receivables.

Recognized by the financial media, including *CFO Asia*, as one of the most innovative financial market transactions in 2006, the deal was arranged by RSA Capital, Citigroup, the Netherlands Development Finance Company (FMO), and the German development bank KfW. Two local banks also invested in the certificates, along with Citibank Bangladesh. Among the most impressive aspects of the transaction is the way it deals with the complexity of a dynamic pool that will contain

about 3.3 million short-term loans with an average outstanding principal of around $95.

The microcredit bond transaction, denominated in Bangladesh taka, will provide BRAC with Tk 12.6 billion ($180 million) in financing over a six-year period. BRAC will received disbursements of Tk 1 billion ($15 million) every six months, with a maturity of one year. Thus the securitization allows BRAC not only to diversify its funding sources but also to disburse more funds to a larger number of microentrepreneurs.

The transaction has brought innovation to funding for the poor, introducing a model that can be replicated in other developing countries. It should also help boost the development of the Bangladesh capital market. The transaction, rated by the Credit Rating Agency of Bangladesh, was the country's first AAA-rated issue of local certificates and was well received by local investors.

Source: Citigroup (http://www.citigroup.com).

the share of households owning their own home is estimated to be less than 30 percent. In 2004 residential property prices in Dhaka were reported to be 16 times the average household income, making the purchase of a home difficult without a long-term mortgage loan (Crimson Capital 2006). But banks and nonbank financial institutions can rarely obtain funding with maturities of more than three years, making it difficult for them to grant long-term loans.

Thus there is a demand for developing mortgage-backed securities in Bangladesh. There are also hurdles: tax and incentive problems, regulatory barriers, and shortages of knowledge and skills.

Credit Rating Industry

Two domestic credit rating agencies operate in Bangladesh, which has had a legislative framework for credit ratings since 1996. The first, Credit Rating Information and Services Limited (CRISL), was set up in 1995 with Rating Agency Malaysia Berhad, JCR-VIS Credit Rating of Pakistan, Prime Commercial Bank of Pakistan, and the government-owned Investment Corporation of Bangladesh as key shareholders. CRISL is a founding member of the Association of Credit Rating Agencies in Asia (sponsored by the Asian Development Bank). The second, established recently, is the Credit Rating Agency of Bangladesh.

International credit rating agencies have had little incentive to be involved in market issues. There have been no sovereign issues in international markets.[4] Domestic government issues have been sold exclusively in the local market and have attracted virtually no investment from abroad. And Bangladesh lacks a well-developed corporate bond market.

Legal and Regulatory Framework

Many government authorities and regulators play complementary roles in the regulation of the Bangladesh securities market (table 2.11). Two of these, the Securities and Exchange Commission and Bangladesh Bank, have overlapping jurisdiction in some areas. The two organizations signed a memorandum of understanding to improve coordination.

Regulation of Capital Market, Private Issuers, and Intermediaries

The Securities and Exchange Commission regulates institutions engaged in capital market activities, exercising powers under the Securities and Exchange Ordinance, 1969 and the Securities and Exchange Commission Act, 1993. Its responsibilities include:

- Regulating stock exchanges and any other securities markets
- Registering and regulating stock brokers, subbrokers, share transfer agents, bankers to an issue, trustees of trust deeds, registrars to an issue, merchant bankers, underwriters, portfolio managers, investment advisers, and any other intermediaries associated in any way with securities markets

Table 2.11 Regulators of the Capital Market and Market Participants, Bangladesh

	Regulator
Government debt securities market	
Primary market	Ministry of Finance, Bangladesh Bank
Secondary market	
OTC segment	Bangladesh Bank
Exchange-traded segment	Securities and Exchange Commission
Primary dealers	Bangladesh Bank
Other markets and intermediaries	
Equity market, corporate bond and debenture market	Securities and Exchange Commission
Insurance companies	Office of the Chief Controller of Insurance

Source: Country authorities.

- Registering, supervising, and regulating collective investment schemes, including mutual funds
- Promoting, regulating, and supervising self-regulatory organizations
- Prohibiting fraudulent and unfair trade practices relating to securities markets
- Promoting the education of investors and the training of securities market intermediaries
- Prohibiting insider trading in securities
- Regulating substantial share acquisitions and company takeovers
- Undertaking inspections, conducting inquiries, and auditing the stock exchanges, intermediaries, and self-regulatory organizations in the securities market

To strengthen its oversight capacity, the Securities and Exchange Commission established Central Depository Bangladesh to operate and maintain a central depository system under the Depositories Act, 1999. In the future, oversight authorities will need to extend their attention to electronic transactions, which seem to be the area of potential expansion for the settlement system.

Market participants fall under the jurisdiction of different laws and institutions, depending on their role. Brokers and dealers operating in the stock exchanges are governed by rules of the Securities and Exchange Commission and the regulations and bylaws of the exchanges. Banks providing custodial services are supervised by Bangladesh Bank and subject to the Bank Companies Act, 1991. As noted, primary dealers operating in the government securities market are also regulated by Bangladesh Bank.

The Securities and Exchange Commission licenses market intermediaries. By June 30, 2007, it had issued licenses to 28 institutions to act in the capital market:

19 merchant banks and portfolio managers and 9 issue managers and underwriters. (Of the 19 licensed merchant banks, 10 have been continuously inactive, and the commission is taking steps to cancel their licenses.)

The Dhaka and Chittagong Stock Exchanges are self-regulatory organizations, falling under the supervision of the Securities and Exchange Commission. Each stock exchange operates its own clearinghouse for the settlement of securities transactions.

To reduce systemic risk in the financial sector, Bangladesh Bank oversees payments settlement systems while the Securities and Exchange Commission oversees securities settlement systems. Bangladesh Bank, deriving this power from Bangladesh Bank Order, 1972, maintains oversight of cash, noncash, and foreign currency settlement systems.

Regulation of Investors

Banks and Nonbank Financial Institutions. Bangladesh Bank, as the central bank, is authorized to license, regulate, and supervise all banks and nonbank financial institutions—microfinance organizations, housing finance banks, leasing companies, venture capital firms—under the Financial Institutions Act, 1993. Microfinance organizations traditionally have operated on a self-regulatory basis. But to ensure effective regulation, a separate regulatory framework has been set up under the Microcredit Regulatory Authority Act, 2006, and all those operating a microcredit business in the country must obtain a license from the Microcredit Regulatory Authority.

Insurance. Regulatory authority over the insurance sector lies with the Office of the Chief Controller of Insurance, operating under the Ministry of Commerce. The regulatory framework includes a range of instruments: the Insurance Act, 1938; insurance rules issued in 1958; the Insurance Corporation (Amendment) Act, 1990, introduced to regulate and promote the growth of the insurance sector; and key investment policy guidelines issued by the Ministry of Commerce in October 2004 to clarify asset exposures for insurance firms.

Yet the regulatory structure for the insurance industry remains underdeveloped and not yet geared toward playing its role in the industry's development. Creating an effective system of monitoring and supervision will be critical in guiding the industry in sound management of its business and thus enhancing its role in the development of the country's financial system.

Mutual Funds. Recognizing the importance of institutional investment in developing the capital market, the Bangladesh government has amended a number of laws with the aim of promoting such investment. Among these are Securities and Exchange Commission laws amended to encourage private-sector-sponsored mutual funds to operate in the market. Another, the Merchant Banker and Portfolio

Manager Act, 1996, facilitates the operation of merchant bankers and portfolio managers. A total of 19 companies are now listed as merchant banks and portfolio managers in Bangladesh. Regulatory authority over the country's 14 mutual funds rests with the Securities and Exchange Commission.

Tax Regulation

The withholding tax on interest income on government bonds was removed in the fiscal 2008 budget. There is no withholding tax on interest income on national savings certificates.

Recommended Actions

The debt securities market in Bangladesh remains at an incipient stage, characterized by a limited supply of debt instruments, particularly long-term ones, and by a lack of liquidity and active trading. The lack of a well-functioning bond market blunts the effectiveness of monetary policy operations: it weakens the transmission of policy measures and thereby prevents the desired effect on the real economy.

Recommended actions for developing the bond market form a broad road map:

- Strengthening the government debt securities market by improving the efficiency and transparency of the secondary market and enhancing its liquidity
- Developing market infrastructure and an enabling environment for the bond market by upgrading the depository, clearing, and settlement arrangements; promoting development of the money market; strengthening the government's cash and debt management capacity; creating an enabling legal and regulatory framework; and strengthening the credit rating industry
- Reforming the national savings scheme by aligning its returns with market expectations, transforming the scheme into a modern retail program equipped with modern information technology, and targeting small investors
- Broadening and diversifying the investor base by promoting pension sector reform, strengthening the insurance sector, adopting reforms to attract foreign investors, and implementing an investor education program
- Promoting development of the corporate bond market by streamlining the Securities and Exchange Commission guidelines on issuance of bonds and debentures, further reducing issuing costs, tapping potential new issuers (such as banks for Tier 2 capital), and creating an enabling environment for asset-backed securitization and infrastructure bonds

Supply Side

Developing the Money Market. Developing a well-functioning money market should be a priority. A country's money market must normally be operating well before a government bond market—with both an efficient primary market and a liquid secondary market—can be fully developed. In a deregulated market economy a well-functioning money market facilitates the conduct of monetary policy through market-based instruments, anchoring the short end of the yield curve and supporting the development of the foreign exchange market. It provides the authorities with better signals of market expectations, allows banks (and their customers) to better manage their liquidity, and strengthens competition in financial intermediation. A well-developed money market also helps promote private issuance of short-term instruments (negotiable certificates of deposit, promissory notes, commercial paper) and thereby supports the development of the longer-term corporate bond market (World Bank and IMF 2001).

Strengthening the Government's Debt and Cash Management Capacity. Effective debt and cash management is key to market-based monetary policy operations and the functioning of the government bond market. Strengthening the government's capacity in debt and cash management should therefore be another priority in developing the Bangladesh bond market. The government, to its credit, has taken steps to strengthen public debt management. But gaps remain. There is no medium-term debt strategy. And the Ministry of Finance lacks the capacity to provide reliable cash flow projections.

Reforming the National Savings Scheme. National savings certificates, with their implied sovereign guarantee, depress potential demand for market-traded instruments. Reforming the national savings scheme to create a level playing field between market-traded instruments and national savings certificates would help reduce the market distortions. Consideration could also be given to replacing the present scheme with market-oriented mechanisms for raising government funds.

Reducing Issuance Costs for Corporate Bonds. High transaction costs have discouraged public bond issues by corporate issuers. Lowering the costs of bond issuance—including the registration fee, stamp duties, annual trustee fees, and ancillary charges—should be part of a long-term plan to develop the corporate bond market.

Demand Side

Broadening the Investor Base. A large and diversified investor base helps ensure strong, stable demand for government securities. Efforts to promote such an investor base should focus on facilitating the development of institutional investors—especially through pension reform and measures to strengthen the insurance sector—and creating an environment conducive to investment in the bond market by both domestic and foreign institutional investors.

Targeting Small Investors. Though aimed at small investors and pensioners, the national savings scheme attracts larger investors as well. Indeed, as noted, small savers account for only 20 percent of the funds mobilized. Transforming the scheme into a modern retail program equipped with modern information technology could help develop a retail investor base.

Market Infrastructure

Increasing Transparency in the Secondary Market. Transparency in the secondary market for government debt securities remains limited. There is no central source of information on trading activity in the OTC market. While Bangladesh Bank receives reports on OTC trading from primary dealers, it does not publish the information. Publishing this information in a timely fashion would help improve transparency in the OTC market and facilitate price discovery.

Improving the Clearing and Settlement System. Because securities transactions in Bangladesh still depend on a manual payment system, securities cannot be settled on a delivery-versus-payment basis. To enhance the transparency and integrity of the market, the clearing and settlement process needs to be improved by moving toward a real-time gross settlement system.

Developing Securitization. The potential for mortgage-backed securities in Bangladesh suggests that these instruments would be a good place to start in developing securitization. An early priority would be to overcome the hurdles to securitization—the tax and incentive problems, regulatory barriers, and shortages of knowledge and skills. Experts from developed financial markets could help familiarize the diverse participants in securitization with its concept and practice.

To increase the popularity of mortgage-backed securities and reduce the cost of issuing these instruments, other steps will also be needed, including introducing a legislative framework governing securitization and standardizing its regulatory and accounting treatment.

Strengthening the Credit Rating Industry. The domestic credit rating agencies have gaps in their capabilities, and the Securities and Exchange Commission has not yet built up adequate expertise in oversight of the rating agencies. As a result, the rating work is of poor quality, impeding the development of the corporate bond market. Measures are needed to strengthen the credit rating industry.

Legal and Regulatory Framework

Creating an Enabling Legal and Regulatory Framework. The regulatory framework for the bond market in Bangladesh is both poorly developed and poorly enforced. Reform of this framework should be aimed at the three complementary objectives critical to sound regulation of securities markets: maintaining fair, efficient, and transparent markets; reducing systemic risk; and protecting investors.

An appropriate set of rules and regulations—commensurate with the level of market development—should be developed to govern the organization of the primary and secondary markets in government debt securities. These rules should also address the roles of different types of market participants.

In addition, regulatory reform should devote attention to clarifying procedures for dealing with the failure of a market intermediary and to strengthening disclosure requirements, transparency, and valuation rules.

To promote the development of the corporate bond market, regulatory efforts could also focus on creating an enabling environment for infrastructure bonds, which offer a potential starting point for developing the corporate bond market.

Strengthening Enforcement to Build Investor Confidence. Gradually establishing the confidence of investors should be an important focus of efforts to develop the corporate bond market. Toward this end, greater efforts are needed to enforce contractual payment terms of debt issues by disciplining issuers that fail to comply with these terms. Enforcing compliance with the disclosure requirements for listings on the stock exchanges would also help build investor confidence.

Annex 2.1   Reforms in the Banking Sector

Bangladesh has pursued a series of legal, policy, and institutional reforms to strengthen the financial sector since the early 1990s:

- Liberalizing interest rates
- Introducing new treasury bills to activate open market operations
- Granting greater autonomy to Bangladesh Bank and strengthening its capabilities and technical skills
    - Launching the Central Bank Strengthening Project, including automation of the clearinghouse
    - Introducing service standards for work in different departments of Bangladesh Bank
- Restructuring the management and internal processes of the nationalized commercial banks with the ultimate aim of privatizing them
- Introducing a requirement, effective January 2007, that all banks obtain a credit rating by a credit rating agency
- Improving prudential regulation and supervision
    - Raising the minimum capital requirement from Tk 400 million to Tk 2 billion in stages
    - Issuing comprehensive risk management guidelines on five core risk areas—credit risk, asset-liability risk, foreign exchange risk, internal control and compliance risk, and money laundering risk
    - Introducing exposure limits for individual customers and groups of customers
    - Imposing stricter measures for loan loss provision and supervisory enforcement of compliance
    - Linking the large-loan limit to banks' nonperforming loan ratio
    - Encouraging banks to form syndications for large loans
    - Introducing stringent loan rescheduling conditions to stop "evergreening" of loans
    - Imposing guidelines on restructuring of loans
    - Introducing an early warning system
    - Adopting the Basel II Capital Accord effective January 2009
- Strengthening corporate governance in the financial sector
    - Improving disclosure and transparency standards
    - Introducing "fit and proper" tests for bank directors, chief executives, and advisers
    - Introducing restrictions on the composition of boards of directors
    - Improving clarity on the roles and functions of the board and management

○ Requiring that all banks form an audit committee with clear guidelines and terms of reference
- Strengthening legal and judiciary processes, including bank loan recovery
- Allowing the entry of new foreign and private banks

Source: Bangladesh Bank.

Endnotes

1. Banks' limited management of liquidity has contributed to a large interest rate spread. According to the Offsite Supervision Department of Bangladesh Bank, the weighted average interest rate spread for all commercial banks in Bangladesh was as high as 5.35 percent in 2007, impeding private sector growth.

2. This discussion draws on Bangladesh Bank (2007c).

3. Bangladesh Stock Market, "Market Capitalization" (http://www.bdstock.com/market capitalization.htm).

4. The Fitch Ratings Web site lists 102 sovereign issuers as of mid-June 2006 (http://www.defaultrisk.com/). The list does not include Bangladesh.

References

Asian Development Bank. 2004. "Bangladesh Country Governance Assessment." Manila.

———. 2007. "Bangladesh Quarterly Economic Update." September. Manila.

Bangladesh Bank. 2006. *Annual Report 2005–2006.* Dhaka.

———. 2007a. *Annual Report 2006–2007.* Dhaka.

———. 2007b. "Monetary Policy Statement." June. Dhaka.

———. 2007c. "Monetary Policy Statement." July. Dhaka.

Balalle, N. B. S. B. 2006. "Reform of the National Savings Scheme in Bangladesh." Study report sponsored by the International Development Association of the World Bank Group, Washington, DC.

Crimson Capital. 2006. "Bangladesh: Study on Development of the Bond Market for Mortgage Backed Securities (MBS)." Study report sponsored by the International Finance Corporation of the World Bank Group, Washington, DC.

IMF (International Monetary Fund). 2006. "Bangladesh: Fifth Review under the Three-Year Arrangement under the Poverty Reduction and Growth Facility and Request for Waiver of Performance Criteria, Extension of the Arrangement, and Rephrasing—Staff Report." Washington, DC.

———. 2007. "Bangladesh: Statistical Appendix." IMF Country Report 07/229. Washington, DC.

INAFI (International Network of Alternative Financial Institutions). 2006. "Harnessing Remittances for Economic Development of Bangladesh." INAFI Bangladesh Working Paper Series, No. 1. Dhaka.

World Bank and IMF (International Monetary Fund). 2001. *Developing Government Bond Markets: A Handbook.* Washington, DC: World Bank and IMF.

3

India

India ranks among the emerging market economies with a deep and well-diversified financial market. The government debt securities market has grown rapidly, driven by sustained budget deficits of the central and state governments over the past two decades that needed to be financed by domestic savings. Policy reforms aimed at developing this market have achieved clear results: the government debt securities market is liquid and deep, with infrastructure comparable to that in developed markets. The corporate bond market, however, has failed to keep pace.

The prospects for further development of India's bond market remain excellent. India has the human capital and other resources needed. A high-level committee has made a number of far-reaching policy, operational, and technical recommendations. Implementing these and other recommendations made and accepted by the government could pave the way to a deep and well-developed bond market.

Introduction

India achieved the second fastest growth, after China, among a sample of major developing (including Asian) economies in 2000–07. It has also reduced inflation substantially; the rate in the present decade is half that of the 1990s (Mohan 2007a).

In the financial sector India has introduced impressive, wide-ranging reforms since the early 1990s. Interest rates have been largely liberalized, capital markets deregulated, restrictions on capital flows gradually eased, and the financial sector opened to competition, both domestic and foreign. These reforms have led to significant structural change in India's financial sector and greatly increased the importance of the financial market.

The reforms of the 1990s transformed the country's financial market from one that was government dominated and consisted mainly of state-owned banks into

Table 3.1   Financial Market Profile, India, 2002–September 2007
Share of total (%)

Indicator	2002	2003	2004	2005	2006	Sept. 2007
Domestic debt securities market	28	25	24	21	19	19
Equity market capitalization	23	34	37	42	47	49
Banking assets	49	41	40	36	34	32
Total	100	100	100	100	100	100
Total market size (US$ billions)	560.6	815.3	1,061.4	1,310.1	1,731.9	2,502.3

Sources: BIS 2007; World Bank, World Development Indicators database; International Monetary Fund, International Financial Statistics database; World Bank staff calculations.
Note: Banking assets include claims by banking institutions on the central government and the private sector.

a broad-based, vibrant market that has achieved tremendous growth. The banking system's expanding network of branches and the growth of credit and deposits indicate continued financial deepening (Mohan 2007b). The equity and equity derivatives markets in India have good liquidity, high trading volumes, and market infrastructure on par with international standards.

From 2003 to the end of 2006 the Indian financial market more than doubled in size to $1.7 trillion, with equities accounting for 47 percent, banking assets for 34 percent, and debt securities for 19 percent (table 3.1). By September 2007 the market had grown further, to about $2.5 trillion. The market is well regulated and supervised by regulatory authorities with adequate statutory powers.

The growth in the financial market has been robust as well as rapid. Equity and debt securities markets have mobilized substantial funds to meet public and private sector financing needs. A range of domestic and foreign currency instruments is traded in the market. Derivatives such as options and futures, introduced in 2000, have allowed investors to hedge their positions and reduce risks. Commercial banks have diversified their activities and improved their performance. Contractual savings institutions are beginning to grow in response to deregulation of the insurance industry and reform of the pension industry. As successful as the reforms have been, however, further reforms are needed to develop the financial market, particularly the corporate bond market.

Banking Sector Reforms

The Indian banking sector has seen many positive developments in the past decade. Today its performance on key banking indicators is comparable to that in developed economies (IMF 2007).

Banks in India can be broadly classified as scheduled and nonscheduled. The vast majority are scheduled banks, those satisfying criteria (such as minimum capital) set by the central bank, the Reserve Bank of India, and entitled to certain privileges. At the end of March 2007 there were 177 scheduled banks: 96 regional rural banks and 81 commercial banks. Scheduled commercial banks include the State Bank of India and its associates (8), nationalized banks (19), foreign banks

(29), private sector banks (24), and a public sector bank (RBI 2007c). Other players in the financial markets include nonbank financial institutions and cooperative banks.

Because of the banking sector's overwhelming dominance in the financial system and its systemic importance, the government introduced reforms first for commercial banks and later extended them to other financial intermediaries such as financial institutions and nonbanking finance companies. The reforms included lowering the once-high statutory reserve requirement, moving toward market-determined interest rates, encouraging competition by allowing new entrants, strengthening prudential regulations and standards, and enhancing transparency and disclosure standards (see annex 3.1).

State-owned banks recorded significant improvements in their fundamentals and financial performance following the reforms, and by March 2007 the government was able to divest part of its equity in 17 of the 19 nationalized banks through public offerings and listings on local stock exchanges. These public sector banks, now listed entities with broad ownership, have come under greater public scrutiny and market discipline, paving the way for sustained improvements in performance and profitability. Indian banks with international presence were expected to comply with the norms of the Basel II Capital Accord beginning March 31, 2008, while the rest will be required to adhere to these norms beginning a year later.

While impressive, the reforms remain limited in coverage. Access to financial services is still limited to 48 percent of the population (World Bank 2006d, 2008). The ratio of deposits to GDP is low compared with that in other Asian countries, as is the ratio of loans to GDP (Mohan 2006). And the cost of bank intermediation remains higher than that in developing markets such as China and Thailand as well as developed ones such as Singapore and the United States (McKinsey & Company 2005). While the onus of change lies mainly with the banks, an enabling policy and regulatory framework will also be critical.

Equity Market Reforms

India's equity market is perhaps one of the most vibrant among emerging markets. While the country has 23 stock exchanges, trading is concentrated in the two largest, the National Stock Exchange and the Bombay Stock Exchange. The past decade has seen a series of reforms, innovation, growth in volumes, and greater sophistication in India's equity market. Market capitalization grew from less than 25 percent of GDP in 1991 to nearly 86.5 percent at the end of fiscal 2007. India's equity market remains much smaller than those of many advanced economies, such as the United States, the United Kingdom, Australia, and Japan. But it is significantly larger than those of many other emerging market economies, including Brazil and Mexico (RBI 2007d).

The primary equity market was very active in 2006–07, raising about Rs 914 billion in those two years (India, Ministry of Finance 2008). Resources mobilized through private placement accounted for about 61 percent of the total; most was raised by private sector (financial and nonfinancial) entities.

Table 3.2 Net Institutional Investments in Equity and Debt Securities, India, Fiscal 2002–07

(Rs billions)

Fiscal year	Foreign institutional investors		Mutual funds	
	Equity	Debt securities	Equity	Debt securities
2002	80.67	6.85	−37.96	109.59
2003	25.28	0.60	−20.67	126.04
2004	399.59	58.05	13.08	227.01
2005	441.23	17.59	4.48	189.87
2006	485.42	−70.65	143.06	368.01
2007	252.36	56.05	90.24	525.48

Source: RBI 2007a.

Institutional investors have played an increasingly important role in the overall financial market. Foreign institutional investors have been particularly active participants, especially in the equity market (table 3.2). The mutual fund industry, which has been growing rapidly, has also been an important investor base.

The reforms in the capital market were initiated in the aftermath of the external payment crisis in 1991. The focus initially was on the development of the equity market, and the Securities and Exchange Board of India (SEBI) was established in 1992 to protect the interests of the investing public, improve corporate governance in the corporate sector, and usher in improvements in the infrastructure of capital markets.

To improve the efficiency and governance of the stock markets, the National Stock Exchange was set up to provide competition to the Bombay Stock Exchange, which enjoyed a near monopoly at the national level. The National Stock Exchange has posted phenomenal growth since starting business in June 1994, thanks to its nationwide reach and use of technology. The exchange has as many as 1,200 corporations listed, trading terminals in more than 1,500 locations across the country, and a market share of more than 65 percent.

The establishment of National Securities Depository Limited in 1996 and Central Depository Services (India) Limited in 1999 has allowed paperless trading in the stock exchanges, facilitated instantaneous electronic transfer of securities, and eliminated the risks to investors arising from bad deliveries and delays in share transfer.

Recent Developments in the Debt Securities Market

India's domestic debt securities market can be broadly divided into two segments—the government debt securities market (encompassing the central government and the 28 state governments) and the corporate bond market (private corporate issuers and financial institutions). Government debt securities domi-

Table 3.3 Composition of Domestic Debt Securities Market, India, 2002–06

(US$ millions)

Issuer	2002	2003	2004	2005	2006	Share of total, 2006 (%)
Government	153,658	200,398	245,306	268,033	304,856	93.6
Financial institutions	242	840	1,406	7,280	15,509	4.8
Corporations	1,879	1,921	2,778	3,812	5,315	1.6
Total	155,779	203,159	249,490	279,125	325,680	100.0

Sources: BIS 2007; World Bank, World Development Indicators database.

nate, accounting for 94 percent of the total outstanding (table 3.3). Corporate debt securities account for only about 6 percent, a marginal share compared with that in other emerging markets such as Malaysia. The corporate sector has been funding itself mainly through bank borrowings at below-prime lending rates, private placement, equity, and other borrowings.

Government Borrowing Trends. The dominance of the government debt securities market—in outstanding issues, amount raised from the primary market, and trading volume—stems from the massive borrowing needs of the government. Before the launch of financial sector reforms the government financed its budget deficit primarily through captive use of banking resources, by setting a high statutory liquidity ratio for commercial banks. Interest rates on these borrowings were set below market levels to keep borrowing costs down. Only 17.9 percent of domestic government borrowings were at market-related rates.

With the financial sector reforms came a new policy, aimed at developing a liquid and efficient government debt securities market. Initiated in fiscal 1992 as part of structural reforms, the policy addressed (among other issues) the high fiscal deficit. The government progressively reduced the deficit, in 2002–06 alone lowering it from 9.6 percent of GDP to 6.4 percent. The government also allowed the interest rate to be determined by market forces, and by fiscal 2003 domestic market borrowing had increased to more than 70 percent of domestic government borrowing. By fiscal 2007 the share had risen to 76.5 percent (figure 3.1).

While direct market borrowing dominates the government's debt liability, its actual debt liability is much larger if central government debt issued to the Reserve Bank under the Market Stabilization Scheme is included. Issuance under the scheme increased substantially during 2004–07. The outstanding internal debt liability of the central government under government debt securities (including the market stabilization bonds) rose from Rs 13.9 trillion (39.0 percent of GDP) in fiscal 2006 to Rs 15.5 trillion in fiscal 2007 (37.7 percent of GDP).

Liabilities of the state governments have also increased steadily. The combined liability of the central and state governments (including external debt) rose from

Figure 3.1 Market Borrowing by Central Government, India, Selected Fiscal Years, 1991–07

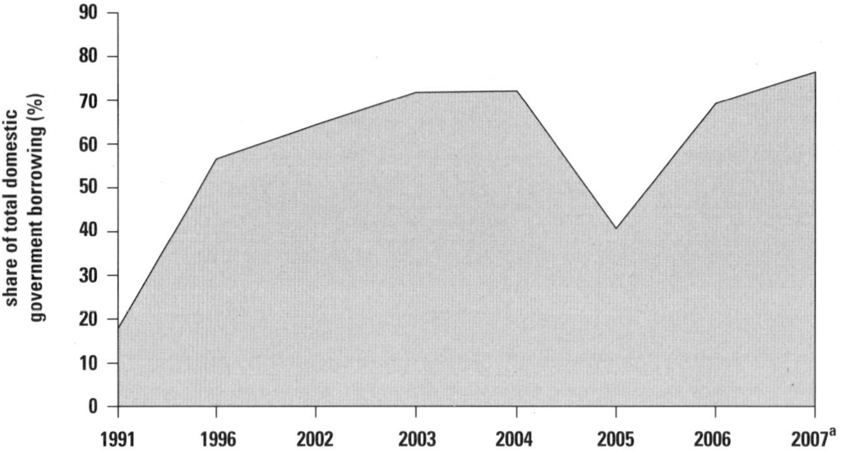

Source: RBI 2006, 2007a.
a. Budget estimate.

Table 3.4 Consolidated Liabilities of Central and State Governments, India, Selected Fiscal Years, 1991–07

Fiscal year	Outstanding liabilities (Rs billions)			Debt-GDP ratio (%)		
	Central	States	Combined	Central	States	Combined
1991	3,145.6	1,281.6	3,688.2	55.3	22.5	64.9
1996	6,062.3	2,508.9	7,282.1	51	21.1	61.3
2001	11,685.4	6,020.7	14,920.3	55.4	28.6	70.8
2002	13,664.1	7,005.2	17,428.1	59.9	30.7	76.4
2003	15,592.0	7,989.2	19,833.0	63.6	32.6	81.0
2004	17,366.8	9,244.2	22,530.0	62.9	33.5	81.6
2005	19,944.2	10,438.1	25,766.5	63.9	33.4	82.5
2006	22,601.0	11,638.0	28,756.0	63.4	32.6	80.5
2007	25,364.0	12,601.0	31,875.0	61.5	30.5	77.0

Source: RBI 2007a.
Note: Data are for the end of the fiscal year, March 31. Under combined liabilities, intergovernmental transactions are netted out.

Rs 28.75 trillion ($729 billion) in fiscal 2006 to Rs 32 trillion ($812 billion) at the end of fiscal 2007 (table 3.4). As a share of GDP, however, the liability declined—from 80.5 percent in fiscal 2006 to 77 percent in fiscal 2007. This change reflected both the improvement in the overall fiscal position and the country's robust economic growth.

Market Reforms. The government debt securities market is slowly adding all the ingredients of a well-functioning market and has improved considerably in the past decade. The Reserve Bank of India, which manages the government's debt and regulates government-issued paper, has gradually introduced reforms since 1991 aimed at increasing transparency, strengthening market intermediation, and reducing settlement risk.[1] The efforts have paid off in a large, deep, and liquid market. At the end of September 2007 outstanding government debt securities amounted to $396 billion.

The government debt securities market has also become sophisticated, with a sovereign benchmark yield curve extending to 30 years. This has enabled the Reserve Bank to conduct monetary policy more effectively and provides a basis for developing the corporate long-term bond market.

GOVERNMENT DEBT SECURITIES MARKET

The impressive growth of the government debt securities market can be traced to a calibrated approach to reforms in the legal framework and market infrastructure. Since 1991 the Reserve Bank has introduced auctions in the primary market to improve price discovery and transparency, introduced primary dealers to strengthen market intermediation, and broadened the array of debt instruments. It has also put into place trading, clearing, and settlement systems that have improved efficiency and reduced costs. Recent enactment of the Payment and Settlement Systems Bill, 2007 represents a major regulatory reform. Thus while further reforms are needed, much has already been achieved. (See annex 3.2 for a chronological summary of the reforms.)

Supply Side

The central and state governments issue debt securities in a range of maturities and for a variety of purposes.

Government Debt Issuance

The central government issues treasury bills through the Reserve Bank with maturities of 91, 182, or 364 days and dated securities with maturities of 2–30 years (table 3.5). Treasury bill auctions are volume driven, with the quantity announced before each auction, and are fully underwritten by the Reserve Bank and primary dealers. The government also issues a range of medium- and long-term securities: zero-coupon bonds, capital-indexed bonds, floating-rate bonds, bonds with call and put options, and "plain vanilla" bonds (the most popular and actively traded).

In addition, the central government has issued oil bonds to the three public sector oil marketing companies to fund the losses on their sales of petroleum products, passing the burden on to future budgets. These tradable securities have

Table 3.5 Participants and Products in Debt Securities Market, India

Issuers	Instruments	Maturity	Investors
Government debt securities market			
Central government	Dated securities	2–30 years	Reserve Bank of India, banks, insurance companies, provident funds, mutual funds, primary dealers
Central government	Treasury bills	91, 182, or 364 days	Reserve Bank of India, banks, insurance companies, provident funds, mutual funds, primary dealers
State governments	Dated securities	5–13 years	Banks, insurance companies, provident funds
Public sector units	Bonds, structured obligations	5–10 years	Banks, mutual funds, insurance companies, provident funds, corporations, individuals
Public sector units	Municipal bonds	1–7 years	Banks, corporations, individuals, trust fund associations, foreign institutional investors, nonresident Indians
Corporate bond market			
Corporations	Debentures	1–12 years	Banks, mutual funds, corporations, individuals
Corporations, primary dealers	Commercial paper	7 days–1 year	Banks, mutual funds, financial institutions, foreign institutional investors, corporations, individuals
Scheduled commercial banks, selected commercial banks	Certificates of deposit	7–10 days[a]	Banks, corporations, individuals, trust fund associations, foreign institutional investors, nonresident Indians
Scheduled banks	Bank bonds	1–10 years	Banks, corporations, individuals, trust fund associations, foreign institutional investors, nonresident Indians

Source: NSE 2006.

a. A certificate of deposit issued by a financial institution has a minimum maturity of one year and a maximum of three years.

fixed coupon rates and maturities of up to 17 years. The government has also issued bonds to the Food Corporation of India toward food subsidies. State governments have issued power bonds to central public sector power generators as a
one-time settlement of payments overdue from state electricity boards. These
bonds, with a maturity of up to 10 years, are not eligible toward the statutory liquidity requirements of banks but they may be traded.

State-owned companies began issuing bonds as subsidies were gradually with-
drawn. Known as public sector undertaking bonds (PSU bonds), these instruments are medium-term debt obligations, with maturities typically ranging from
3 to 10 years. Some issues are guaranteed by the central or state government. PSU
bonds generally pay a semiannual, fixed coupon with bullet redemption; varia-
tions include floating-rate bonds, step-up coupon bonds, and zero-coupon bonds.
Most are issued through private placement.

Sovereign Yield Curve

For most of the 1990s the maturity of debt securities issued by the central government ranged up to 10 years. The limited range led to potential redemption pressure and refinancing risk. This, as well as the need to develop the yield curve for
longer maturities, prompted efforts to lengthen the maturity of government bond
issues. The Reserve Bank, since 2002, has progressively increased the maturity to
30 years (figure 3.2). The weighted average maturity of bonds outstanding at the
end of fiscal 2006 was about 17 years (see annex 3.3). Thus the Reserve Bank has
succeeded in building a risk-free sovereign yield curve across the broad spectrum.
The yield curves are quoted daily in Bloomberg and by several news services in
India, online and in real time.

During fiscal 2006 yields in the government debt securities market hardened in
line with the general increase in international interest rates. Yields for longer-term
maturities increased less than those for shorter-term maturities, reflecting a flat-
tening yield curve and expectations of relatively stable inflation. Intrayear movements in yields were influenced by domestic liquidity conditions, inflationary expectations, volatility in crude oil prices, and movements in the yields for U.S.
government securities.

The yields on five-year AAA-rated corporate bonds increased during fiscal
2006 in line with the higher yields for government debt securities. In addition, the
yield spread for five-year AAA-rated bonds over the corresponding government
debt security has been increasing over the years, rising from 64 basis points in fiscal 2005 to 106 basis points in fiscal 2007 (RBI 2007a).

The yield on government securities with 5–6 years' remaining maturity changed
by 56 basis points from April 2005 to March 2006, while the yield on comparable
corporate bonds changed by 125 basis points. For government securities with 9–10
years' remaining maturity the yield movement was 45 basis points, while the corresponding change for corporate bonds was 74 basis points. And for government securities with more than 10 years' remaining maturity, the yield movement was just

Figure 3.2   Yield-to-Maturity Curve in Government Bond Market, India, November 13 and 14, 2007

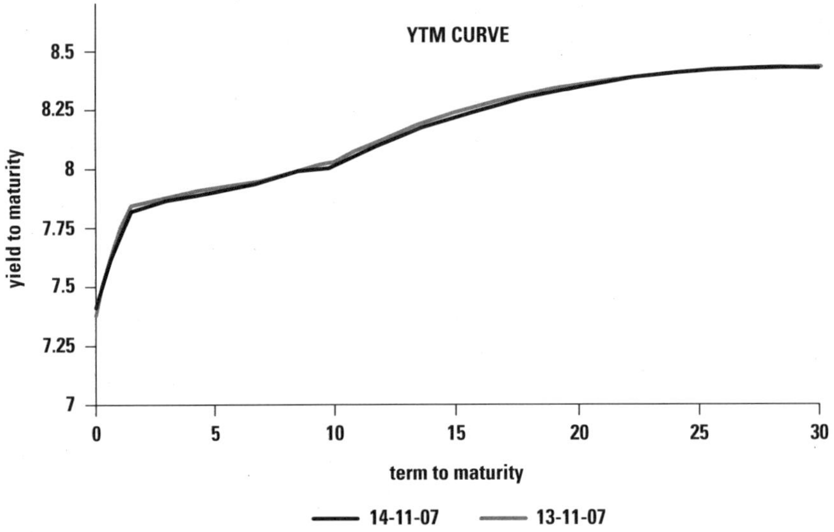

Source: Clearing Corporation of India Limited (CCIL).

10 basis points, while the corresponding change for corporate bonds was 42 basis points (NSE 2006). The yield spread did not remain constant, and since trading in corporate bonds with maturities longer than 5 years is sporadic, the spreads are merely indicative.

Demand Side

Domestic entities are the major investors in government securities. In December 2006 banks held 44 percent of central government debt securities, insurance companies 27 percent, pension and provident funds 6 percent, and primary dealers 6 percent. For banks and insurance companies most of the holdings are to meet statutory investment requirements.

Banks

As noted, banks buy sovereign bonds to meet statutory requirements, though they also buy them for trading purposes. The Banking Regulation Act, 1949 set the statutory liquidity ratio at 25 percent, meaning that scheduled banks are required to maintain at least 25 percent of their net demand and time liabilities in liquid assets such as cash, gold, and unencumbered government securities or other approved securities. (Some banks have faced lower statutory liquidity ratios, depending on their line of business and the size of their liabilities.) Recently the Banking

Table 3.6   Resource Mobilization by Mutual Funds, India, Fiscal 2006–07
(Rs billions)

Segment	2006		2007	
	Net mobilization[a]	Net assets[b]	Net mobilization	Net assets
Private sector mutual funds	429.77	1,815.15	790.38	2,620.79
Public sector mutual funds	98.02	503.48	149.47	642.13
Total	527.79	2,318.63	939.85	3,262.92

Source: RBI 2007a.
Note: Data are for the end of the fiscal year, March 31.
a. Net of redemptions.
b. Including UTI Mutual Fund.

Regulation Amendment Act, 2007 removed the minimum limit of 25 percent for the statutory liquidity ratio for scheduled banks, giving the central bank more flexibility in monetary management.

Mutual Funds

The rapid growth of mutual funds has expanded the investor base. The assets under management by mutual funds more than doubled between March 2005 and March 2007, from Rs 1.5 trillion to Rs 3.3 trillion (table 3.6). By the end of November 2007 the assets had grown to about Rs 5.5 trillion ($139 billion). About half these assets are invested in fixed-income securities, mainly money market instruments and government debt securities.

Pension Funds

The pension and provident fund industry holds assets of about Rs 1.4 trillion ($31 billion), much of which is invested in government debt securities. As new reforms take effect, these funds are expected to play an increasingly important role in the debt securities market.

Until recently the mandatory pension system consisted mainly of an essentially pay-as-you-go system for central and state government employees and employees' provident funds (and related insurance and annuity funds) for other formal sector employees. Altogether, these have about 21 million contributors and assets of more than 4 percent of GDP. By regulation, provident funds are required to invest a minimum of 40 percent of additional contributions each year in PSU bonds, 25 percent in government debt securities, and 15 percent in state government securities. They are allowed to invest no more than 10 percent in rated private sector debentures.

Reforms now being put into place by the government involve setting up a legal framework for defined-contribution pension schemes for new government employees and other contributors. A new pension regulator, the Pension Fund Regulatory and Development Authority, began operating in January 2004 to promote old-age income security. The authority is charged with establishing, developing, and regulating pension funds and protecting the interests of pension fund contributors. It will also establish guidelines for managing and investing pension fund assets. These are expected to allow pension funds the freedom to allocate resources to corporate bonds rather than investing their assets entirely in government securities and PSU bonds.

Retail Investors

The Indian government has taken steps to encourage retail participation in the government debt securities market. Starting in December 2001 small and medium-size investors were allowed to participate in primary auctions by submitting noncompetitive bids through their financial institution. Bids can range from a minimum of Rs 10,000 to a maximum of Rs 20 million. The government reserves up to 5 percent of the issuance for eligible noncompetitive bidders.

In addition, since January 2003 the government has allowed its debt securities to be traded on the stock exchanges, to enable small investors to participate in the government debt securities market. The minimum order size is Rs 1,000. Bond trading through the stock exchanges has failed to take off, however, because of the preference of Indian savers for bank deposits and money market mutual funds.

Foreign Institutional Investors

Foreign institutional investors are allowed to invest in a variety of debt instruments in the local market, subject to limits. Since 1997 SEBI has permitted registered foreign institutional investors to invest in Indian government debt securities under certain guidelines. More recently foreign institutional investors have also been permitted to invest in treasury bills and to hedge their currency exposure arising from investment in fixed-income instruments in the onshore market. In addition, at the end of March 2007 the limit on cumulative investment in all government debt securities by foreign institutional investors was raised from $2.6 billion to $3.2 billion.

Even so, the investment limit for foreign institutional investors remains small relative to the size of the domestic debt securities market and the level of foreign exchange reserves. Raising the limit could be expected to accelerate the deepening and broadening of the bond market.

Market Infrastructure

Through a series of reforms India has put into place all the infrastructure required for an efficient government debt securities market. An important milestone in developing the financial market infrastructure was the establishment of the Clearing Corporation of India Limited (CCIL) in 2002, with the active support of the Reserve Bank, to minimize settlement risks in the money, government securities, and foreign exchange markets. In addition, the Reserve Bank has put into place a screen-based trade reporting platform, an anonymous order-matching trading system, and, more recently, real-time gross settlement to minimize payment risk.

Primary Dealers

India has a well-functioning system of primary dealers that has played an important part in deepening and widening the government debt securities market. The system was introduced in 1995 with liquidity support and incentives for underwriting primary issues of government securities. Primary dealers are expected to provide two-way quotes in the secondary market and thereby help develop the retail market. The scale, scope, and regulation of the primary dealer network in India are generally consistent with best practices.

At one time India had 17 stand-alone primary dealers in operation; today that number has fallen to 8. Because of rising yields and the resulting heavy depreciation in their holdings, many primary dealers opted to merge with their parent bank. Nine banks now conduct primary dealer business through a department as a result of such changes, and an additional bank was authorized to undertake primary dealer business in April 2007 (RBI 2007f).

Primary dealers fall under the regulatory framework of the Reserve Bank. In 2003 they were brought under the oversight of the Board for Financial Supervision. This move recognized their substantial stake in the government debt securities market. It also recognized their highly leveraged portfolios funded with short-term funds that account for a significant position in the money market and thus pose systemic risk. The Reserve Bank conducts on-site inspections of each primary dealer as well as off-site supervision.

In view of their essential function as dealers in money market instruments and government debt securities, primary dealers enjoy certain regulatory advantages. These include liquidity support extended to stand-alone primary dealers. Half the liquidity support is divided equally among these primary dealers and the other half extended on the basis of their performance in the primary auctions and turnover in the secondary market. Primary dealers are also permitted to borrow and lend in the money market. And unlike banks, primary dealers are exempt from Reserve Bank regulations relating to asset classification, income recognition, nonperforming assets, and provisioning and exposure norms.

In response to the Fiscal Responsibility and Budget Management Act, 2003, which requires the Reserve Bank to withdraw from participation in the primary market for central government debt securities, the Reserve Bank revised the system for underwriting in primary auctions. The new program, launched in April 2006, entrusts the primary dealers with underwriting the entire issue: a requirement to meet an underwriting commitment replaced the earlier requirement of a bidding commitment and voluntary underwriting. Primary dealers have a minimum underwriting commitment (3 percent of the issue size in each auction) and can bid for additional commitment in an auction. The success of the auction related to the additional competitive underwriting determines their underwriting commission.

In fiscal 2007, when there were 33 primary auctions of dated government securities, the amount subscribed by investors fell short in only 3 of the auctions, leading to a need to allocate the undersubscription to primary dealers. Thus the twin policy measures of expanding the primary dealer system to include banks and revising the underwriting scheme have contributed to successful debt management.

To help ensure that the business model for primary dealers is financially viable, in July 2006 the Reserve Bank permitted stand-alone primary dealers to diversify their activities beyond their core business of dealing in government debt securities, subject to limits. Primary dealers may now divide their operations into core and noncore activities. Core activities involve dealing in government debt securities and other fixed-income securities. Noncore activities include investing and trading in equity and equity derivatives, investing in equity-oriented mutual funds, underwriting public issues of equity, and providing such services as professional clearing, portfolio management, issue management, private equity management, project appraisal, loan syndication, debt restructuring, and merger and acquisition advisory services.

Secondary Market Trading Platforms

The Reserve Bank provides an electronic platform for all eligible members (most of which are its regulated entities) to facilitate reporting and trading in government debt securities and money market instruments. The negotiated dealing system (NDS) in which all trades are reported, interfaces with CCIL for clearing and settlement of all transactions in government debt securities, including repurchase agreements (repos).

To further facilitate trading in government debt securities, in August 2005 the Reserve Bank introduced an electronic, anonymous, order-matching trading system, known as the NDS-OM (negotiated dealing system–order matching, developed and managed by CCIL). The system improves liquidity, increases transparency, and allows better price discovery. All trades on the system are automatically routed to CCIL for guaranteed settlement.

Early on, the NDS-OM supported trading in central government dated securities and state government securities, allowing T+1 (next day) settlement. It has since been extended to cover trading in treasury bills and the "when issued" market (in which market participants are allowed to buy and sell the security for delivery on the date of the auction, which aids price discovery before trading starts).

Before the advent of the anonymous trading platform, most secondary market trades in government debt securities were carried out in the over-the-counter (OTC) market through negotiation between the key market participants (primary dealers, banks, mutual funds, financial institutions). Most market participants have now switched over to the NDS-OM. This system now accounts for about 82 percent of trades, while those conducted with the help of stock exchange brokers have dropped below 12 percent. The rest are direct bilateral deals between participants.

Secondary market trades in government debt securities that are negotiated only through a National Stock Exchange broker are reported to the electronic platform of the exchange's Wholesale Debt Market. The Wholesale Debt Market, which the National Stock Exchange has been operating since June 1994, is a fully automated, screen-based reporting platform for high-value transactions in the debt securities market. Its participants include banks, institutions, corporations, and other intermediaries. It is a stand-alone reporting system that is not connected to any settlement system, and market participants must settle deals between themselves. However, all deals in government debt securities, whether transacted directly or through brokers, are settled through CCIL.

Because the negotiated dealing system is restricted to entities that hold current accounts and securities with the Reserve Bank (banks, primary dealers, financial institutions, and so on), market participants such as brokers and provident funds, which play an active role in the Wholesale Debt Market, are not yet part of this system. The result is fragmentation and inefficient price discovery.

Secondary Market Liquidity

Secondary market trading in dated government securities is very active in maturities up to 15 years, though 30-year securities also are regularly traded. The average daily outright trading volume for all government securities fell from about Rs 39 billion in fiscal 2005 to Rs 32 billion in fiscal 2006, then rose to Rs 42 billion in fiscal 2007 (table 3.7). State government bonds are not traded in significant volumes. Primary dealers, banks, and insurance companies are the main participants

Table 3.7 Liquidity in Government Debt Securities Market, India, Fiscal 2003–08

(Rs billions except where otherwise specified)

Fiscal year	Outright trades settled		Market capitalization	Turnover ratio (%)[a]
	Annual volume	Daily average		
2003	10,761.5	36.23	6,580	163.5
2004	15,751.3	53.58	9,593	164.2
2005	11,342.2	38.84	10,061	112.7
2006	8,647.5	32.15	10,597	81.6
2007	10,215.4	41.87	11,893	85.9
2008[b]	8,382.9	57.81	15,269	54.9

Source: CCIL, *Rakshitra,* various issues.
Note: Data are for both central and state government debt securities.
a. Calculated as the ratio of volume to market capitalization.
b. Data through September 2007.

in the secondary market and account for most of the trading in the government debt securities market.

At the end of September 2007 there were 129 central government debt securities with an outstanding amount of Rs 12,731 billion along with 10 floating-rate bonds (Rs 446 billion) and treasury bills (Rs 1,474 billion). Of these, 65 securities with outstanding issues of Rs 100 billion or more accounted for a major share of the total amount outstanding.

The bid-ask spreads of the liquid securities are comparable to those of the most liquid markets in the world. The spreads declined substantially after introduction of the anonymous order-matching system.

Short Sale in Government Debt Securities

The volume of trading in government debt securities declined notably in fiscal 2006 because of rising interest rates: banks preferred to hold securities rather than trade them because of the lack of derivative instruments to manage interest rate risk. In response, the Reserve Bank took several measures aimed at addressing such risk. Among these measures was first allowing short sales (sales of securities not owned by the seller), then extending the duration of short sales from one day to five.

Without instruments that allow players to take a view on interest rates and hedge their exposures, the markets are generally active and liquid when the rates fall but tend to become illiquid when the rates rise. Low volumes make markets shallow and susceptible to price manipulations. Short sales enable market participants to manage their interest rate risk more efficiently and to impart liquidity to the markets even when interest rates are rising.

In February 2006 the Reserve Bank permitted banks and primary dealers to engage in intraday short selling: undertaking the outright sale of dated government securities that they do not own as long as the securities are covered by outright purchase from the secondary market within the same trading day. In January 2007 the Reserve Bank relaxed this rule, extending the short sales period for these entities from intraday to five days subject to certain conditions. It also allowed the delivery of borrowed securities from repo transactions. If short selling is to help deepen the market, however, a securities borrowing and lending program may also have to be allowed.

Clearing and Settlement

The Reserve Bank acts as the depository and clearinghouse for government debt securities and treasury bills through its subsidiary general ledger system, where banks and institutions hold bond ledgers and current accounts with the Reserve Bank. Clearing and settlement are done through a delivery-versus-payment system.

CCIL provides clearing and settlement for all government bond transactions, both outright and repo. CCIL is owned by banks, primary dealers, and other financial institutions that are also its main users.

Acting as a central counterparty, CCIL provides guaranteed settlement, removing all risks associated with settlement failures arising out of nonperformance or failure of any of the parties to the settlement. It has in place risk management systems to limit settlement risk and operates a settlement guarantee fund backed by lines of credit from commercial banks to take care of liquidity needs. Its risk management practices adhere to internationally accepted standards.

In May 2005 the settlement system for transactions in government debt securities was standardized to the T+1 cycle to provide participants with more processing time and to allow better management of funds, securities, and risk. The security settlement by CCIL is also linked to the real-time gross settlement system, which provides for interbank and customer-based interbank funds transfer. By June 2006 real-time gross settlement was being provided by 96 banks at almost 22,000 branches.

All transactions in government debt securities that are concluded or reported on the negotiated dealing system necessarily have to be settled through CCIL. CCIL also provides a dealing platform for transactions in its own money market instrument, the collateralized borrowing and lending obligation, and in foreign exchange (FX-CLEAR) through its wholly owned subsidiary Clearcorp Dealing Systems (box 3.1). And as noted, it manages the NDS-OM as well as NDS-CALL (an electronic order-matching system for call money transactions) owned and operated by the Reserve Bank.

Box 3.1 A New Instrument for India's Money Market

A major development in India's government debt securities market was the introduction in 2003 of a new money market instrument by the Clearing Corporation of India Limited (CCIL). Approved by the Reserve Bank, the collateralized borrowing and lending obligation (CBLO) is dealt through an anonymous order-matching system for lending and borrowing.

The CBLO is a variant of the held-in-custody and triparty repurchase agreement (repo); the approved government debt securities used for borrowing are held with CCIL, which acts as a central counterparty and guarantees the settlement of all CBLO transactions. The instrument in the electronic form can be traded on the trading platform provided by CCIL and thus provides an exit, not normally available in ordinary repo trades.

Initially the CBLO market was not liquid. Market participants needed time to develop an understanding of the product. But since March 2005 the CBLO has overtaken competing products such as call and repo, establishing itself as the leading money market product. Today the CBLO is used not only by banks and financial institutions but also by large corporations, which can borrow against both liquid and illiquid bonds. These nonbanks are connected to the CBLO system by the Internet and settle their deals through approved settlement banks.

The trading volume for the CBLO often exceeds the combined volume for normal repo and call money transactions. The average daily volume for the CBLO rose from Rs 2.6 billion in fiscal 2004 to Rs 227.2 billion on September 28, 2007. Rates on the CBLO, as a leading product in the market, provide direction for other short-term rates in the market.

Source: Data from CCIL 2007.

Dissemination of Market Information

India has a well-developed system for disseminating market information. In the primary market the Reserve Bank has produced an issuance calendar for dated securities since 2002, enabling institutional and retail investors to better plan their investments and improving the efficiency of the government debt securities market. To improve the flow of information to the market, the Reserve Bank announces results soon after each auction. And all transactions settled through subsidiary general ledger accounts are announced on the same day through press releases on the Reserve Bank's Web site.

To ensure transparency in debt management operations and secondary market activity, statistical information on the primary and secondary market for government debt securities is disseminated in real time by news agencies, CCIL, and the stock exchanges. Information on debt securities and the money market is distributed through press releases or the Reserve Bank's publications (such as the monthly *RBI Bulletin* and the *Weekly Statistical Supplement*). To provide wider access to the data and transparency in the market, the trade data and other data captured by the negotiated dealing system have been disseminated to the general public through the Reserve Bank's Web site since October 2002. The data on transactions in government debt securities settled daily at the Public Debt Office in Mumbai are also posted on the Web site.

With NDS-OM and NDS-CALL in operation, real-time trading information is now available to market participants on their trading terminals. Trading information is also disseminated by financial data providers such as Reuters and Bloomberg, which obtain their data from CCIL.

Changes in the Legal Framework

Recent and pending changes in the legal framework have potential implications for India's debt securities market. The Fiscal Responsibility and Budget Management Act, 2003, enacted by the government, is expected to have a positive impact on the development of the corporate bond market. The government's financing requirements are large, at 90 percent of GDP, and its borrowings through bond issuance can be seen as crowding out the private debt securities market. The Fiscal Responsibility and Budget Management Act calls on the central government to reduce the gross fiscal deficit by at least 0.3 percent of GDP each fiscal year, bringing it down to 3 percent of GDP in 2008 (the target year has since shifted to 2009). As noted, the act also requires the Reserve Bank to withdraw from participation in the primary market for central government securities.

Enactment of this law is considered to be one of the most important changes in the Indian bond market. It imposes fiscal discipline on the central government and excludes automatic financing by the central bank. And it calls for significant changes in the monetary, debt management, and regulatory policies of the Reserve Bank.

The Government Securities Act, 2006 is intended to replace the Public Debt Act, 1944. Although passed in August 2006, the act has yet to come into force, pending notification of rules under it. The act is aimed at consolidating and amending the law relating to the issuance and management of government debt securities by the Reserve Bank. It includes the provisions of the Public Debt Act relating to issuance of new loans, payment of semiannual interest, retirement of rupee loans, and all matters pertaining to debt certificates and registration of debt holdings. In addition, the new act provides flexibility for holding government securities in depositories while at the same time specifically excluding government securities from the purview of the Depositories Act, 1996.

The act allows lien marking and pledging of securities for raising loans against government securities, recognizes electronic record keeping, enlarges the dematerialization facility through the bond ledger account, and liberalizes norms relating to nomination and legal representation. The act also gives the Reserve Bank substantive powers to design and introduce an instrument of transfer suited to the computer environment, issue duplicate securities, issue new securities on conversion, consolidate government securities with similar ones, subdivide the securities, and renew, strip (separately for interest and principal), or reconstitute the securities.

The Payment and Settlement Systems Bill, 2007, passed by both houses of parliament in December 2007, seeks to designate the Reserve Bank as the authority to authorize, regulate, and supervise all payment and settlement systems. It also provides for settlement and netting to be final and irrevocable at the determination of money, securities, or foreign exchange payable by participants.

CORPORATE BOND MARKET

Developing a corporate bond market in India has become increasingly important. Indian corporations no longer have access to long-term funding from development finance institutions, the traditional (mostly government-owned) providers of long-term project loans. And banks are more inclined toward retail lending, where the risks are much lower. Moreover, banks' willingness to make long-term loans is also limited by the asset-liability mismatch on their balance sheets. The likelihood of a large fiscal deficit in the foreseeable future leaves banks little flexibility to provide long-term funding for infrastructure, industry, and agriculture.

Thus companies wanting to finance expensive investments through long-term borrowings in local currency face a dearth of adequate institutional sources. The absence of a deep and liquid corporate bond market at the longer end of the maturity spectrum causes corporations to turn to rolling shorter-maturity borrowings, which tend to be more expensive, or to foreign borrowings, which pose exchange rate risks. Developing an active local corporate bond market would allow firms to issue debt securities that better match the timing and currency of their cash flows, reducing their costs and vulnerabilities associated with balance sheet mismatches and exchange rate risks.

Moreover, corporate bond markets are a principal vehicle for corporations to raise long-term financing for infrastructure to support economic growth. The growing need for investment in infrastructure and the huge financing gap that already exists imply that private funding will have to play a significant role. As infrastructure policy and regulatory frameworks emerge and reforms advance, a better-developed financial system, particularly a long-term domestic bond market, can accelerate access to finance by infrastructure projects. If the financial system fails to develop rapidly enough, it will be unable to respond quickly to changing financial requirements, especially for long-term financing, and it is likely to slow reform in infrastructure and economic growth overall.

The corporate bond market has been much more difficult to develop than the equity or government debt securities market in all countries, developed or developing. Building up adequate liquidity for corporate bonds is generally difficult, since there is much greater heterogeneity in corporate debt issues. But there are East Asian countries, such as Malaysia and the Republic of Korea, that have been very successful, and their experience is worth reviewing.

India already has in place or is implementing some of the elements of an enabling environment for a corporate bond market. One example is the relatively liquid benchmark yield curve of up to 30 years for government debt securities. Ongoing efforts to improve the liquidity of the repurchase market are also important for the corporate bond market. And while local securities markets can provide an alternative to the banking sector, especially during banking crises, a sound and well-regulated banking system can be a necessary complement to the development of local bond markets.

The issues relating to corporate bonds in India have been studied in great depth by the World Bank (2006a). There are issues related to supply, demand, and market infrastructure. Many of the factors impeding the growth of the corporate bond market have also been brought out in the report of the High Level Expert Committee on Corporate Debt and Securitization headed by Dr. R. H. Patil (Patil Committee 2005). The Indian government has accepted the findings of the committee and agreed to implement the recommendations in its report (see annex 3.4 for a summary of the suggested reforms).

Supply Side

Raising debt through a public issuance in India entails substantial costs, both those associated with regulatory compliance and direct issuance costs. These high costs have hampered the development of the corporate bond market by in effect discouraging the supply of bonds. Smaller corporations in particular are likely to opt for bank loans, which tend to be cheaper because of the high liquidity in the banking system.

Table 3.8   Costs of Bond Issuance through Private Placement, India, 2006
(Rs except where otherwise specified)

Item	One-time cost	Annual cost
Rating	1,000,000	100,000
Listing (National Stock Exchange)	7,500	50,000
Trustees	50,000	50,000
Registrar and share transfer agent	25,000	25,000
Arranger fees	2,500,000	n.a.
Stamp duty on secured debentures (assuming mortgage in Mumbai)[a]	1,000,000	n.a.
Total cost	4,582,500	225,000
Total cost as share of issue (%)	0.46	0.02

Source: World Bank staff estimates based on interviews with investment bankers.
Note: Assumes an issue size of Rs 1 billion. Costs are indicative. All costs other than the stamp duty are subject to negotiation.
a. For unsecured debentures the stamp duty would be 0.375 percent of the amount issued. The stamp duty also varies depending on the state in which the mortgage is created.
n.a. = Not applicable.

For corporations issuing debt, the choice has often been the easier route of private placement of bonds. Private placement involves less stringent regulatory requirements than public issuance. Moreover, private debt placements can be tailored to the issuer's needs. For example, many of the privately placed bonds include put options and are equity linked.

Raising funds through private placement is also much cheaper because the issuer can avoid the costs related to filing a prospectus as well as such expenses as legal, accounting, and underwriting fees. Consider the costs of a hypothetical private placement (table 3.8). In India all debt issues for Rs 1 billion or more must be rated, and smaller issues must be rated if the securities are to be placed with institutional investors. The cost of the rating is roughly 0.1 percent of the size of the issue. The stamp duty on the issuance of debt securities varies depending on the type of investor and the state in which the charge for the mortgage is created.

For a frequent issuer the total cost for an issue of Rs 1 billion through private placement is a little less than 0.5 percent, far less than the estimated 3–4 percent of issue size for public issuance. Moreover, private placement is a much speedier process than public issuance.

The strong preference of the Indian corporate sector for private placement of debt is clear. In fiscal 2007 there were 1,677 privately placed debt issues, involving Rs 1,455 billion, while there were only 3 publicly placed debt issues, amounting to Rs 8.5 billion (table 3.9). In addition, there has been a surge in euro issues by Indian companies. In fiscal 2007 there were 40 such issues, amounting to Rs 170.1 billion.

SEBI is simplifying debt issuance with a view to reducing costs and enhancing transparency. The changes center on introducing an integrated disclosure regime

Table 3.9   Resources Mobilized through Public and Private Placement, India, Fiscal 2005–07

	2005		2006		2007	
Type of issuance and issuer	Issues	Amount (Rs billions)	Issues	Amount (Rs billions)	Issues	Amount (Rs billions)
Public placement						
Private sector						
Financial	12	57.1	11	77.46	9	24.20
Nonfinancial	42	77.7	120	134.08	109	291.80
Total	54	134.8	131	211.54	118	316.00
Public sector						
Public sector undertakings						
Government companies	1	26.8	1	3.7	0	0
Banks and financial institutions	4	57.3	6	54.1	1	7.82
Total	5	84.1	7	57.9	1	7.82
All public placements						
Equity	54	180.2	136	267.0	116	315.35
Debt	5	38.7	2	2.5	3	8.47
Total	59	218.9	138	269.4	119	323.82
Private placement						
Private sector						
Financial	255	209.7	375	264.63	649	513.21
Nonfinancial	462	148.2	571	147.27	890	330.66
Total	717	357.9	946	411.90	1539	843.87
Public sector						
Financial	124	255.3	137	391.65	108	490.26
Nonfinancial	69	220.8	32	161.19	31	121.58
Total	193	476.1	169	552.84	139	611.84
All private placements						
Equity	—	—	1	1.50	1	0.57
Debt	—	—	1,114	963.23	1,677	1,455.14
Total	910	834.1	1,115	964.73	1,678	1,455.71
Euro issues[a]	15	33.5	48	113.52	40	170.05

Sources: RBI 2006, 2007a.
a. American depository receipts and global depository receipts.
— = Not available.

with the help of an electronic platform that would provide up-to-date information on each listed company. This system would enable listed entities to launch a debt issuance by providing only the additional information required for the transaction. In addition, the disclosure requirements for listing will be substantially trimmed. The changes should greatly reduce the time required and the difficulties faced in accessing the capital market for debt.

Demand Side

Lack of sufficiently developed long-term investors is a major impediment to developing the corporate bond market in India. Institutional investors have a growing volume of assets under management. But in the debt securities market they mainly hold "safe" paper, such as government securities, government-guaranteed paper, and highly rated corporate paper.

Investment Restrictions on Institutional Investors

Because major institutional investors confine their investment in corporate bonds to top-rated ones, most of the debt paper issued in recent years has been in the AA rating class and above (table 3.10). For the corporate bond market to grow in size and to become deep and liquid, greater participation by a wider range of investors willing to explore the risk-reward matrix is needed. That will require addressing regulatory restrictions that get in the way of active participation by banks and other institutional investors.

Banks, insurance companies, and pension and provident funds are all constrained by regulatory and investment guidelines requiring that they invest a large share of their funds in government debt securities. They are allowed little flexibility to invest in nongovernmental, private sector corporations, particularly lower-rated ones. (By contrast, in more mature markets, pension funds and insurance

Table 3.10 Outstanding Issues of Corporate Bonds, India, August 25, 2005

Rating class	Number of issues	Issue size (Rs billions)	Market capitalization Rs billions	Market capitalization Market share (%)
AAA/MAAA	955	926.09	938.72	69.68
AA+/LAA+/MAA+	320	196.05	198.21	14.71
AA/LAA/MAA	175	132.48	136.92	10.16
AA–/LA–	31	12.72	13.22	0.98
A+/LA+	16	15.45	15.59	1.16
A/LA/MA	16	15.12	15.29	1.13
A–	12	10.63	10.65	0.79
BBB+	11	8.33	8.77	0.65
BBB/LBBB	8	7.22	7.25	0.54
B	6	2.57	2.57	0.19
Total	1,550	1,326.66	1,347.19	100.00
No rating available	82	9,906	9,916	

Sources: Patil Committee 2005; National Stock Exchange (Wholesale Debt Market).

companies have greater flexibility in managing their portfolios and do not face explicit ceilings on the debt securities in which they can invest.) In addition, mutual funds are unwilling to hold lower-rated, relatively illiquid bonds because they need to invest in instruments that can be redeemed at any time.

Foreign institutional investors participating in the Indian market have the risk appetite to invest in bonds across the credit spectrum. They also find this investment approach attractive because of the expected appreciation of the currency. But regulatory caps on their debt investments in India prevent them from holding larger portfolios.

Accounting and Investment Rules for Banks

While Indian banks stand ready to make loans to corporations, they keep away from active participation in the corporate bond market. This is in part because of current accounting norms and in part because of regulatory requirements relating to corporate bond investments. Because banks are the largest investors in corporate bonds in India, it is useful to examine the obstacles they face in increasing these investments.

When bonds (government and corporate) form a significant part of banks' balance sheets, as they do in India, the question of their valuation becomes important. As financial systems have become largely market based, regulators increasingly have required that bonds be marked to market value, making their apparent worth more volatile. In India a bond may be marked to market if considered part of a trading portfolio but valued at cost if held as a long-term investment (and many banks often hold bonds to maturity).[2] Corporate bonds must be marked to market, but government debt securities receive preferential treatment: while banks face a 25 percent limit on the share of investments that can be allocated to the held-to-maturity category, they can exceed that limit as long as the excess consists only of securities eligible toward the statutory liquidity requirements—largely government debt securities.

Corporate bonds are also at a disadvantage relative to loans made to corporations (table 3.11). Banks are required to adopt an internal rating system before investing in bonds issued through private placement, a system that involves time-consuming procedures and many approvals and technicalities. Financing corporations through loans entails less stringent procedures and capital requirements. Moreover, while a bank has full control in setting the terms of a loan to a corporation, it has less control over the terms of a bond, which is a more standard commodity.

Also skewing the incentives in favor of loans are restrictions relating to the credit quality of the corporation being financed. Banks may invest only in bonds of investment-grade quality, while they can (and regularly do) make loans to corporations of varying credit quality. In addition, recent guidelines issued by the Reserve Bank restrict banks' investment in unlisted securities not eligible toward the statutory liquidity requirements to 10 percent; the guidelines also require a minimum investment-grade rating. These restrictions prevent banks from investing in bonds of lower-rated corporations (such as, typically, infrastructure companies).

Table 3.11   Disparities in Treatment of Bonds and Loans in Bank Regulations, India

Regulation	Bonds	Loans
Minimum rating criteria	External credit rating required. Minimum investment grade.	None.
Limits on holdings	Cannot invest in unrated securities. Limit on holdings of unlisted securities (10 percent of portfolio).	None.
Accounting treatment	Marked to market if in held-for-trading and available-for-sale category, but not if in held-to-maturity (HTM) category. But banks are prohibited from adding fresh investments in corporate bonds to the HTM category.	Accrual basis (similar to HTM category for corporate bonds).
Loan loss provisioning	Where interest or principal is 90 days overdue, classified as a nonperforming investment. Provisioning is similar to that for nonperforming assets. This is in addition to marked-to-market loss based on market rates.	Detailed norms for recognition of asset as nonperforming. Provisioning guidelines based on the asset category (substandard, doubtful, loss).
Capital requirement	Capital for market risk on investments based on the Reserve Bank's prescribed methodology. In addition, capital is to be provided for on a risk-weighted-assets basis.	Capital provision on risk-weighted assets.

Source: Compiled by the authors.

These restrictions also apply to loans to state governments and state-level enterprises. Until recently all state government bonds were issued as a basket with a sovereign credit rating. But state-level enterprises that had the same credit quality as the corresponding state government had bonds that reflected the state government's "actual" rating. If this rating was not investment grade, a bank could not invest in the bonds. This led to situations in which a bank held the bonds of a state government but not those of the same state government's enterprises.

Market Infrastructure

Among the main factors in the spectacular development of the equity market in India have been the advances in market infrastructure, taking the form of an automated nationwide trading facility and depository settlement. These developments have yet to take place in the corporate bond market. Risk transfer markets also remain at an early stage of development.

Trading, Clearing, and Settlement Practices

Trading, clearing, and settlement practices in the corporate bond market are far less developed than in the government debt securities market. Trades are carried out over the counter and are reported to the exchange if a broker is involved. There is almost no trading of corporate bonds on the electronic exchange.

In 2007, to improve transparency and the availability of information on corporate bonds traded by any investor, whether through a broker or not, regulators called for the development of a reporting platform for corporate bond trading. The two stock exchanges and an industry body, the Fixed Income Money Market and Derivatives Association of India (FIMMDA), have since put trade reporting platforms into operation. While all the trades in corporate bonds on an exchange are captured by that exchange's reporting platform, OTC transactions can be reported on any of these platforms. Aggregated trade information is disseminated by FIMMDA on its Web site. In addition, the exchanges started order-driven trading platforms in July 2007. Nevertheless, trading continues to be largely over the counter (Reddy 2007).

The secondary market infrastructure needs to be thought through at a more conceptual level, particularly in the light of the experience of mature markets in the euro area and the United States. The feasibility of setting up an interdealer electronic brokerage platform needs to be examined. The present framework for the secondary debt securities market is essentially an equity framework that emphasizes the need for an exchange trading environment. But the debt securities market, because of the illiquidity of corporate bonds, requires the active participation of dealers not only to provide liquidity but also to act as the main source of distribution. That requires a more decentralized infrastructure, with OTC transactions making up an important part of the secondary market activity. The undefined recognition of OTC transactions in the present regulatory framework for debt securities, however, makes it difficult for such a dealer structure to develop. This issue needs to be addressed to develop a market infrastructure for the corporate debt securities market that will be acceptable to the majority of the participants in this market—institutional investors.

Constraints on Secondary Market Activity

The secondary market for corporate bonds is hampered both by the lack of incentives for trading and by the lack of an enabling environment.

Credit Derivatives. India has no credit derivatives market. The central bank is considering permitting the introduction of credit derivatives, however, and has begun consultations with market participants on this issue. Credit derivatives would allow investors to hedge credit risk and interest rate risk and thus help to expand the pool of institutional investors that could invest in corporate bonds.

Database. The lack of comprehensive data relating to the debt on issue and the outstanding stock of debt for corporate issuers is a serious handicap in the Indian market. Data on public bond issues are available. But as noted, most corporate debt issues in recent years have been in the private placement market, which until recently had little oversight and few reporting requirements for issuers and arrangers.

Now that the reporting of debt on issue by listed companies has been somewhat streamlined, the reporting is expected to gradually improve.

Even so, data on outstanding debt are still difficult to compile. There is no comprehensive repository of information to track a corporate bond through its entire life cycle—from issuance until redemption. Data on bond issues, size, coupon, latest credit rating, underlying corporate performance, secondary trading experience, and default histories of companies are sparse and usually are not available from one source. (This is not uncommon, however; the corporate bond market worldwide has historically suffered from limited disclosure and lack of credit rating information.) The lack of sufficient, timely, and reliable information on bonds has muddied the corporate bond market and created barriers to active trading and pricing. The trade reporting platforms might address some of these gaps, though it is still too early to evaluate how effective they will be in improving information on corporate bonds.

Taxation. The tax treatment of different debt securities varies, even for those issued by the same corporation. That creates financial distortions and makes it difficult for investors to price different instruments. An added complication for investors is the withholding tax (tax deduction at source).

Withholding on corporate bonds is deducted on accrued interest at the end of the fiscal year. A withholding tax certificate is issued to the registered owner at the end of the fiscal year with interest payment made on the interest payment date, to the registered holder, after deducting the withholding tax due. When multiple trades take place in a corporate bond, physical exchange of cash needs to occur to account for the withholding tax. Investors subject to withholding find it difficult to sell the bond to investors not subject to the tax.

In 2000, in an effort to encourage secondary trading of government securities, a similar withholding tax was abolished. To promote a deeper and more liquid bond market in India, interest payments on corporate bonds and securitized assets similarly need to be exempt from the withholding tax (Patil Committee 2005).

Securitization

The securitization market in India is still at an early stage of development, with all transactions being carried out through private placement. Asset-backed securities (backed by such assets as cars, commercial vehicles, construction equipment, two-wheelers, and personal loans) and mortgaged-backed securities are popular, however, and the portfolio of such securities was estimated at about $6.3 billion in fiscal 2005 (Patil Committee 2005).

The Patil Committee report (2005) includes recommendations for developing the securitized bond market that center mainly on taxation of special-purpose vehicles, stamp duties on the issuance of securitized instruments, and regulations limiting the scope for securitized debt.

Figure 3.3 Securitization Transactions, India, Fiscal 2003–07

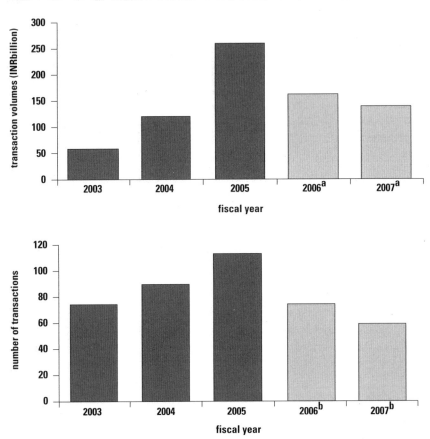

Source: Dalla 2007.
a. Estimated.
b. Expected.

Development of the Market. Securitization initiatives started in India in 1991 but picked up only after the enactment of the Securitization Act in 2002. Most issues have been AAA-rated notes because of the limited investor base and the regulatory restrictions relating to below-investment-grade debt instruments. The secondary market for securitized paper is almost nonexistent. Most investors in securitized paper plan to hold it to maturity.

The volume and number of securitized transactions grew rapidly in fiscal 2002–05 because of the rapid growth in the Indian economy and in lending for automobiles, motorcycles, housing, and other consumer goods (figure 3.3). In fiscal 2005 transactions in asset-backed securities accounted for almost two-thirds of the total volume of about $5 billion. Auto loan transactions were the most popular category. The short tenor of these loans, and of the associated securitized paper, is popular with Indian investors, who are interested in short- and medium-term instruments. The market in residential mortgage-backed securities is growing slowly. The longer tenors required in this market and the attendant interest rate risk have been constricting growth in the segment.

The issuer base is concentrated. Among the new private sector banks, non-banking finance companies, and housing finance companies that have originated structured finance transactions, the top five account for almost 80 percent of the issue volume. The investor base is also small, limited to banks and a few mutual funds.

In the light of differing market practices and concerns relating to accounting, valuation, and capital adequacy treatment, the Reserve Bank issued guidelines on securitization of standard assets in February 2006. The guidelines clarify some ambiguities in the Securitization Act and impose more stringent requirements for intermediaries on capital and profit recognition. Growth in the market stopped temporarily as market participants realigned their financial statements to comply with the guidelines. The new guidelines also encourage third parties to participate in transactions. Third-party enhancement providers now receive preferential capital treatment over originators providing the same service.

Impediments to Growth. Further development of securitization in India faces several impediments, including the stamp duty, the investor base, and foreclosure laws. The stamp duty imposed at national and state levels increases the cost of securitization. The stamp duty ranges from 0.1 percent to 8 percent, varying across states and by assets. In several states the process of transferring receivables from an originator to a special-purpose vehicle involves a stamp duty that can make securitization commercially unviable. Depending on the transaction structure, a stamp duty may also be levied on the issue of securitized instruments to investors by the special-purpose vehicle. In addition, many states do not distinguish between the conveyance of real estate and that of receivables and levy the same rate of stamp duty on both.

The institutional investor base in India, though growing fast, remains relatively small and, as noted, faces regulatory restrictions prohibiting investment in below-investment-grade instruments. Since securitized instruments are not traded in the secondary market, they also involve a valuation issue. A two-pronged approach of educating investors and making these instruments more liquid and attractive would increase the investor base over time. Foreign institutional investors are not yet permitted to invest in securitized debt instruments because they are not listed on the stock exchange. But the Securities Contracts (Regulation) Amendment Act, 2007, enacted in May 2007, provides a legal framework to allow listing and trading of securitized debt instruments, including mortgage-backed debt. Draft regulations have been prepared for public comment.

Despite the rapid growth in housing lending during fiscal 2002–07, mortgage-backed securities have grown slowly. The reasons for this include the foreclosure norms and recovery against mortgages. Enforcement of mortgages is difficult because of the litigation process. This problem has been partially addressed under the Securitization and Reconstruction of Financial Assets and Enforcement of Security Interest Act, 2002, which provides for sale of property without the intervention of the court.

Future Prospects. Securitization can play an important part in financing infrastructure projects in India, where the needs are enormous. Developing urban infrastructure and improving basic services as part of the National Urban Renewal Mission in 60 large cities was expected to cost more than Rs 1 trillion during fiscal 2000–07. The National Highways Development Program requires an estimated investment of about Rs 1.9 trillion through the end of 2012. The development of ports and modernization of airports also will require substantial investments. Securitization could also play a part in the financing or refinancing of existing infrastructure project debt. And receivables from rail, utilities, airports, toll roads, telecommunications, and the like have the potential to be securitized in the future.

Financial Derivatives

India's market for equity derivatives is among the most active in the world. The Bombay and National Stock Exchanges both began trading stock index futures in 2000. Since then the market has expanded to include single-stock futures, stock index options, and single-stock options. Derivatives for debt instruments have developed much more slowly, and this market remains at an early stage of development.

Exchange-traded derivatives for interest rates were introduced by the National Stock Exchange in 2003 but failed to take off, largely because of a flawed contract design. Another reason cited is the Reserve Bank's not allowing banks to take a trading position in this market. Interest rate derivatives are traded primarily over the counter. While any domestic money or debt market rate may be used as a benchmark rate, the Mumbai interbank offered rate and Mumbai interbank forward offered rate are those widely used.

While both interest rate swaps and forward rate agreements are available for managing interest rate risks, interest rate swaps are by far the more preferred. Data gathered from the balance sheets of banks show growth of more than 30 percent in this market between 2005 and 2006, with about Rs 31.85 trillion outstanding at the end of March 2007.

In the absence of an exchange-traded futures market, the trading is concentrated in the interest rate swap market. The overnight interest swap market is about Rs 120 billion a day. According to a directive of the Reserve Bank, all swap deals by entities that it regulates must be reported to the reporting platform of CCIL.

Even though the yield curve stretches out to 30 years, maturities of up to 5 years are the most liquid in the overnight interest swap market, though swaps of up to 10 years' maturity also are regularly traded. The concentration in 5-year swaps reflects the lack of counterparties for longer maturities and the lack of risk management tools for interest rate exposures exceeding 5 years. The risks in OTC derivatives for interest rates in India are manageable because most counterparties have investment-grade rating.

The OTC market is likely to continue to grow even if an exchange-traded futures and options market comes into being, as has happened in most developed markets. While the OTC market is functioning reasonably well, there is a clear need to start guaranteed settlement of OTC trades through CCIL, as recommended by the Reserve Bank of India Working Group on Rupee Derivatives (RBI 2003). A settlement system for the derivatives markets would greatly reduce the systemic risks inherent in such a market through centralized settlement, enhanced risk management, and multilateral netting. Also needed are exchange-traded futures and options for interest rates as an efficient mechanism for trading and hedging.[3]

Credit Rating Agencies

India has a well-developed credit rating industry, with four credit rating agencies now operating. The dominant player is CRISIL, whose majority equity stake is held by Standard & Poor's. Following is ICRA, in which Moody's has a significant equity stake. The other two are Fitch Ratings and CARE Ratings.

The Patil Committee (2005) placed substantial importance on the credit rating agencies, since it is on the basis of their certification that corporate debt will be listed on the stock exchanges.

Legal and Regulatory Framework

India has a well-designed legal and regulatory framework for its financial system and the securities market. Still, there are regulatory gaps and overlaps that will need to be addressed. As financial markets become more open and complex, issues of overlapping jurisdiction often increase, adding to the challenge of regulation and supervision.

Regulatory Framework

India has a complex regulatory structure for its financial system, necessitated by the country's vast size and the many intermediaries operating at the national and state level. Ensuring the safety and soundness of the financial markets requires close coordination among several regulators. At the apex is the Reserve Bank, which bears overall responsibility for supervising the financial system, including banks and nonbank financial institutions. The Reserve Bank also has responsibility for regulating the government debt securities, foreign exchange, and money markets, while SEBI is responsible for regulating nongovernment securities markets such as those for equity, equity derivatives, and corporate bonds. The Department of Economic Affairs and the Department of Company Affairs provide broad principles for companies. The Insurance Regulatory and Development Authority regulates insurance companies, and SEBI regulates mutual funds.

A coordinated approach to supervision is made possible through the High Level Coordination Committee on Financial Markets, chaired by the governor of the Reserve Bank. The committee, a high-level forum to allow interaction among the financial sector regulators, includes the chiefs of SEBI, the Insurance Regulatory and Development Authority, and the Pension Fund Regulatory and Development Authority and other senior officials of the Ministry of Finance.

As the government's debt manager, the Reserve Bank is responsible for supervising the primary dealers participating in the government debt securities market. The primary dealers are supervised both directly by the Reserve Bank and through its Board for Financial Supervision, formed as a committee of the central board of the Reserve Bank in November 1994. The Board for Financial Supervision is headed by the governor of the Reserve Bank, with a deputy governor as vice chairperson and other deputy governors and four directors of the central board as members. The Board for Financial Supervision provides ongoing direction on regulatory policies and supervisory practices.

Legal Framework

Corporate debt and equity securities are governed by four main laws: the Securities and Exchange Board of India (SEBI) Act, 1992; the Companies Act, 1956; the Securities Contracts (Regulation) Act, 1956; and the Depositories Act, 1996.

The SEBI Act empowers SEBI to protect the interests of investors in securities, promote the development of the securities market, and regulate that market. Its regulatory jurisdiction extends over corporations in the issuing of capital and all intermediaries and individuals associated with the securities market. It can conduct inquiries, audits, and inspections of all participants and adjudicate offenses under the act. It has powers to register and regulate all market intermediaries and can penalize them for violations of the act and related rules and regulations. SEBI has full autonomy and authority to regulate and develop an orderly securities market. In addition, the act provides for the establishment of one or more appellate tribunals to exercise appellate powers over the decisions it hands down.

The Securities Contracts (Regulation) Act provides for direct and indirect control of virtually all aspects of securities trading, including the running of stock exchanges, with the aim of preventing undesirable transactions. It gives the central government regulatory jurisdiction over stock exchanges, through a process of recognition and continued supervision; contracts in securities; and the listing of securities on stock exchanges. The stock exchanges frame their own listing regulations in consonance with the minimum listing criteria set out in their rules. The Securities Contracts (Regulation) Act has recently been amended to consider securitized debt as a tradable instrument.

The Depositories Act provides for the establishment of depositories for securities. With a view to ensuring rapid, accurate, and secure transfer of securities, the act provides for making securities of public limited companies freely transferable subject to certain exceptions; dematerializing the securities in the depository mode; and maintaining ownership records in book-entry form. To streamline settlement, the act also provides for transferring ownership of securities electronically by book entry.

The Companies Act deals with the issue, allotment, and transfer of securities and aspects of company management. It defines standards of disclosure for public issuance, particularly on company management and projects, other listed companies under the same management, and management perception of risk factors. It also regulates underwriting, the use of premium and discounts on issues, rights and bonus issues, payment of interest and dividends, and the supplying of annual reports and other information.

Regulatory Gaps and Overlaps

The multiple regulators in the financial sector pose challenges for regulatory coordination. For example, banks and similar entities have many business activities and would fall under the jurisdiction of different regulators depending on the market segment. To avoid regulatory overlaps, India has adopted the concept of lead or principal regulator: lead responsibility for a regulated entity lies with a principal regulator, to which the entity would report all its activities, while the entity falls under the jurisdiction of a secondary regulator only for the business it undertakes in that regulator's market segment (see Patil Committee 2005 for a detailed discussion of these issues).

To support this concept, a system for exchange of information among the regulators has been put into place. In addition, the lead regulator, along with other regulators, holds periodic discussions with the chief executive officer of the regulated entity.

Despite this structure, there is a concern that the overlap in regulation and the different focus of each authority tend to inhibit the development of new products and innovation in the design of debt securities markets. There is also a perceived need for better harmonization of regulatory principles. And the effectiveness of the exchange of information among regulators is a matter of debate. Even so, creating a unified regulatory and supervisory framework by melding the financial sector regulators into one entity may encounter resistance, whatever the inherent advantages and disadvantages of such an approach.

Regulatory Jurisdiction and Coordination. The regulatory and supervisory roles of the Ministry of Finance, the Reserve Bank, and SEBI in the debt securities markets are not sufficiently delineated. Overlapping regulatory roles and powers can diffuse regulatory authority and create uncertainty for market participants.

The Reserve Bank (government debt securities market) and SEBI (corporate bond market) sought to clarify the demarcation of their responsibilities following an amendment to the securities legislation in 2000 and, more recently, following the Patil Committee report (2005). But some market fragmentation remains, because regulatory jurisdiction is still based on the maturity of debt instruments. The Reserve Bank regulates the issuance of money market instruments, while SEBI regulates the issuance of longer-term corporate debt instruments. This division, which exists in many countries, led to regulatory overlap in the oversight of mutual funds: while mutual funds normally fall under SEBI's purview, they came under the Reserve Bank's control when they offered money market investments. In 2000 it was decided that SEBI would regulate money market mutual funds.

Regulatory confusion also arises because while SEBI is the primary regulator of the markets, the Reserve Bank regulates the primary investors (banks) and primary dealers. The regulations and stipulations that the Reserve Bank issues relating to banks' participation in the corporate bond market can have a significant impact in the market.

Overlap Due to Definitions of Terms. Overlap also arises in the applicability of such terms as *securities, repos, bonds,* and *derivatives,* used in multiple laws. Moreover, the practice of defining terms inclusively leads to lack of clarity, especially where multiple authorities have the ability to regulate a similar space.

An examination of the entire legislative landscape is warranted. Once legislators have a clear idea of how the regulatory jurisdiction should be carved up between SEBI and the Reserve Bank, it is important that appropriate amendments be made to the definitions of the terms used loosely across statutes. Using the same term to define instruments over which multiple authorities have regulatory jurisdiction is best avoided unless absolutely necessary, and then a clear hierarchy of control could be laid down to avoid overlaps in jurisdiction. And where two authorities have similar power over different segments of the debt securities market, care should be taken to use distinct terms to describe their scope of authority.

That said, a recent example shows better interagency coordination in rule setting. SEBI, in consultation with the Reserve Bank, recently prepared and issued guidelines on the issuance and trading of privately placed corporate debt. The Reserve Bank, to complement SEBI's action, issued guidelines on investment in the private placement market for such investors as banks and primary dealers. This coordination in rule setting was meant to encourage greater transparency in the issuance of privately placed corporate debt.

Recommended Actions

India has a well-developed government bond market thanks to the concerted efforts of the government, the Reserve Bank, and key market participants, both public and private sector. But development of the corporate bond market lags far behind. Huge potential remains for developing a market that is deeper and more active and provides a much broader range of instruments.

Following are recommended actions that could further develop India's bond market. Some draw on the recommendations of the High Powered Expert Committee on Making Mumbai an International Financial Centre. The committee, which has critically examined constraints on financial sector development in India, has made far-reaching recommendations on financial regime governance and regulation, the development of "missing" or weak markets, the development of globally competitive institutions and financial firms, and other policies relating to the financial system and its growing needs for qualified human capital (India, Ministry of Finance 2007a).

Supply Side

Further Developing Sovereign Interest Rate Benchmarks. Indian authorities have done an outstanding job in building sovereign interest rate benchmarks across the spectrum of maturities up to 30 years. The yield curves up to 30 years are published daily by CCIL and by international firms active in the bond market. But liquidity remains limited to maturities ranging up to 10 years because of the relatively small institutional investor base requiring long-term debt instruments.

Beyond the measures already taken by the government, expanding securities borrowing and lending to institutional investors would also help improve liquidity. This step, mentioned in the fiscal 2008 union budget (India, Ministry of Finance 2007b), also would provide an additional source of revenue for institutional investors and increase business opportunities for primary dealers. Malaysia's experience here should be of interest to Indian authorities (see box 1.1 in chapter 1).

Broadening the Range of Issuers. The situation in India's debt securities market—with the government as the dominant issuer and the corporate bond market at an early stage of development—is not unusual. Other countries, developed as well as developing, have had a similar experience. Yet Malaysia and Korea, for example, have been very successful in developing their corporate bond markets. In Malaysia there are many large corporate issuers, and they prefer issuing in the local market because of its cost-effectiveness and the demand from a long-term investor, the Employees' Provident Fund. In India, by contrast, large issuers have ready access to the international market at a lower cost than the local market, and the institutional investor base is relatively small. The corporate bond market will need time to grow.

The Patil Committee report (2005) makes several recommendations to accelerate development of the corporate bond and securitization markets that, if implemented, would broaden the range of issuers. One of the committee's recommendations is to recognize securitized debt as tradable debt under the Securities Contracts (Regulation) Act, 1956. (As noted, the Securities Contracts [Regulation]

Amendment Act, 2007 provides a legal framework to allow listing and trading of securitized debt instruments, though the regulations are still in draft.) Another is to put the limits on foreign institutional investment in asset-backed securities issued by asset reconstruction companies on par with those for listed debt securities.

The Deepak Parekh Committee (2007), which focuses on infrastructure financing and has carried forward the Patil Committee's recommendations, has proposed confining private placement to qualified institutional buyers and doing away with the restriction on the number of those participating. It has also proposed lowering the minimum rating required for qualification as an approved investment to BBB for bonds, hybrid instruments, and securitized paper issued by infrastructure companies. Similarly, it has suggested allowing infrastructure schemes of equity mutual funds to qualify as approved investments.

Beyond the corporate sector, there should be room for issuers involved in infrastructure projects. Financing requirements for infrastructure projects over the next decade are estimated at close to Rs 3 trillion. Structured finance in different forms could play a key part in meeting those needs. The understanding of structured finance products among Indian banks is limited, however, and encouraging public sector banks to participate actively in this market would require considerable training.

Other potential issuers of debt securities include cities and municipalities. India now has more than 35 cities with a population of more than a million. These large municipalities, all needing to finance investment in basic infrastructure, could be potential issuers in the domestic bond market. Supporting infrastructure such as credit rating and bond insurance will be needed. But municipalities will also need reforms so that they can access the financial market. They have poor financial records and depend largely on state government grants and budgetary allocations.

Encouraging Consolidation of Privately Placed Bonds. Corporate debt issuers should be encouraged to consolidate their bond issues into a few large ones that can serve as benchmarks. Consolidating debt issuance would create large floating stocks and enhance liquidity in the market. It would also make cash management easier for both issuers and investors and reduce back-office work by reducing the number of bond series to be managed. Consolidation would also bring discipline to the market.

The many small issues from single issuers is the result of the historical indifference to secondary market trading. As long as there was no secondary market trading, the size of an issue did not matter, and issuers preferred to raise whatever funds they needed at a particular time. The government debt securities market faced the same problem of poor liquidity stemming from fragmented debt issues. The problem was addressed by reissuing securities with the coupon and maturity of a similar but more liquid security.

A similar effort is required for benchmark issues in the corporate bond market. But amendments to existing law will be needed to encourage reissuance and consolidation. Reissuance is not legally recognized. Instead, it is considered a fresh issuance of securities and therefore attracts stamp duty, making the process commercially infeasible. Since no fresh securities are being issued, however, there should be no additional stamp duty.

Demand Side

Broadening the Investor Base for the Bond Market. The relatively small size of the institutional investor base remains a major weakness in the Indian capital market. In the past household savings went primarily to banks. The contractual savings sector is still small relative to those in East Asia.

India has been very successful in developing its mutual fund industry, however, which had assets under management amounting to about $80 billion at the end of March 2007. Reforms in the insurance sector since 2000 have been well received, and the market share of the state-owned Life Insurance Corporation of India has gradually declined as a number of private insurance companies have entered the market. But there is room for further reform in the insurance industry to increase the coverage and range of products for Indian households. Pension and provident funds have also shown notable growth, with total assets of $31 billion at the end of March 2006. Further reforms being considered by the government in the pension industry are steps in the right direction.

Market Infrastructure

Developing a Central Database on Corporate Bond Issues. While data on bonds are available in India, there is no central database. The information is available only in fragmented form. Thus investors lack the information they need to make considered investment decisions.

A central, publicly available database on all corporate bonds issued, including credit rating information and credit migration history, is essential for the development of the corporate bond market. The database should be available free of cost to all investors.

Stock exchanges would be best suited to maintaining such a database, since they would receive most of the information needed at the time of listing. They could obtain any subsequent rating updates from the rating agencies. Since the purpose of creating such a database is to ensure wider dissemination of information, the exchanges should be required to ensure that the data are available on a real-time basis on their Web sites as well as through the media and other information providers.

Reducing Risk in Over-the-Counter Transactions in Corporate Bonds. All transactions in corporate bonds take place in the OTC market. Since these are bilateral arrangements, they involve higher settlement risks. Enforcing contracts can be difficult if disputes arise. The lower courts are not conversant with financial markets and the practices followed. Moreover, there is no codified law governing securities transactions in the OTC market. The OTC contracts are based on market convention. For all these reasons, the legal process to enforce them is costly and time consuming.

To reduce these risks, market practices relating to OTC trades may need to be acknowledged by law as valid and enforceable. Since most trades in the wholesale corporate bond market are done by phone, there may be no legal document in place when the deals are struck. In derivatives trading, by contrast, banks and market participants enter into standard agreements based on the conventions of the International Swaps and Derivatives Association before initiating any trade. A similar legally enforceable document for OTC trades in the corporate bond market may help in dispute resolution.

Nurturing the Growth of Risk Management Products. Derivatives for debt instruments have been slow to develop in India, and while the interest rate swap market has grown rapidly, most transactions take place in the OTC market. There is a clear need for developing an exchange-traded derivatives market to reduce systemic risk and improve transparency. Singapore's experience in developing such a market may be of interest. A vibrant debt derivatives market would foster the development of risk management products that would in turn further deepen the Indian bond market.

A broad derivatives market that includes exchange-traded as well as tailored derivatives for the management of currency, interest rate, and credit default risk is one of the "missing" markets identified by the High Powered Expert Committee on Making Mumbai an International Financial Centre. Another is a spot currency trading market.

Besides emphasizing the need for rapid development of these markets, the High Powered Expert Committee has suggested as a high priority establishing a currency trading exchange in Mumbai, with a minimum transaction size of Rs 10 million (roughly $225,000). This wholesale currency spot market, the committee recommends, should be accompanied by a rupee cash-settled currency derivatives market, offering such products as currency futures, currency options, and currency swaps, traded on India's established exchanges. The currency derivatives market should be open to all (including foreign institutional investors).

Since currency and interest rates are not "securities" as defined by the Securities Contracts (Regulation) Act, legislation allowing currency and interest rate derivatives to be traded in established stock exchanges will need to be in place. Regulatory clarity will also be needed, since stock exchanges are regulated by SEBI while currency and interest rates are the purview of the Reserve Bank. Allowing currency futures trading by all would also require the introduction of full capital convertibility.

Legal and Regulatory Framework

Improving Financial Regime Governance. Another set of recommendations by the High Powered Expert Committee centers on improving financial regime governance to meet the best standards of regulatory practices applied around the world. The committee has emphasized increasing the efficiency of the legal system in expeditiously resolving conflicts and disputes, clearing the backlog of cases in the civil system, and reducing the time and thus the cost required to resolve disputes. Its recommended regulatory reforms would also require strengthening the legal and regulatory framework by clarifying oversight responsibilities among the regulatory agencies for the debt securities market, and modernizing laws governing creditors' rights and corporate governance.

Annex 3.1   Reforms in the Banking Sector

- The banking sector reforms in India started in 1991 with the lowering of the statutory reserve requirement and a move to market-determined interest rates through gradual deregulation and rationalization of the administered interest rate structure.

- Competition was encouraged in the banking sector by allowing the entry of new private banks and foreign banks. Ten new private banks and more than 30 foreign banks have been licensed since 1991. Competition has also been encouraged among the public sector banks.

- The equity base of most public sector banks has been expanded by infusing private equity, with the government continuing to retain the majority shareholding.

- The government introduced a set of prudential measures to ensure the safety and soundness of the banking sector and bring prudential rules and standards closer to international best practices (risk-based capital standards, income recognition, asset classification and provisioning requirements for standard loans and nonperforming loans, exposure limits for single and group borrowers, international accounting rules, investment valuation norms). As a transitory measure the government recapitalized some of the state-owned banks to meet the prudential norms. To allow speedy enforcement of bank-related financial claims on borrowing entities, special courts (debt recovery tribunals) were set up in important cities. Lenders' rights were further enhanced by passage of the Securitization and Reconstruction of Financial Assets and Enforcement of Security Interest Act, 2002, which permits enforcement of security interests without court intervention.

- To enable banks to realize greater value from nonperforming assets, new rules allow them to sell their distressed assets to privately owned asset reconstruction companies. The government has permitted foreign direct investment of up to 49 percent of the equity capital in the asset reconstruction companies to tap the expertise and resources of foreign institutions with international experience in managing distressed assets.

- To ensure compliance with the standards and norms, regulation and supervision have been strengthened through an on-site inspection and off-site surveillance mechanism and greater accountability for external auditors. The Board for Financial Supervision was formed in November 1994 to pay focused attention to bank supervision.

- To help improve credit risk management by commercial banks, the Credit Information Bureau (India) Limited (CIBIL) was set up in January 2001 to collect, collate, and share information on all borrowers.

- In 2004 the Reserve Bank put into place the real-time gross settlement system, allowing faster, more efficient, and more secure settlement of large-value payments.
- Greater transparency and stronger disclosure standards have been introduced in the banking system and gradually expanded to promote market discipline.
- Greater transparency and disclosure standards were introduced in the rupee derivatives market by creating a central reporting system for all rupee derivatives transactions (swaps, forward rate agreements) by regulated entities such as banks and financial institutions.

Source: Reserve Bank of India.

Annex 3.2   Reforms in the Government Debt Securities Market

Date	Reform	Objective	Outcome
June 1992	Auction method introduced for issuance of central government debt securities.	To make yields on government securities market determined.	Price discovery has improved over time.
January 1994	Zero-coupon bond issued for the first time. Securities Trading Corporation of India (STCI) commenced operations.	To add new instruments and intermediaries.	The STCI and other primary dealers have become important intermediaries in the government debt securities market.
August 1994	Agreement reached between the Reserve Bank and the government on limiting issue of ad hoc treasury bills.	To do away with automatic monetization.	Cash management of the government has improved.
March 1995	Primary dealer system introduced.	To strengthen market intermediation and support primary issuance.	The primary dealer system has become an important segment of the government debt securities market.
July 1995	Delivery-versus-payment system in government debt securities introduced.	To reduce settlement risk.	The transition from settlement on a gross basis (DVP I) to settlement on a net basis (DVP II) has been made.
September 1995	Floating-rate bonds introduced.	To add more instruments.	The bonds were discontinued after the first issuance for lack of market interest. They were reintroduced in November 2001 but discontinued again in October 2004.
January 1997	Technical Advisory Committee formed.	To advise the Reserve Bank on developing government securities, money, and foreign exchange markets.	Committee plays a pivotal role in implementing the Reserve Bank's reform agenda on the basis of a consultative approach.
March 1997	System of Ways and Means Advances introduced for central government.	To discontinue automatic monetization.	Transparency and pricing have improved, and autonomy in monetary policy making has increased.
April 1997	Fixed Income Money Market and Derivatives Association of India (FIMMDA) established.	To introduce self-regulation and develop market practices and ethics.	Market practices have improved.
July 1997	Foreign institutional investors permitted to invest in government debt securities.	To broaden the market.	Foreign institutional investors have become important players in the market, particularly in the treasury bill segment.

Date	Action	Outcome
December 1997	Capital-indexed bonds issued.	To help investors hedge inflation risk.	Efforts are being made to revitalize this product.
April 2000	Sale of securities allotted in primary issues on the same day.	To improve secondary market.	Management of overnight risk has improved.
February 2002	Clearing Corporation of India Limited (CCIL) established.	To act as a clearing agency for transactions in government debt securities.	Stability in the market has improved, greatly mitigating the settlement risk.
June 2002	Primary dealers brought under the jurisdiction of the Board for Financial Supervision.	To improve integration of market supervision.	Primary dealers are periodically reporting their market position to the Board for Financial Supervision.
October 2002	Trade data from the negotiated dealing system made available on the Reserve Bank's Web site.	To improve transparency.	The measure is helping small investors as well.
January 2003	Retail trading of government debt securities permitted on stock exchanges.	To facilitate easier access and wider participation.	This program has not taken off. Efforts are being made to improve the position.
February 2003	Regulated entities permitted to participate in repo markets.	To widen the market.	Activity in the repo market has improved.
June 2003	Interest rate futures introduced.	To facilitate hedging of interest rate risk.	These futures have not taken off.
July 2003	Government debt reissuance implemented.	To reduce the government's interest burden and help banks offload illiquid securities.	Debt buyback introduced.
March 2004	Third phase of delivery-versus-payment system (DVP III) introduced.	To achieve netting efficiency and allow rollover of repos.	Running successfully.
April 2004	Real-time gross settlement system introduced.	To provide real-time, online, large-value interbank payment and settlements.	Running successfully.

Annex 3.2   Reforms in the Government Debt Securities Market *(continued)*

Date	Reform	Objective	Outcome
August 2005	Anonymous order-matching system (NDS-OM) established, allowing straight-through processing.	To provide members of the negotiated dealing system with a more efficient trading platform.	More than 60 percent of transactions in government debt securities take place through the NDS-OM. Odd-lot trading on NDS-OM began in May 2007 with a view to encouraging retail trading. Sale of repurchase agreements (repos) simultaneously permitted.
February 2006	Intraday short selling permitted.	To improve liquidity in the market, particularly when interest rates are rising.	Extended to five trading days effective January 31, 2007.
August 2006	"When issued" trading commenced.	To allow efficient price discovery and distribution of auctioned stock.	Extended to newly issued securities in November 2006.
August 2006	Government Securities Act, 2006 passed by parliament and approved by the president of India.	To facilitate wider participation in the government debt securities market and create enabling provisions for the issuance of separately traded registered interest and principal securities (STRIPS).	December 1, 2007, set as the date on which the act would come into force.

Source: RBI 2006b (with updates by authors).

Annex 3.3   Maturity Profile of Central Government Debt Securities

The Indian government has lengthened the maturity profile of its debt securities and now issues bonds of 30 years' maturity in addition to others. This effort has helped in developing a yield curve for longer maturities. The weighted average maturity of outstanding central government debt securities increased from 14.13 years in fiscal 2005 to 16.90 in fiscal 2006 before falling to 14.72 in fiscal 2007, in part because of the hardening of interest rates. The weighted average interest rate rose from 6.11 percent in fiscal 2005 to 7.34 percent in fiscal 2006 and to 7.89 percent in fiscal 2007. The average interest on government debt securities moved up to 8.23 percent by August 2007 (table A3.1).

The Reserve Bank pursued a policy of passive consolidation in fiscal 2004–07, reissuing existing securities and issuing very few new ones. The outstanding stocks of existing securities have steadily grown, helping to improve liquidity in the market. Of the 30 issues of dated securities in fiscal 2006, 29 were reissues; the single new security was issued to provide a benchmark for a 30-year maturity. The share of reissues in the total debt securities issued increased from 82.1 percent in fiscal 2005 to 97.7 percent in fiscal 2006. During fiscal 2005 there were just two new issues of fixed-rate securities.

To impart greater liquidity to the government debt securities market, the Reserve Bank's Internal Technical Group on Central Government Securities recommended a policy of active consolidation: buying back a large number of small, illiquid issues of central government debt securities from the holders and issuing a smaller number of liquid debt securities in exchange. The resulting availability of a smaller number of large issues, held across a wider base of market participants, is expected to increase the floating stock and thus the trading interest. The central government approved the scheme of active consolidation and provided $641 million in the fiscal 2008 union budget toward the premium payments.

Table A3.1 Profile of Central Government Market Loans, India, Fiscal 1998–08

Fiscal year	Range of yields to maturity at primary issuance (%)			Weighted average yield at primary issuance (%)	Range of maturities of new loans (years)	Weighted average maturity of loans (years)	Weighted average maturity of outstanding stock (years)	Weighted average coupon of outstanding stock (%)
	<5 years	5–10 years	>10 years					
1998	10.85–12.14	11.15–13.05	n.a.	12.01	3–10	6.60	6.50	—
1999	11.40–11.68	11.10–12.25	12.25–12.60	11.86	2–20	7.70	6.30	—
2000	n.a.	10.73–11.99	10.77–12.45	11.77	5–19	12.60	7.10	—
2001	9.47–10.95	9.88–11.69	10.47–11.70	10.95	2–20	10.60	7.50	—
2002	n.a.	6.98–9.81	7.18–11.00	9.44	5–25	14.30	8.20	10.84
2003	n.a.	6.65–8.14	6.84–8.62	7.34	7–30	13.80	8.90	10.44
2004	4.69	4.62–5.73	5.18–6.35	5.71	4–30	14.94	9.78	9.30
2005	5.90	5.53–7.20	4.49–8.24	6.11	5–30	14.13	9.63	8.79
2006	n.a.	6.70–7.06	6.91–7.79	7.34	5–30	16.90	9.92	8.75
2007	7.69–7.94	7.06–8.29	7.43–8.75	7.89	4–30	14.72	9.97	8.55
2008[a]	n.a.	7.58–8.44	8.34–8.64	8.23	6–30	14.32	10.39	8.46

Source: RBI 2007a.
Note: Excludes issuance under the Market Stabilization Scheme.
a. Through August 10, 2007.
n.a. = Not applicable (no issues made).
— = Not available.

Annex 3.4   Regulatory and Market Reforms for the Corporate Bond Market Recommended by the Patil Committee

Reform	Responsible entities
Regulatory reforms	
Reforms affecting issuers	
Streamline procedures for public issuance of debt. Extend shelf registration to all types of corporate borrowers.	Securities and Exchange Board of India (SEBI), Ministry of Company Affairs
Strengthen the debenture trustee system by providing protection from default by the company in timely payment of interest.	SEBI
Rationalize the stamp duty among different classes of investors and states.	Ministry of Finance, state governments, Reserve Bank of India
Reforms affecting investors	
Relax and amend regulations for permitting pension and provident funds to invest in corporate debt.	Ministry of Finance, Income Tax Department, Ministry of Labor, Employees' Provident Fund Organization
Modify the investment guidelines for insurance companies to allow investment in instruments with a rating of less than AA with adequate safeguards to protect the soundness of the investor.	Insurance Regulatory and Development Authority
Relax regulatory caps on banks' investments in unlisted corporate bonds (now limited to 10 percent of their total investments not eligible toward the statutory liquidity ratio) as well as the minimum rating (investment grade) required for investments in corporate bonds.	Reserve Bank of India, Ministry of Finance
Provide capital for the interest rate risk in the entire balance sheet rather than just the marked-to-market part of the book. This would ensure similar treatment of bonds and loans with respect to interest rate risk.	Reserve Bank of India, Ministry of Finance
Remove the artificial distinction between investments and advances in the regulatory regime. Guidelines and rules for a given credit should be similar whether the credit is held as a loan or a bond.	Reserve Bank of India, Ministry of Finance
Further raise the investment ceiling on corporate bonds for foreign institutional investors. As a first step the cap could be relaxed for longer-term investment (more than three years) in the corporate bond market.	Ministry of Finance, Reserve Bank of India, SEBI
Professionalize fund management services. Pension and provident funds and insurance companies need access to professional fund management services, and adequate risk management systems need to be put into place to preserve the soundness of these investors.	SEBI, Insurance Regulatory and Development Authority, Employees' Provident Fund Organization
Reforms affecting the legal and regulatory framework	
Improve existing regulatory practices. Regulation of the corporate bond market should be put under one regulator.	High Level Committee on Capital Markets, Ministry of Finance, Reserve Bank of India, SEBI

(Table continues on next page)

Annex 3.4 Regulatory and Market Reforms for the Corporate Bond Market Recommended by the Patil Committee *(continued)*

Reform	Responsible entities
Enforce recently amended bankruptcy laws that clearly define creditors' rights and borrowers' responsibilities; promote adequate corporate governance practices; and ensure timely and accurate public disclosure of financial information.	Ministry of Company Affairs, Ministry of Finance, Reserve Bank of India, SEBI
Market infrastructure reforms	
Improve the comprehensiveness and accessibility of corporate credit and trade information.	SEBI, Ministry of Company Affairs *Secondary responsibility:* credit rating agencies, stock exchanges, Clearing Corporation of India Limited (CCIL), or Fixed Income Money Market and Derivatives Association of India (FIMMDA)
Improve trading and settlement systems. Efficient systems are critical for providing liquidity, efficient price discovery, and an exit route for debt investments in infrastructure.	SEBI, Reserve Bank of India, stock exchanges, CCIL, Ministry of Finance
Develop new product structures (credit enhancement, bond insurance) and hedging mechanisms.	SEBI; Reserve Bank of India; stock exchanges; CCIL; Ministry of Finance; self-regulatory organizations such as FIMMDA, Association of Mutual Funds of India, Primary Dealers Association
Permit short selling in government securities, because it will help in refining the pricing mechanism for corporate bonds and help investors hedge their risks effectively.[a]	Reserve Bank of India, Ministry of Finance
Remove differential tax treatment of different classes of corporate bonds.	Ministry of Finance, Central Board of Direct Taxes

Source: Patil Committee 2005.
a. Short selling was permitted in February 2006 and extended from intraday to five days (subject to certain conditions) in January 2007.

Endnotes

1. The government plans to create a separate debt management office, allowing the Reserve Bank to focus on monetary policy.

2. Reserve Bank regulations require that at least 75 percent of the investment portfolio be marked to market. Banks value their portfolios according to a model for valuation prescribed by the Reserve Bank or by the Fixed Income Money Market and Derivatives Association of India (FIMMDA). Consistent with current risk management principles, the market values of bonds must be estimated on a regular basis to ensure that the correct amount of capital is set aside.

3. For comprehensive discussion of the development of derivatives markets in India, see World Bank and FICCI (2007).

References

ADB (Asian Development Bank). 2005. *Bond Market Settlement and Emerging Linkages.* Manila: ADB.

Arnone, Marco, and George Iden. 2003. "Primary Dealers in Government Securities: Policy Issues and Selected Countries' Experience." IMF Working Paper WP/03/45, International Monetary Fund, Washington, DC.

BIS (Bank for International Settlements). 2006. *Quarterly Review.* December. Basel.

———. 2007. *Quarterly Review.* September. Basel.

CCIL (Clearing Corporation of India Limited). 2007. "CCIL Market Update." September 28. Mumbai.

———. Various issues. *Rakshitra.* http://www.ccilindia.com/index.html.

Dalla, Ismail. 2003. *Harmonization of Bond Market Rules and Regulations.* Manila: Asian Development Bank.

———. 2006. "Asset Securitization Markets in Selected East Asian Countries." In *East Asian Finance: Selected Issues,* ed. Ismail Dalla. Washington, DC: World Bank.

———. 2007. "Indian Bond Market." East Asia and Pacific Region, World Bank, Washington, DC.

Deepak Parekh Committee. 2007. "The Report of the Committee on Infrastructure Financing." Ministry of Finance, New Delhi.

Deutsche Bank. 2004. "Asian Bond Market Insights." Singapore.

Faulkner, Mark. 2004. *An Introduction to Securities Lending.* International Securities Lending Association.

Fitch Ratings. 2006. "Indian Securitisation Market Q&A." New York.

IMF (International Monetary Fund). 2004. *Emerging Local Securities and Derivatives Markets: Recent Developments and Policy Issues.* World Economic and Financial Surveys Series. Washington, DC: IMF.

———. 2007. *Global Financial Stability Report 2007.* Washington, DC: IMF.

India, Ministry of Finance. 2005. *Union Budget 2006–07.* New Delhi.

———. 2007a. *Report of the High Powered Expert Committee on Making Mumbai an International Financial Centre.* New Delhi: Sage India.

———. 2007b. *Union Budget 2007–08.* New Delhi.

———. 2008. *Economic Survey 2007–08.* New Delhi.

India, Planning Commission. 2008. "Draft Report of the Committee on Financial Sector Reforms." New Delhi.

McKinsey & Company. 2005. "India Banking 2010: Towards a High Performing Banking Sector." New Delhi.

Mohan, Rakesh. 2006. "Financial Sector Reforms and Monetary Policy: The Indian Experience." *RBI Bulletin* (June).

———. 2007a. "India's Financial Sector Reforms: Fostering Growth While Containing Risk." *RBI Bulletin* (December 3).

———. 2007b. "Reforms, Productivity and Efficiency in Banking: The Indian Experience." *RBI Bulletin* (March).

NSE (National Stock Exchange of India). 2006. *Indian Securities Market: A Review.* Vol. 9. Mumbai: NSE.

OECD (Organisation for Economic Co-operation and Development). 2002. *Debt Management and Government Securities Markets in the 21st Century.* Paris: OECD.

Patil Committee. 2005. *Report of the High Level Expert Committee on Corporate Bonds and Securitization.* New Delhi: Ministry of Finance.

RBI (Reserve Bank of India). 2003. *Report of the Working Group on Rupee Derivatives.* Mumbai.

———. 2006. *Annual Report 2005–06.* Mumbai.

———. 2007a. *Annual Report 2006–07.* Mumbai.

———. 2007b. *Macroeconomic and Monetary Developments: Third Quarter Review 2006–07.* Mumbai.

———. 2007c. *A Profile of Banks, 2006–07.* Mumbai.

———. 2007d. *Report on Currency and Finance 2005–06: Development of Financial Markets and Role of the Central Bank.* Mumbai.

———. 2007e. *Report on Equity and Corporate Debt Market.* Mumbai.

———. 2007f. *Report on Trend and Progress of Banking in India, 2006–07.* Mumbai.

Reddy, Y.V. 2007. "Developing Debt Markets in India: Review and Prospects." Remarks by the governor of the Reserve Bank of India at a meeting of central bank governors of Asia and Latin America and the Caribbean, Washington, DC, October 18.

SEBI (Securities and Exchange Board of India). Various years. *Annual Report.* Mumbai.

Trilegal. 2007. "The Indian Corporate Debt Market: Legal and Regulatory Issues." Draft. Mumbai.

World Bank. 2005. *Global Development Finance 2005: Mobilizing Finance and Managing Vulnerability.* Washington, DC: World Bank.

———. 2006a. "Developing India's Corporate Bond Market." South Asia Region, Washington, DC.

———. 2006b. *East Asian Finance: The Road to Robust Markets.* Washington, DC: World Bank.

———. 2006c. *Global Development Finance 2006: The Development Potential of Surging Capital Flows.* Washington, DC: World Bank.

———. 2006d. *World Development Indicators 2006.* Washington, DC: World Bank.

———. 2008. *Finance for All: Policies and Pitfalls in Expanding Access.* Washington, DC: World Bank.

World Bank and FICCI (Federation of Indian Chambers of Commerce and Industry). 2007. *Developing Markets for Long-Term Finance.* New Delhi: FICCI; Washington, DC: World Bank.

World Federation of Exchanges. 2006. *Annual Report and Statistics 2005.* Paris.

4

Nepal

Nepal's bond market remains at an early stage of development. In a pattern common in South Asia, government debt securities dominate, and corporate bond market activity is negligible, reflecting a lack of both issuers and investors. In addition, the institutional investor base is minute, and the market infrastructure largely inadequate for meeting the needs of a functioning bond market.

The slow growth of the Nepalese bond market can be attributed to a range of factors, not least the conflict that has been hampering the country's economic growth for the past decade. With civil unrest dominating policy makers' concerns, developing the bond market has not been a top priority. Doing so will require addressing a multitude of issues.

Introduction

Nepal's economic performance has deteriorated in recent years, with GDP growth slowing from 3.5 percent in fiscal 2004 to 2.3 percent in fiscal 2005 and 2006. Future economic prospects depend on the resolution of civil unrest in the country. In this environment of uncertainty Nepal's financial sector also has grown slowly. The moderate growth has been driven mainly by a rapid increase in the number of nonbank financial institutions, from 104 in fiscal 2002 to 176 at the end of fiscal 2006 (table 4.1).

Recent Financial Sector Reforms

Until 2006 the country's central bank, Nepal Rastra Bank, had been implementing a series of reforms aimed at promoting the development of the financial sector. Significant steps included removing controls on interest rate spreads and relaxing those on compulsory lending: priority sector lending (which amounted to 12 percent of banks' loan portfolios, including 3 percent for deprived sector lending) had

Table 4.1   Financial Institutions by Type, Nepal, Selected Years, 1990–07

Type of institution	1990	1995	2000	2005	2006	2007
Commercial banks	5	10	13	17	18	20
Development banks	2	3	7	26	29	38
Finance companies	0	21	45	60	70	74
Microcredit development banks	0	4	7	11	11	12
Savings and credit cooperatives	0	6	19	20	19	17
NGOs	0	0	7	47	47	47
Total	7	44	98	181	194	208

Source: Nepal Rastra Bank.
Note: Data are for the end of the fiscal year, July 15.

gradually been phased out and was completely abolished at the end of fiscal 2007, while deprived sector lending (loans amounting to less than Nrs 300,000) remains set at 3 percent of banks' loan portfolios.

In addition, exchange rate controls have been lifted. The price of the Nepalese rupee is now market determined (except for the exchange rate with the Indian rupee, which remains fixed), a move aimed at enhancing competitiveness and credibility in international markets.

Most important has been enactment of the Nepal Rastra Bank Act, 2006, to strengthen the central bank's supervisory and regulatory powers. In addition, new banking regulations have been implemented to bring Nepal up to international standards and conform to the Basel Capital Accord provisions. Nepal Rastra Bank has expressed an intention to adopt a simplified form of the Basel II Capital Accord and has set up the Accord Implementation Group to move forward with this plan. All banks covered by Basel II will be required to adopt the prescribed approaches by mid-July 2008 (NRB 2007b).

Finally, the Banks and Financial Institutions Act, 2006 has replaced all earlier acts regulating banks and financial institutions. The act classifies institutions in four categories—commercial banks, development banks, finance companies, and microcredit development banks—and has prescribed performance parameters and mechanisms for upgrading and downgrading institutions on the basis of these performance yardsticks. The act also addresses governance issues: it provides for "fit and proper" tests for board members and required the withdrawal of all Nepal Rastra Bank representatives from the boards of commercial and development banks.

Transparency remains low across the financial system, however. Disclosure standards are generally poor (though they are improving for banks and financial institutions), and such practices as related-party lending are believed to be rampant, signaling a need for further reforms.

Table 4.2   Financial Market Profile, Nepal, 2002–07
(US$ billions except where otherwise specified)

Segment	2002	2003	2004	2005	2006	2007	Percentage of GDP		
							2005	2006	2007
Domestic debt securities market	0.94	1.14	1.20	1.19	1.27	1.55	16.1	15.1	14.1
Equity market capitalization	0.41	0.50	0.65	0.96	1.31	2.86	13.0	16.3	25.9
Banking assets	2.37	2.90	3.40	3.67	4.33	7.56	49.7	53.8	68.5
Total	3.72	4.54	5.25	5.82	6.91	11.97	78.7	85.2	108.5

Sources: BIS 2007; World Bank, World Development Indicators database; International Monetary Fund, International Financial Statistics database; World Bank staff calculations.
Note: Banking assets include claims of banking institutions on the government of Nepal, nonpublic financial institutions, the private sector, and other financial institutions.

Financial Market Trends

The banking system, with assets amounting to 68 percent of GDP, dominates the Nepalese financial system (table 4.2). The equity market has grown, however, with market capitalization increasing from $0.41 billion in 2002 to $2.86 billion in 2007.

The bond market, by contrast, has had no noticeable growth in recent years. It remains of secondary importance in the Nepalese financial system and, at a mere 14 percent of GDP at the end of 2007, is the second smallest in the region (see table 1.3 in chapter 1).

Against the backdrop of political uncertainty and the resulting lack of long-term government or corporate projects, the Nepalese government has devoted only limited attention to developing the bond market. Though its history dates to 1961, when the first government bond issue took place (box 4.1), the market remains underdeveloped. This status points to companies' overreliance on the banking system for funding, the government's lack of medium- and long-term funding needs for infrastructure and development projects, and corporate entities' lack of interest in publicly issuing debt.

Supply Side: Debt Instruments and Issuers

Government debt securities dominate the country's bond market, accounting for more than 98 percent of outstanding debt. Public debt management centers on meeting immediate financing needs, and the issuance calendar (when followed) gives no indication of volumes. Issuance tends to be erratic, undermining the government's credibility as a borrower and depriving the bond market of the volume of liquid debt instruments needed to develop a sovereign benchmark. Activity in the corporate bond market is negligible.

Money Market

One encouraging development in Nepal's financial market was a sharp increase in activity in the interbank market, which helps banks regulate their liquidity and

---

Box 4.1 Chronology of Bond Market Development in Nepal

- 1961: First government bond issue takes place.
- 1976: Securities Market Center is established.
- 1981: Securities Market Center starts government bond trading at par.
- 1983: Securities Exchange Act is implemented.
- 1986: Bottlers Nepal issues first corporate bond with a coupon rate of 18 percent.
- 1988: Treasury bill auction system is introduced.
- 1991: First issue of Nepal Rastra Bank bills takes place.
- 1993: First amendment to the Securities Exchange Act establishes the Securities Board of Nepal (SEBON) and converts the Securities Market Center to the Nepal Stock Exchange (NEPSE).
- 1994: NEPSE is converted into a full-fledged stock exchange.
- 1997: Second amendment to the Securities Exchange Act provides for dealer registration.
- 2005: SEBON introduces the Government Securities Trading Management Bylaws.
- 2006: EPSE starts secondary market trading of government bonds based on yield to maturity.

Sources: Nepal Merchant Banking & Finance 2007; Bambang 2005.

---

evens out interest rates among banks through arbitrage. Activity in the interbank exchange market grew particularly strongly in fiscal 2005. Since then, however, the market has been developing slowly and has even shown signs of deceleration. Discussions with market participants suggest that greater excess liquidity has depressed activity.

The Nepalese banking system has been experiencing excess liquidity as a result of lack of viable investment opportunities, diminishing private sector demand for funds, and an increase in remittances from abroad. Excluding cash reserve ratios, commercial banks held Nrs 16.41 billion in excess liquidity in mid-July 2006, up from Nrs 14.34 billion in mid-July 2005.

In an effort to mop up the excess liquidity, Nepal Rastra Bank began conducting open market operations in fiscal 2005. In fiscal 2006 it conducted 1 repurchase agreement (repo) auction (Nrs 450 million), 9 reverse repo auctions (Nrs 650 million), 15 outright sale auctions (Nrs 13.5 billion), and 2 outright purchase auctions (Nrs 830 million; table 4.3).

In fiscal 2006 Nepal Rastra Bank shortened the maturity period for borrowings from the Standing Liquidity Facility from five days to three to prevent misuse of the facility, which is provided to commercial banks to meet short-term liquidity requirements. Limits on borrowings from the facility for each bank are set on the basis of its holdings of treasury bills and the longer-term Development Bonds. As a result of the shortened maturity and excess liquidity in the system, use of the facility fell from Nrs 49.31 billion in fiscal 2005 to Nrs 9.88 billion in fiscal 2006.

While activity in the interbank market has fluctuated, the volume increased from Nrs 153 billion in fiscal 2005 to Nrs 176 billion in fiscal 2006, in part because

**Table 4.3   Open Market Operations by Nepal
Rastra Bank, Fiscal 2005–06**

(Nrs millions)

Type of operation	2005	2006
Outright purchase auction	1,310	830
Outright sale auction	1,500	13,510
Repo auction	688	450
Reverse repo auction	5,270	650

Source: Nepal Rastra Bank.

Table 4.4   Interbank Transactions, Nepal, Fiscal 2005–06

Month	2005		2006	
	Amount (Nrs millions)	Rate (%)	Amount (Nrs millions)	Rate (%)
August	4,309	1.02	20,554	2.47
September	13,165	0.39	24,671	3.87
October	12,145	0.83	12,021	3.18
November	9,056	2.24	10,369	2.36
December	11,018	3.54	15,533	0.96
January	11,030	3.49	11,256	1.22
February	12,710	3.95	14,541	2.48
March	9,500	4.33	20,075	2.84
April	18,162	4.50	15,654	1.97
May	13,050	4.28	7,970	3.52
June	18,334	4.11	10,245	1.77
July	20,359	4.71	12,862	2.13
Total	152,838		175,751	

Source: Nepal Rastra Bank.

of the shortening of maturities for borrowings from the Standing Liquidity Facility (table 4.4). More recently, however, activity in the interbank market has decelerated. Transactions increased by only 3 percent in the first eight months of fiscal 2008 compared with the same period in the previous fiscal year.

Government Debt Issuance

To meet the government's short-term financing needs, Nepal Rastra Bank issues domestic short-term public debt in the form of treasury bills on an auction basis. The share of treasury bills in domestic government debt has been growing steadily, rising from 56 percent at the end of fiscal 2002 to 75 percent at the end of fiscal 2007 (table 4.5). Nepal Rastra Bank bills, with a maximum maturity of 91 days, can be issued as part of the central bank's open market operations when

Table 4.5   Composition of Domestic Government Debt, Nepal, Fiscal 2002–07

Share of total (%)

Type of debt instrument	2002	2003	2004	2005	2006	2007
Treasury bills	55.8	57.7	57.4	58.7	70.0	74.97
Development Bonds	15.1	16.1	20.4	22.8	20.0	19.31
National savings certificates	15.7	13.1	10.5	7.5	4.3	1.53
Citizens savings certificates	0.9	1.1	1.4	1.6	1.9	1.40
Special Bonds	12.6	11.9	10.4	9.3	3.9	2.79

Sources: Nepal Rastra Bank; World Bank staff calculations.
Note: Data are for the end of the fiscal year, July 15.

treasury bills do not suffice to absorb excess liquidity in the market. The benchmark 364-day treasury bill rate has been consistently decreasing over the past five years, with the annual weighted average moving from 5.20 percent in 2002 to 2.48 percent in January 2007. Interest rates at the longer end of the market have also shown a downward trend, reflecting sluggish aggregate demand.

The government also meets its financing needs by issuing long-term debt instruments. Development Bonds accounted for 19 percent of outstanding domestic debt in July 2007. These bonds are issued at face value and at predetermined interest rates, with maturity ranging from 3 to 20 years, and they are available to all investors in the market. The share of these instruments in total outstanding debt has fallen since 2003, reflecting the decline in financing of long-term government projects. Special Bonds account for another 2.8 percent of outstanding public debt. These are issued for special purposes, as requested by the government, and only to institutions that have import requirements. (One such purpose has been to pay duty drawbacks, though the Public Debt Management Department of Nepal Rastra Bank indicates that this practice has been abolished.)

The government issues two types of nonmarketable and tax-exempt instruments to the retail public: national savings certificates, with maturities ranging from 3 to 15 years, which accounted for 1.5 percent of outstanding domestic debt at the end of fiscal 2007; and citizens savings certificates with a maturity of 5 years, which accounted for 1.4 percent (see table 4.5). These certificates are sold at face value with a predetermined interest rate and are restricted to individual investors and nonprofit organizations. In 2007 the issuance of national savings certificates was interrupted and replaced by the issuance of citizens savings certificates. Nepal Rastra Bank also started issuing 12-year instruments known as Peace Bonds, with a coupon rate of 6.5 percent.

The price mechanism plays little part in allocating funds in the public debt market. The government does not assume the role of a price taker in auctioning either short- or long-term instruments. Auctions remain driven by yields rather than by announced volumes, with the Public Debt Management Department deciding on cutoff rates.

The government's outstanding domestic debt increased by 10.2 percent between mid-July 2005 and mid-July 2006, to Nrs 94.19 billion (16.2 percent of GDP). In fiscal 2006 the total liability on treasury bills increased by Nrs 11.58 billion, while the liability on Development Bonds declined by Nrs 2.04 billion and that on citizens savings certificates by Nrs 2.70 billion (NRB 2006a).

Sovereign Yield Curve

Nepal lacks an established sovereign yield curve. The yield of the 91-day treasury bill was 3.25 percent in July 2006, and the yield of the 364-day treasury bill 4.04 percent. Without trading data on longer-term bonds, however, it is difficult to establish a yield curve.

The benchmark short-term interest rate since 1998 has been the auction-based 364-day treasury bill rate. The medium-term benchmark is the return on the 5-year Development Bonds, and the long-term benchmark the return on the 10-year Development Bonds. But lack of a reliable issuance calendar, minimal volumes in the primary market, and negligible liquidity in the secondary market all contribute to the lack of a liquid sovereign benchmark.

Public Debt Management

Nepal Rastra Bank lacks a coherent cash management strategy to guide decisions on the volume and maturity of each issuance of government debt securities. A committee of Nepal Rastra Bank and Ministry of Finance representatives develops the issuance calendar for short- and long-term debt securities at the beginning of each fiscal year. Decisions on volume and maturity are made throughout the year on the basis of immediate financing needs. For treasury bills the Public Debt Management Department often decides on issuance on the basis of monthly forecasts of excess liquidity in the market and requests from commercial bankers. For long-term instruments the volume of the issue is determined on the basis of the projected fiscal deficit for the year and divided into four quarters.

Recently, as political instability continued to impede long-term projects, no capital expenditure was planned, and the government ran a budget surplus that reached a peak of Nrs 18 billion in May 2007. As a result, the Public Debt Management Department decided to cancel the issuance calendar and repay principal on maturing outstanding securities rather than roll these debts over.

To strengthen debt management, Nepal will need to initiate reforms aimed at establishing proper governance arrangements, internal processes, resources, and staff capacity. Putting these into place would allow the government to develop a medium-term debt management strategy with yearly updates, based on a sound analysis of cost and risk and taking into account macroeconomic and market constraints. It would also provide the means to execute the strategy efficiently while ensuring prudent management of operational risk. In addition, a risk management system should be developed to monitor and evaluate risks inherent in the structure of government debt.

An additional source of concern is the mix of domestic and external debt. According to the most recent data available, Nepal's public debt amounted to an estimated 61 percent of GDP at the end of fiscal 2004. Nearly 75 percent of this, roughly $3.25 billion, is external debt, 90 percent of which is owed to multilateral institutions and has a high degree of concessionality. While concessionality lowers the government's cost of borrowing, effective management of exchange risk remains a challenge. Achieving an optimal mix of domestic and external debt would reduce that risk, and developing the local currency bond market could help the government reduce the cost of domestic debt.

The fragmentation of public debt issues also merits attention. The proliferation of primary issues of treasury bills, Development Bonds, Special Bonds, and savings certificates not only pushes up the issuance cost; this fragmentation of issues also leads to illiquidity and hinders the development of the secondary market. Consolidating these securities and introducing the practice of reopening issues would improve liquidity in the secondary market. The proposed listing of government debt securities on the stock exchange, along with electronic trading, would provide a further boost to the development of the bond market.

Separating public debt management from the conduct of monetary policy would also be beneficial. Doing so would establish clear accountability and responsibility for debt management.

Corporate Bond Market

The corporate bond market in Nepal amounts to a mere 0.21 percent of GDP. Only nine issues have taken place in the past 10 years (table 4.6). The issues were mainly by banks, to meet Tier 2 capital requirements, and were for the most part

Table 4.6   Corporate Debenture Issues, Nepal, Fiscal 1997–07

Issuer	Fiscal year	Public offering	Private placement	Maturity (years)	Coupon rate (%)
		Issue amount (Nrs millions)			
Shree Ram Sugar Mills	1997	93	0	4	14
Himalayan Bank	2002	100	260	7	8.50
Nepal Investment Bank	2003	100	200	7	7.50
Everest Bank	2004	50	250	7	6
Bank of Kathmandu	2005	50	150	7	6
Nepal Investment Bank	2006	80	170	7	6
Nepal Industrial and Commercial Bank	2006	50	150	7	6
Nepal SBI Bank	2006	150	50	7	6
Nepal Investment Bank	2007	50	20	7	6.25

Source: Nepal Stock Exchange.

Table 4.7   Cost of Bond Issuance, Nepal, 2007

Item	Share of issue (%)	Nrs
Securities and exchange commission registration	0.225	450,000
Publication of prospectus	0.013	26,000
Printing of prospectus and applications	0.001	2,266
Printing of certificates; postissue expenses; postage	0.003	6,000
Listing fee	0.075	150,000
Annual stock exchange fee	0.025	50,000
Issue manager or underwriter	0.100	200,000
Trustee fee	0.025	50,000
Credit rating; bankers; legal and audit	0.040	80,000
Broker commission	0.200	400,000
Total cost	0.707	1,414,266

Source: Country authorities and market information.
Note: The size of the bond issue is assumed to be Nrs 200 million.

privately placed with other banks. Debt issues are unsecured, with maturities ranging from four to seven years and semiannual interest payments.

The conspicuous absence of corporate debentures from the Nepalese capital market can be attributed to several factors. First, the first two debenture issues in Nepal, by two major corporate entities in the late 1980s and the 1990s, ended in default (on both interest and principal repayments), eroding the confidence of Nepalese investors. Second, lack of corporate governance standards, poor transparency in companies' financial statements, and lack of a credit rating system make investing in corporate debt a leap in the dark—one that investors have understandably avoided making. Third, on the issuer side, the conflict and instability have put business expansion, and thus long-term financing needs, on hold. Short-term financing needs are met through the banking system.

Two debenture issues are in the pipeline, a salt trading company and a state-owned hydropower project. As agreed with some donor agencies, the government has refrained from providing explicit guarantees to lenders for borrowings by enterprises that it owns. In lieu of such guarantees, however, these state-owned enterprises plan to offer investors seniority over existing cash flows from other projects.

One constraint on the development of the corporate bond market is the cost of bond issuance. In Nepal this cost hovers around 0.70 percent of the issue size (table 4.7). There is room for reducing the cost.

Demand Side: The Investor Base

The major investors in the government debt securities market are commercial banks and Nepal Rastra Bank (figure 4.1). Holding more than 80 percent of

Figure 4.1   **Distribution of Holdings of Government Bonds and Treasury Bills, Nepal, 2002–06**

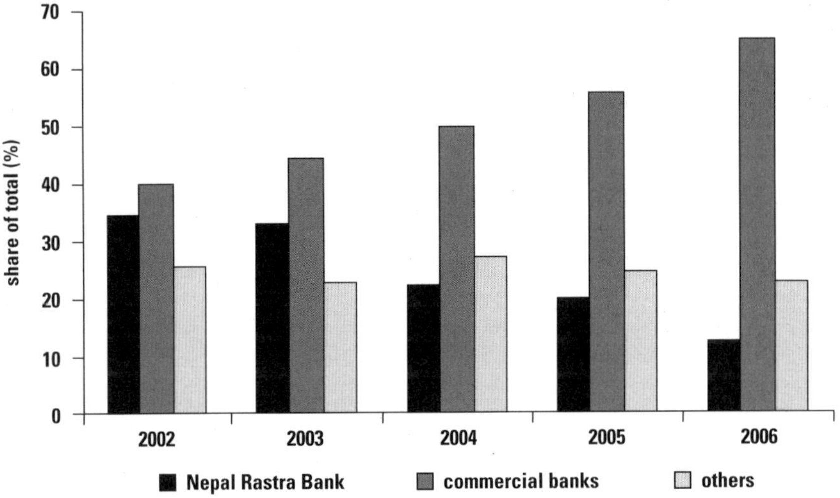

Sources: Nepal Rastra Bank; World Bank staff calculations.
Note: Data are for the end of the fiscal year, July 15.

outstanding treasury bills, commercial banks are the dominant players in the treasury bill market, which they use for short-term liquidity management. Nepal Rastra Bank absorbs an additional 15 percent, while other investors account for a meager 4 percent. At the longer end of the market the investor base also includes financial institutions, insurance companies, the Employees' Provident Fund, and high-net-worth individuals. These investors together account for less than a quarter of all investments in government debt securities, however.

Provident Funds

The Citizen Investment Trust, an entity supervised by the Ministry of Finance and responsible for operating all nongovernment retirement schemes, invests more than 60 percent of its assets in fixed deposits with banks. It invests less than 30 percent in government debt securities, and places the other 10 percent in the equity and corporate debt securities market (table 4.8). The decisions of its investment committee are approved by a government-nominated board that is not allowed to undertake any investment in securities not covered by a government guarantee. Because these guarantees are no longer issued for corporate debt, the entity's investments in fixed-income instruments will increasingly gravitate toward government paper.

The Employees' Provident Fund, a funded and contributory scheme for government and semigovernment employees with 415,000 members, also limits its

Table 4.8   Investment Portfolio of Citizen Investment Trust, Nepal, 2002–06

(Nrs millions)

Type of investment	2002	2003	2004	2005	2006
Government debt securities	766	1,496	1,707	1,705	1,474
Fixed deposits	229	223	1,006	1,763	3,222
Shares and debentures	61	138	154	148	494
Total	1,056	1,858	2,866	3,616	5,190

Source: Citizen Investment Trust.
Note: Data are for the end of the fiscal year, July 15.

Table 4.9   Investment Portfolio of Employees' Provident Fund, Nepal, 2002–07

(Nrs millions)

Type of investment	2002	2003	2004	2005	2006	2007
Government debt securities	3,493	3,914	5,198	5,089	4,229	4,337
Pokhara Awaas[a]	6	1	11	7	5	6
Shares	231	231	255	311	391	405
Fixed deposits	14,917	15,256	16,096	15,630	18,520	19,325
Total	18,647	19,402	21,560	21,036	23,145	24,073

Source: Nepal Rastra Bank.
Note: Data are for the end of the fiscal year (July 15) except for 2007, for which the data are for January.
a. Shares in a real estate development company.

participation in the country's capital market. The fund holds more than 80 percent of its investment portfolio (totaling about Nrs 24 billion) in fixed deposits with banks. It invests only 18 percent in government debt securities and less than 2 percent in the equity market (table 4.9). The fund's investment decisions are guided by its policy of providing its members with the greatest possible return at the lowest possible risk, and it benefits from a government guarantee of a minimum return of 3 percent on members' investments. Under the prevailing market conditions, fixed deposits with banks provide the highest rate of return and are thus an obvious choice for the fund's investment managers.

Mutual Funds

Mutual funds are conspicuously absent from the Nepalese market. NIDC Capital Markets attempted to establish one in 1994, but it shut down the fund in 2004 in the face of restrictions on the scope and size of its investments, an obligation to pay a minimum 5 percent dividend, a ban on foreign investments, an investment ceiling of 10 percent of the fund in any company, and unclear tax and regulatory regimes.

Banks have been deterred from creating trusts by the ban they face on investing in other banks' equity. While this restriction has the welcome effect of avoiding excessive concentration of ownership in the country's financial system, it drastically reduces the range of viable investment opportunities for banks in this segment of the market.

Another constraint is the lack of a trust act that would enable Nepal Rastra Bank to issue operating licenses. Some positive steps have recently been taken in this direction, however. In May 2007 the Ministry of Finance set up a working group to formulate guidelines for the introduction of mutual funds in Nepal. The consultations of the working group led to a detailed report that included a proposed regulatory act for mutual funds. The report suggests that regulation of the mutual fund industry could fall under the jurisdiction of the Securities Board of Nepal. In view of the low interest rates in the country, it also suggests allowing the funds to invest up to 50 percent of their assets abroad, a suggestion that found favor in the mid-July 2007 budget speech by the minister of finance.

Foreign Investors

Foreign investors are not allowed to participate directly in the domestic bond market. However, they may establish a presence in the country's financial system by entering into a joint venture agreement with a Nepalese entity.

Market Infrastructure

Nepal lacks several of the elements critical for a well-functioning bond market, including a scripless securities settlement system and a credit rating industry.

Issuance Procedures

There is no primary dealer system in the Nepalese market. As noted, treasury bills are sold on an auction basis. While the bidding is normally open to any interested party, commercial banks and financial institutions dominate the market.

Auctions have a two-tier structure. Bidders are classified as competitive—commercial banks for treasury bills; commercial banks, development banks, and finance companies for long-term bonds—or noncompetitive. In any auction at least 15 percent of the issue is allocated to noncompetitive bidders.

The process for both treasury bills and bonds is entirely paper based. For treasury bills bidders use a standard form provided by Nepal Rastra Bank and submit their offer by placing the form in a tender box along with 2.5 percent of the bid price as earnest money. The box is opened at the end of the day, and the bid forms verified and registered in record-keeping books.

For long-term instruments the sale is announced in a national daily newspaper, and potential buyers fill out an application form. If an issue is oversubscribed, bonds are allocated pro rata at the same rate. Certificates are then prepared for each investor and distributed accordingly.

Secondary Market

In fiscal 2004 Nepal Rastra Bank initiated a secondary market for treasury bills. Commercial banks and financial institutions are licensed to function as market makers, offering two-way quotes. Treasury bills represent the most liquid segment of the market—they are issued in the form of promissory notes, and ownership can be transferred simply by endorsement—though lack of coordination in data recording makes estimating trading volumes difficult.

In 2007 the Public Debt Management Department designated 51 market makers for the retail sale of citizens savings certificates. These entities are obligated to buy back securities sold prematurely by the holders (in exchange for a fee for the premature sale).

Trading in Development Bonds is almost nil, as investors tend to hold these bonds until maturity. The bonds have been listed on the Nepal Stock Exchange (NEPSE), and the trading that has taken place has been conducted at par through three market makers, appointed by NEPSE in consultation with Nepal Rastra Bank and the Securities Board of Nepal.

Clearing and Settlement System

The clearing and settlement system is by any standards inadequate to support a well-functioning bond market. All bonds and debentures listed and traded through NEPSE are cleared through the exchange's clearing unit, which uses domestically developed spreadsheet-based software. Processing information on transactions takes 10–15 days on average, and there are no electronic links for sharing information with Nepal Rastra Bank departments for the purposes of debt management.

All debt instruments are issued in paper form. That not only adds to the time and cost of transactions; it also makes the securities vulnerable to theft, forgery, and destruction. Introducing a scripless security system is essential for efficient clearing and settlement of traded securities and recording of information.

Introducing an electronic book-entry system is vital to the development of the primary and secondary markets for government debt securities. There has been little progress on this front, however. Nepal Rastra Bank is developing a transitional system with the aim of moving to a paperless (dematerialized) treasury bill market, but this effort remains at the first stage.

Moreover, the benefits of having a dematerialized treasury bill market will not be fully realized until a modern, automated payment system is in place for interbank payments. To complete these payments today, banks must physically deliver checks at a dedicated branch of the central bank. The ability to complete purchase and sale transactions without physical exchange of paper will not be enough for developing the secondary treasury bill market as long as the cash leg of the transaction continues to rely on paper instructions. Developing automated payment and settlement systems remains essential.

Nepal Rastra Bank recently acquired a debt recording and management software system (CS-DRSM 2000+) from the Commonwealth Secretariat, which was expected to be implemented in late 2007. The system would expedite the recording of transactions and facilitate the provision of information for debt management. But no concrete steps toward implementing the system have been taken yet because the system needs to be tailored to the needs of domestic debt management in Nepal. Meanwhile, Nepal Rastra Bank is also considering a comprehensive upgrade of information technology as part of the ongoing financial sector reform project.

Credit Rating Industry

No credit rating agency operates in Nepal. As a result, debt instruments are issued without being rated, limiting the ability of investors to make informed investment decisions.

Under the present circumstances in Nepal it is unlikely that a credit rating agency will be established. Lack of accounting and auditing standards, poor disclosure requirements, and lack of corporate governance guidelines make credit rating a difficult endeavor. Moreover, at this stage of market development prospective credit rating agencies may not find enough business to make the venture commercially viable.

Legal and Regulatory Framework

Recent laws provide a legal and regulatory framework for oversight of the Nepalese debt securities market, though resources for oversight appear to fall short of what is needed. Substantial weaknesses remaining in corporate governance and accounting and auditing standards undermine investor confidence. In addition, the tax system lacks harmonization across instruments and asset classes.

Oversight of the Financial Market

Nepal Rastra Bank is responsible for overall supervision of the financial market in Nepal, while its Public Debt Management Department is responsible for oversight of domestic government debt and the issuance of debt instruments.

The Domestic Debt Act, 2002 provides the framework for the issuance and servicing of the government's domestic debt securities. The Ministry of Finance has responsibility for managing foreign debt, while the Public Debt Management Department implements the domestic debt strategy. Nepal Rastra Bank's holdings of government securities cannot exceed 10 percent of the government's revenue in the previous year, with three exceptions: securities purchased at the time of primary issuance to maintain the desired market liquidity, securities purchased in the secondary market as part of open market operations, and securities purchased before enactment of the Domestic Debt Act in 2002.

The government debt securities market is also regulated by the Government Securities Trading Management Bylaws, 2005 and the Banks and Financial Institutions Act, 2006. Their joint stipulations deal mainly with capital requirements, qualifications, and licensing of market makers and brokers.

The issuance of corporate debt is governed by the Company Act, 2006, which replaced the Company Ordinance, 2005. The act prohibits unlisted companies from publicly issuing debt. It also includes corporate governance guidelines, though enforcement of these has been lacking.

The Securities Exchange Act, 2006 regulates the securities market in Nepal. It names the Securities Board of Nepal as the apex regulatory body for the country's capital market, to function in coordination with NEPSE, Nepal Rastra Bank, the Insurance Board, and the Company Registrar's Office. But while the Securities Board bears the ultimate responsibility for oversight of the capital market, its resources appear to be inadequate for that role.

Corporate Governance Standards

Lack of corporate governance standards remains one of the biggest obstacles to developing the corporate bond market. Most private businesses in the country are family owned, with boards consisting mainly of family members. Adding to the problem are the inadequate accounting and auditing standards, which make evaluating the financial health of these companies a difficult exercise. And in the event of default, the judicial system is unable to guarantee quick and efficient bankruptcy procedures. The Banks and Financial Institutions Act established minimum corporate governance guidelines, but so far these have been applied only to the banking sector.

Accounting Standards

Nepal has yet to develop a coherent set of accounting standards. While the Institute of Chartered Accountants of Nepal has developed a number of local standards, these are rarely followed, and manipulation of financial statements is widespread in the corporate sector. The lack of accounting standards, by undermining transparency and making it impossible to monitor publicly listed companies, has been a major impediment to the development of the corporate bond market.

Tax Regime

The tax regime provides for different treatment of different classes of investors and assets. Capital gains are taxed at 10 percent for individuals and 15 percent for institutions. Tax treatment also varies for different types of government securities (some being taxable, and some tax exempt). Each bond certificate sets out specific tax provisions.

All interest income from corporate bonds and taxable government bonds is taxed at 6 percent if the bondholder is an individual and at 15 percent if the holder is an institutional investor. This differential tax rate rules out cross-trading between institutions and the retail public, further limiting the possibilities for secondary market activity.

Recommended Actions

Just as efforts are under way to resolve the domestic conflict in Nepal, so too should efforts be under way to prepare the country for the long-term projects it will need to undertake once political conditions permit. Developing the bond market will need to be part of this. Doing so will require addressing many issues; outlined here are those warranting immediate consideration.

Supply Side

Further Improving the Money Market. One priority should be to establish the well-functioning money market that must normally be in place before a government bond market—with both an efficient primary market and a liquid secondary market—can be fully developed. Nepal Rastra Bank's liquidity management efforts, while noteworthy, have been hampered by the lack of a sound framework for cash and debt management.

Developing a Reliable Issuance Calendar and Improving Cash Management. Nepal's poorly functioning and illiquid market in domestic government debt securities makes building a sovereign yield curve difficult. To help create a benchmark, Nepal Rastra Bank should devote serious attention to developing an issuance calendar that specifies the volumes of issues. As part of this, cash management practices will need to be revised and a cash management strategy developed.

Demand Side

Broadening the Investor Base. Developing collective investment schemes deserves high priority. The country's existing schemes—the Employees' Provident Fund and Citizen Investment Trust—are negligible in size, and they invest most of their funds in fixed deposits for lack of better investment opportunities. In addition, with no mutual funds, the country lacks a vehicle for small investors to pool funds and thus participate in the debt securities market.

The proposal to promote a mutual fund industry in the country should be given serious consideration: mutual funds would provide both an engine for deepening and broadening the investor base and a stable source of domestic demand for the local debt securities market. In addition, qualified foreign institutional investors should be invited to participate in the debt securities market to provide access to additional sources of capital.

Market Infrastructure

Establishing a Primary Dealer System. While Nepal Rastra Bank appoints market makers to facilitate the trade of government debt securities, primary dealers are also needed. These roles should be entrusted to established financial institutions with adequate capital and infrastructure. Primary dealers would have the exclusive right to deal with Nepal Rastra Bank as counterparty in the primary and secondary markets for government securities. In return, they would be expected to subscribe to a minimum amount of government securities during auctions while acting as market makers by providing two-way quotes in the secondary market.

Introducing a Scripless Securities Settlement System. Physical delivery of paper certificates not only is time consuming and inefficient; it also entails risks of loss, theft, damage, forgery, and delivery errors. Developing a scripless securities settlement system will be crucial in efforts to upgrade the Nepalese bond market.

Legal and Regulatory Framework

Enhancing Corporate Governance. The weak corporate governance and equally weak disclosure system are major obstacles in developing the country's corporate bond market. While steps have been taken toward improving governance standards, transparency remains minimal. Effective steps should be taken to strengthen governance standards across the entire financial system.

Strengthening Regulatory and Supervisory Oversight. The Securities Board of Nepal should be vested with the necessary powers to enforce the rules it frames on corporate governance, disclosure, and accounting standards.

Developing Accounting Standards. The Institute of Chartered Accountants of Nepal needs to devote attention to developing a comprehensive set of accounting standards, and the Securities Board of Nepal should be made responsible for enforcing those standards.

Implementing a Clear Tax System. The differences in tax treatment among asset classes should be eliminated. In reviewing the Income Tax Act, the Ministry of Finance should pay particular attention to creating a level playing field for all market participants.

References

Bambang Kusmiarso. 2005. "The Development of Domestic Bond Market and Its Implications to Central Banks: Country Experience." South East Asian Central Banks (SEACEN) Research and Training Centre, Kuala Lumpur.

BIS (Bank for International Settlements). 2007. *Quarterly Review.* September. Paris.

IMF (International Monetary Fund). 2007. "Nepal: Article IV Consultation." Washington, DC.

Nepal Merchant Banking & Finance. 2007. "Study on South Asian Domestic Debt Markets—Nepal." Consultant's note prepared for the World Bank, Kathmandu.

Nepal, Ministry of Finance. 2006. *Economic Survey, Fiscal Year 2005/2006.* Kathmandu.

NRB (Nepal Rastra Bank). 2006a. *Annual Report, 2005/06.* Kathmandu.

———. 2006b. *Banking and Financial Statistics, No. 47.* Banks and Financial Institutions Regulation Department, Kathmandu.

———. 2007a. *Annual Report, 2006/07.* Kathmandu.

———. 2007b. *Annual Supervision Report 2006.* Kathmandu.

5

Pakistan

Pakistan's bond market remains at an early stage of development, depriving the economy of an important avenue for the efficient allocation of capital. As in other South Asian countries, government debt securities dominate. Yet the government bond market lacks depth, breadth, and liquidity. Among the impediments to its development are national savings instruments offering more attractive terms than market-based instruments that are otherwise comparable. The corporate bond market remains tiny.

A recent proposal by the Pakistani government sets out several strategies aimed at both ensuring effective public debt management—borrowing at the lowest cost while keeping risks in check—and developing an efficient government debt securities market.

Introduction

Pakistan posted an impressive economic performance in 2002–07. Real GDP growth averaged a robust 7 percent a year. The growth momentum in 2006–07 was broad based, with strong performance in all three major sectors—agriculture, industry, and services. Aided by the lifting of sanctions, foreign investment inflows, including those deriving from privatization, hit record highs. Inflation declined marginally. The current account deficit rose to nearly 4 percent of GDP, but government borrowing from international markets on favorable terms more than covered the larger deficit, resulting in a balance of payments surplus of more than $1 billion.

The momentum is expected to continue, though moderated by the effects of tighter monetary policy, high international oil prices, and slow export growth. Moving forward, the key challenges will be containing inflation and the current account deficit, as well as maintaining political stability, sound macroeconomic management, and structural reforms.

Table 5.1   Financial Market Profile, Pakistan, 2002–06

(US$ millions)

Segment	2002	2003	2004	2005	2006
Domestic debt securities market	28,403.0	30,905.0	31,495.0	33,964.0	33,361.9
Equity market capitalization	10,199.7	16,629.3	29,149.8	45,906.1	45,414.7
Banking assets	26,984.3	33,296.4	36,958.3	44,915.1	50,697.6
Total	65,587.1	80,830.7	97,603.2	124,785.2	129,474.3

Sources: BIS 2007; World Bank, World Development Indicators database; International Monetary Fund, International Financial Statistics database; World Bank staff calculations.

Despite concerns about recent political instability, market players remain confident about the country's growth prospects. Financial sector performance has been strong. Following sector reforms launched by the government in the late 1990s as part of wide-ranging structural reforms, the banking industry has undergone enormous structural changes and posted significant improvements. The stock market has had remarkable growth, with market capitalization rising from about $10 billion in 2002 to more than $45 billion by the end of 2006. By contrast, the debt securities market saw little growth and accounted for less than half the total securities market capitalization at the end of the period (table 5.1).

Banking Sector Reforms

Reforms in the banking sector have been extensive. The central bank, the State Bank of Pakistan, liberalized foreign investment in banks and encouraged consolidation in the industry in the late 1990s. There has been a shift in the ownership structure: local private banks have emerged as the leading players, accounting for nearly 81 percent of banking system assets in 2007. More than 14 banks have foreign shareholders, and a few are either fully or partially foreign owned. Today the banking sector consists of 20 private sector commercial banks, 6 foreign banks, 6 microfinance banks, 5 Islamic banks, 5 specialized banks, and 4 public sector commercial banks (State Bank of Pakistan 2008).

Banking sector reforms have also strengthened the regulatory and supervisory framework, including corporate governance standards. Other major reform initiatives have included developing a road map for implementing the Basel II Capital Accord, improving financial information systems, and raising the minimum capital requirement to $100 million for banks and development finance institutions effective December 31, 2009 (see annex 5.1).

The impact of all these reforms has been far reaching. Banking assets (at 27 percent of GDP in 2002 and 35 percent in 2006) have kept pace with the country's economic growth. The equity market has also benefited from the positive impact of the reforms: banks now constitute almost 25 percent of market capitalization at the Karachi Stock Exchange. And the banking sector's performance has improved across a range of indicators, including nonperforming loans, capital adequacy, and return on assets.

Thanks to these improvements, Pakistan's banking sector maintained its ranking among the top half in a group of 44 emerging market economies on indicators of capital adequacy and asset quality (IMF 2006). Moreover, it moved close to the top of the ranking on profitability—up from a position near the bottom in 2001.

Development of the Debt Securities Market

While Pakistan's financial system has grown in depth and breadth, there continues to be excessive reliance on the banking system. Developing the long-term bond market, particularly the corporate bond market, and further strengthening the equity market will go a long way toward achieving stability in the financial markets.

Compared with other emerging markets in Asia, Pakistan's debt securities market remains small in both relative and absolute terms. At the end of fiscal 2006 it amounted to a mere 26 percent of GDP, substantially smaller than regional counterparts at similar income levels (see table 1.3 in chapter 1). As in other South Asian countries, the slow growth of the domestic bond market in Pakistan can be attributed to the heavy reliance on the banking sector for funding needs. It can also be traced to the nationalization policies of the 1970s and 1980s, when the government met its borrowing needs through captive sources of funding. An auction-based market for treasury bills was established only in 1991, and long-term government debt securities did not appear until 1992. The corporate bond market followed a few years later, in 1995.

Beyond the small size of the market, the dominance of government debt raises concerns about the depth of Pakistan's financial markets and about the ability of the bond market to contribute to the economy's financial strength and development.

Supply Side: Debt Instruments and Issuers

Government debt securities accounted for more than 97 percent of those outstanding at the end of fiscal 2006 (table 5.2). Debt instruments issued by corporations and financial institutions accounted for a mere 1.7 percent and 1.2 percent. Issuance of corporate debt securities has recently picked up because of liquidity pressures, but the corporate bond market remains negligible in size compared with the government debt securities market.

The modest growth of the Pakistani bond market can be traced to several constraints on the supply side. Perhaps the greatest one has been the lack of a government debt management strategy geared toward developing the bond market as a whole rather than using debt instruments as an immediate source of government financing. Nonmarketable debt instruments issued through the government-subsidized national savings schemes accounted for 37 percent of domestic government debt at the end of fiscal 2006. The national savings instruments have had

Table 5.2   Composition of Debt Securities Market, Pakistan, 2006

Issuer	Amount (US$ millions)	Share of total (%)
Government	32,410.0	97.1
Financial institutions	392.5	1.2
Corporations	559.4	1.7
Total	33,361.9	100.0

Sources: For government, BIS 2007; for financial institutions and corporations, national authorities and World Bank staff calculations.
Note: Data are for the end of the fiscal year, June 30.

a heavily distorting effect on the market. In addition, the government debt securities market lacks depth and liquidity, and the bond market lacks a credible sovereign benchmark.

Money Market

The money market in Pakistan consists mainly of the treasury bill market, overnight interbank call money market, and repurchase agreement (repo) market. The State Bank uses the six-month treasury bill auction rate as the policy signal rate. It also uses this rate as one of its main instruments for open market operations, apart from adjustments in bank reserve requirements to control aggregate money supply.

The interbank call money market is not yet well established, primarily because of the lack of credit information on counterparties. The repo market is very active, however, and meets more than 60 percent of the liquidity requirements of the interbank money market (table 5.3).

The State Bank continued its tight monetary policy during fiscal 2007, taking care to both maintain price stability and support attainment of the economic growth target. Robust growth in deposit mobilization and larger central bank purchases of U.S. dollars from the interbank market added to the rupee liquidity in the banking system. Excess liquidity in the interbank market, primarily from external and government sectors, led to some temporary dips in the interbank overnight repo rate—with large deviations from the discount rate—though for short durations. The overnight repo market saw less volatility than in fiscal 2006, and the three-day State Bank repo rate rose by 50 basis points to reach 9.5 percent.

In the second half of fiscal 2007 the State Bank sterilized rupee liquidity through auctions while still effectively using open market operations to manage interbank liquidity (table 5.4). Thanks to banks' greater interest in longer-term treasury bills, the State Bank was able to sterilize liquidity for a longer period.

To contain inflationary pressures and restrain the easing of monetary conditions, in August 2006 the State Bank raised the reserve requirements for banks and

Table 5.3   Trading Volume in Repo Market, Pakistan, Fiscal 2006–07

	Volume (PRs billions)		Share of total (%)	
	2006	2007	2006	2007
By market				
Outright	1,104.20	1,532.40	10.4	11.6
Repo	7,442.49	8,563.63	70.0	65.1
Call	1,151.53	1,810.60	10.8	13.8
Clean	926.90	1,257.40	8.7	9.6
Total	10,625.12	13,164.03	100.0	100.0
By category				
Collateralized	8,546.69	10,096.03	80.4	76.7
Uncollateralized	2,078.43	3,068.00	19.6	23.3
Total	10,625.12	13,164.03	100.0	100.0

Source: State Bank of Pakistan, Domestic Market and Monetary Management Department.
Note: The trading volume in each market represents the lending volume.

Table 5.4   Net Outflow through Treasury Bill Auctions and Open Market Operations, Pakistan, Fiscal 2007

(PRs billions except where otherwise specified)

Period	Auctions		Open market operations		Net outflow
	Maturity (days)	Net acceptance	Number of operations	Net absorption	
July–Dec. 2006	403.7	−28.6	43	539.5	510.9
Jan.–June 2007	241.9	271.4	26	324.5	595.9
Fiscal 2007	645.6	242.7	69	864.0	1,106.8

Source: State Bank of Pakistan, Domestic Market and Monetary Management Department.

hiked the policy rate by 50 basis points to 9.50 percent. In August 2007 it raised the rate by another 50 basis points, to 10 percent. As a result, treasury bill yields rose (in both the primary and the secondary market), and other rates also responded with an upward movement in the first quarter of fiscal 2008. At the same time the State Bank continued to drain excess liquidity from the interbank market and kept the overnight rates close to the discount rate through most of fiscal 2007. Weighted average lending rates showed a rising trend. Tight liquidity conditions in the interbank market moderated speculative demand for credit.

Government Debt Issuance

The Pakistani government issues domestic debt securities in a range of maturities. But it has yet to take the role of a price taker. Auctions are driven by price rather

Table 5.5   Results of Treasury Bill Auctions, Pakistan, Fiscal 2002–07

Fiscal year	Auctions	Offer (PRs billions)	Accepted (PRs billions)
2002	26	615.3	317.2
2003	26	1,551.0	642.7
2004	26	1,021.8	514.5
2005	26	1,616.6	1,051.3
2006	26	1,124.4	738.1
2007	26	1,094.8	888.3

Source: State Bank of Pakistan, Domestic Market and Monetary Management Department.

than by volume: the government decides the cutoff yield for the securities rather than accepting the market-determined price. Moreover, auctions of long-term securities remain irregular.

In addition to issuing domestic debt securities, the government accessed the international capital market in fiscal 2006 for the first time, through an issuance of euro bonds with tenors of 10 years ($500 million) and 30 years ($300 million). Besides meeting the government's funding needs, this issuance may help in establishing a long-term sovereign benchmark and facilitating access to global markets for local corporations.

Treasury Bills. The State Bank conducts treasury bill auctions every two weeks. These instruments have maturities of 3, 6, and 12 months, with the 6-month yield being the benchmark short-term rate. The primary market for treasury bills, particularly for short-term bills, has remained robust, and the acceptance ratio has been improving (table 5.5).

In fiscal 2007 the government set the cutoff acceptance yields in the range of 8.64–8.69 percent for 3-month treasury bills, 8.81–8.90 percent for 6-month bills, and 9.00–9.05 percent for 12-month bills. In August 2007, however, the government moved the rates up to 9.09 percent, 9.14 percent, and 9.16 percent. The choice of the 6-month treasury bill rate as the target for the State Bank's open market operations intensifies the short-term rate volatility caused by the government's unpredictable liquidity needs.

Pakistan Investment Bonds. The State Bank auctions Pakistan Investment Bonds, longer-term instruments with maturities ranging from 3 to 20 years, on an ad hoc basis. Although initial issues met with success, issuance of these bonds has been erratic: the government remained reluctant to issue these instruments during most of fiscal 2005 and 2006. More recently, however, there have been some fresh issues (figure 5.1; table 5.6).

Figure 5.1   Issuance of Pakistan Investment Bonds, Fiscal 2001–07

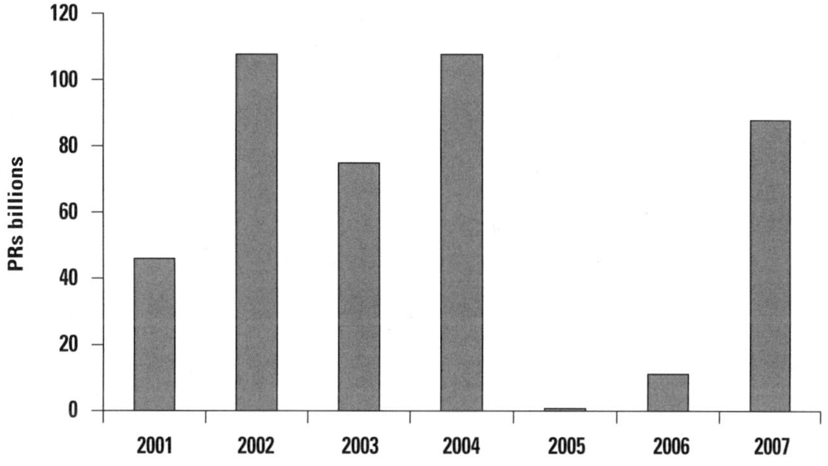

Source: Pakistan, Ministry of Finance 2007.
a. Data are for end-November 2006.

Table 5.6   Results of Pakistan Investment Bond Auctions, Fiscal 2001–07

Fiscal year	Auctions held	Bids		Amount (PRs billions)		Acceptance	
		Offer	Accepted	Offer	Accepted	As % of offer	As % of target
2001	6	261	182	58.8	46.1	78.4	94.1
2002	13	1,374	486	238.4	107.7	45.2	115.8
2003	7	1,595	323	212.0	74.8	35.3	113.4
2004	7	1,273	626	221.3	107.7	48.6	85.4
2005	3	126	17	8.0	0.8	9.6	8.6
2006	1	182	133	17.1	11.2	65.8	112.4
2007	5	898	430	199.0	87.9	39.0	90.4

Source: State Bank of Pakistan, Domestic Market and Monetary Management Department.

Pakistan Investment Bonds are allocated on the basis of cutoff yields decided by the government rather than by market-determined prices. When the market has demanded higher yields than the government was willing to pay, auctions have been canceled. This was the case for all Pakistan Investment Bond auctions initiated between 2004 and 2006. The supply constraints in these long-term instruments restricted their liquidity and, because trading activity was so limited, led to a situation in which long-term yields did not reflect market conditions. The limited issues also create constraints for financial institutions in managing gaps between their long-term assets and liabilities. Moreover, they deprive the market of a current benchmark as well as hamper the emergence of credible benchmark rates for long-term financing.

In May 2006 the government again began issuing Pakistan Investment Bonds at regular intervals. It also reopened the earlier issues to increase the supply of on-the-run issues. The State Bank held five auctions in fiscal 2007 by reopening previous issues as well as making new issues, including 30-year bonds.

Sovereign Yield Curve

The government's resumption of regular bond issues and the issuance of 30-year bonds represent a major breakthrough toward extending the yield curve and developing a benchmark. But even as these steps offer promise for developing the bond market, another government decision may hamper its development: a reversal of an earlier decision to ban institutional investments in the national savings schemes (see following section).

Rising short-term interest rates have placed upward pressure on the shorter end of the yield curve, which has thus assumed an increasingly flatter shape in recent years. In addition, the practice of basing auctions on yields rather than on announced volumes undermines the government's credibility as a borrower. For these reasons, Pakistan lacks a sovereign benchmark that would provide guidance to market players.

National Savings Schemes

The national savings schemes are perhaps the single biggest impediment to developing the bond market in Pakistan. These schemes offer long-term, government-subsidized instruments with both high yields and an inherent cost-free put option—investors are able to resell the instruments before maturity without incurring penalties. The schemes are run by the Central Directorate of National Savings, a department of the Ministry of Finance, which is responsible for the sale of the products to the retail public through a network of 376 branches across the country.

The national savings schemes are useful for accessing retail sources of funding. But they work to the detriment of government debt management because they provide an on-tap source of financing over which the government has no effective control. Moreover, because of the higher yields and the inherent cost-free put option that the national savings products offer, market-based instruments that are otherwise comparable, such as Pakistan Investment Bonds, immediately become a less attractive investment option. This again hinders the establishment of a long-term benchmark.

At the end of June 2006 the outstanding balance of national savings instruments totaled PRs 934 billion, equivalent to 37 percent of domestic government debt (table 5.7). The balance showed an increasing trend by April 2007, reflecting a change in policy. In March 2000 the government had taken the positive step of

Table 5.7 Outstanding Balance of National Savings Schemes, Pakistan, Fiscal 2002–06

(PRs millions)

Type of instrument	2002	2003	2004	2005	2006
Accounts	56,755	73,821	82,296	105,668	119,372
Certificates	686,742	778,688	742,320	670,232	649,354
Prize Bonds	103,130	129,970	152,812	164,057	165,496
Total	846,627	982,479	984,428	939,957	934,222

Source: State Bank of Pakistan.
Note: Data are for the end of the fiscal year, June 30.

banning institutional investors from accessing national savings instruments for purposes of portfolio management. But it reversed that decision in October 2006, without previous consultation with market participants.

Some unlisted state-owned enterprise bonds (carrying the guarantee of the federal government) also offer very high returns. Offloading these bonds to the capital market would provide an immediate impetus to its development by creating competition for the national savings instruments. More critically, it would also save important revenue for the government. In addition, a number of revenue bonds could be floated on the exchanges, increasing their depth.

Composition of Domestic Government Debt

Domestic government debt falls into three main categories: floating debt (short-term debt such as treasury bills), permanent debt (long-term borrowings such as Pakistan Investment Bonds), and unfunded debt (instruments offered through the government's national savings schemes, including long-term bonds and deposit facilities; table 5.8).

The structure of domestic government debt has shifted since fiscal 1999. Floating (short-term) debt has been increasing as a share of the total, while permanent (long-term) debt and unfunded debt have been decreasing (figure 5.2). A rise in

Table 5.8 Composition of Domestic Government Debt, Pakistan, Fiscal 2002–06

(PRs millions)

Type of debt	2002	2003	2004	2005	2006
Permanent	367,989	427,908	536,800	500,874	499,775
Floating	557,807	516,268	543,443	778,163	940,233
Unfunded	792,138	909,500	899,215	854,044	859,161
Total	1,717,934	1,853,676	1,979,458	2,133,081	2,299,169

Source: State Bank of Pakistan.
Note: Data are for the end of the fiscal year, June 30.

Figure 5.2 Structure of Domestic Government Debt, Pakistan, Fiscal 2002–06

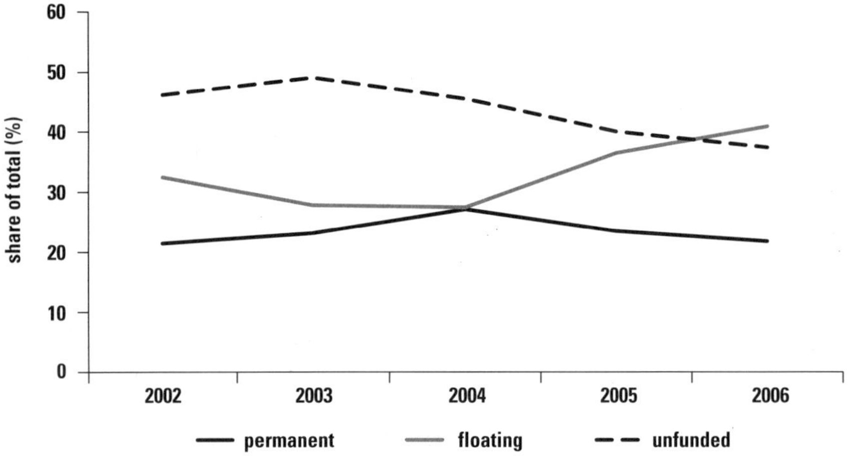

Source: Pakistan, Ministry of Finance 2007.

the stock of treasury bills was the primary reason for the increase in overall domestic government debt in fiscal 2005–06.

Reliance on short-term debt increased for two main reasons. First, there was limited issuance of long-term debt (Pakistan Investment Bonds) between 2004 and 2006 because of unstable interest rates. Second, net investment in national savings instruments was lower than expected in fiscal 2004–06. As noted, however, growth in the outstanding balance for these instruments showed an upward trend in fiscal 2007 because of the reversal of the government's earlier decision prohibiting institutional investment in them.

Public Debt Management

In recent years total government debt in Pakistan has steadily declined as a percentage of GDP, evidence of improved potential for debt repayment (see annex 5.2). The government's debt management practices, however, leave room for improvement. An effective cash management system is lacking. Financing needs are approximated quarterly, and no formal forecasts are produced. In the absence of effective forecasting the Budget Wing of the Ministry of Finance keeps a surplus amount in the treasury account hosted by the State Bank. When deficits occur, the State Bank issues short-term paper and credits the treasury account with the corresponding amount. The lack of predictability makes the task of building a credible and efficient sovereign benchmark difficult.

Responsibility for decision making in debt management lies with three different agencies: the State Bank for short- and long-term government securities, the

Central Directorate of National Savings for the national savings schemes, and the Economic Affairs Division for foreign currency borrowing. To strengthen coordination among these three entities, the government in 2003 set up the Debt Policy Coordination Office to prepare a debt reduction strategy and maintain records of government debt and guarantees. Before any auction of government debt securities the Debt Policy Coordination Office, the Ministry of Finance's Budget Wing, and the State Bank's Exchange and Debt Management Department meet to discuss the volume and maturity of each issue.

The government of Pakistan recently proposed strategies to achieve the twin objectives of ensuring effective public debt management—borrowing at the minimum cost while keeping risks in check—and developing an efficient local currency sovereign debt securities market (Pakistan, Ministry of Finance 2007). Key strategies include these:

- Having the Debt Policy Coordination Office publish a quarterly analytical report on debt
- Reducing the share of floating debt to reduce the interest rate risk
- Following a regular calendar for Pakistan Investment Bond auctions (probably quarterly) with targets
- Limiting the number of tenors in Pakistan Investment Bond issues to create an adequate size to promote secondary market trading
- Revamping the primary dealer system for Pakistan Investment Bond auctions
- Reconsidering the held-to-maturity category for sovereign bonds
- Reducing the stock of treasury bills at a measured pace by issuing Pakistan Investment Bonds
- Making national savings instruments more market based
- Developing a comprehensive external borrowing strategy
- Tapping the global capital market through regular issuance of bonds (conventional and Islamic) to ensure a steady supply of sovereign paper and establish a benchmark for Pakistan
- Developing a framework for assessing the revaluation of debt arising from changes in exchange rates
- Closely monitoring external debt on a floating rate basis
- Developing a framework to assess the risks arising from developments in global capital markets

Corporate Bond Market

Corporate bonds first appeared in Pakistan in 1995, though the Companies Ordinance had allowed the issuance of corporate debt since 1984. The debut issue of the securities, known as term finance certificates, was by Packages Limited for PRs 250 million.[1] The catalysts for this first issue were the establishment of Pakistan's

Table 5.9   New Equity and Corporate Debt Issuance, Pakistan, Fiscal 2000–06

Fiscal year	Equities		Term finance certificates	
	Companies listed	Paid-up capital (PRs millions)	Issues floated	Amount subscribed (PRs millions)
2000	3	2,035.03	3	862.87
2001	3	2,884.70	5	5,694.94
2002	4	6,318.25	16	11,366.83
2003	6	4,562.56	6	4,590.20
2004	17	66,837.04	5	5,377.24
2005	19	30,090.28	8	10,849.77
2006	9	14,789.76	3	3,413.56

Source: Karachi Stock Exchange.

first credit rating agency and the reduction of the stamp duty from 1 percent to 0.15 percent.

The corporate debt securities market failed to take off until 2000, however, when the first issues of Pakistan Investment Bonds started providing a long-term indication of rates and the government decided to ban institutional investors from participation in the national savings schemes (table 5.9). The ban gave rise to an enormous pool of funds suddenly made available to the corporate sector.

At the end of June 2006 outstanding corporate debt amounted to about $952 million, or 0.8 percent of GDP. Activity in the corporate bond market dropped substantially in October 2006, when the ban on institutional investment in national savings schemes was lifted. The corporate bond market has continued to grow, however: the excess liquidity in the market has increased the demand for investment opportunities, and a booming mutual fund industry provides a strong investor base for term finance certificates. The growing issuance of these debt securities has led to an increase in secondary market activity. Most transactions occur in the over-the-counter (OTC) market and are not registered with the Karachi Stock Exchange, hampering estimates of the volumes traded.

Market Trends. The largest issue of term finance certificates was by Pakistan International Airlines for PRs 15.4 billion, in February 2003. Excluding that jumbo issue, the average size is PRs 660 million. The coupon rates on term finance certificates followed a declining trend from 1995 until January 2006, when there was a reversal in the trend. The rates track trends in other important rates, including the discount rate and the Karachi interbank offered rate (KIBOR). The returns closely follow those on Defense Savings Certificates, which compete for the same funds at the retail level (Hameed 2006).

As the amount of term finance certificates has continued to grow, there has been an apparent shift in the type of firms tapping the market for these securities, with nonbank financial institutions (including leasing firms) playing an increasingly large role. While nonfinancial term finance certificates have remained stagnant since the middle of 2004, financial ones have grown as a share of both the number and the amount of issues, mainly because banks tap this market to raise their Tier 2 capital.

An additional departure from previous trends has been a shift from fixed to floating rates. Until 1999 all term finance certificates were issued at fixed interest rates. Starting in 2001, however, most were issued at floating rates because of the rising trend in interest rates and the need to hedge against interest rate volatility.

The underlying benchmark rates for floating-rate term finance certificates have also changed over time. Beginning in 2003 most of these were linked to the weighted average yield of the five-year Pakistan Investment Bond, while others were tied to the cutoff yield of the last auction or an average of previous auctions. Issuers expected that a robust secondary market for Pakistan Investment Bonds would ensure that the yields on these bonds reflected long-term market rates. The secondary market for the bonds has not developed enough to serve this purpose, however, and as a result the markets have shifted to using the six-month KIBOR as the benchmark. Most new term finance certificates issued in 2005 and 2006 were linked to that rate.

The corporate debt securities market saw a few new issues in fiscal 2007, amounting to PRs 14.2 billion (table 5.10). Both the number of issues and the amount mobilized exceeded levels in the previous year. Most of the issues were from the financial sector.

Impediments to Developing the Market. There are a number of impediments to developing the corporate bond market in Pakistan. A major one is the lack of a credible benchmark for long-term paper. Because the interest rate on government paper is not entirely market determined, it does not serve as a benchmark for pricing corporate issues. In addition, the limited volume of sovereign paper in the secondary market undermines its benchmarking role. Lacking credible benchmarks, the corporate bond market, as mentioned, has moved to issuing long-term paper on floating rates linked to KIBOR.

Crowding out by government borrowing is another impediment. The corporate bond market and the government compete for the same pool of savings. The government taps retail savings through the national savings schemes, while it accesses institutional investment funds through Pakistan Investment Bonds and treasury bills. Sovereign papers, shorn of credit risk, have an obvious advantage. The national savings instruments have a particularly strong advantage, scoring not only on credit risk but also on pricing with their built-in put option.

The high cost of issuance is a serious deterrent to accessing the corporate bond market. Preliminary data suggest that this cost, which includes listing charges,

Table 5.10 New Issues of Term Finance Certificates, Pakistan, Fiscal 2007

Company	Issue date	Coupon rate	Tenor (years)	Amount (PRs millions)
Mobilink 2	May 31, 2006	6-month KIBOR + 2.85%[a]	7	3,000
First International Investment Bank	July 11, 2006	6-month KIBOR + 2.25%[a]	5	500
UBL 3	Aug. 9, 2006	12.11% (KIBOR + 1.7%)	5	2,000
JS & Co. 3	Nov. 21, 2006	6-month KIBOR + 2.50% 6.00% floor, 16.00% cap	5	1,000
JS ABAMCO (A & B)	Jan. 17, 2007	6-month KIBOR + 2.00% 6.00% floor, 16.00% cap	7	700
Bank Al-Habib Limited (II)	Feb. 7, 2007	12.61% (KIBOR + 1.95%)	8	1,500
Escort Investment Bank	Mar. 15, 2007	6-month KIBOR + 2.50% 8.00% floor, 17.00% cap	5	500
Orix Leasing Pakistan	May 25, 2007	6-month KIBOR + 1.50%	5	2,500
Total				14,200

Source: State Bank of Pakistan.
a. No floor and cap.

Table 5.11 Cost of Bond Issuance, Pakistan, 2007

Item	Share of issue (%)	PRs
Publication of prospectus	1.021	2,041,354.88
Listing fee	0.070	140,000.00
Annual stock exchange fee	0.500	999,065.60
Issue manager or underwriter	3.800	7,600,000.00
Credit rating; bankers; legal and audit	0.750	1,500,000.00
Central depository fees	0.299	597,372.80
Broker commission	1.000	2,000,000.00
Total cost	7.439	14,877,793.28

Source: Country authorities and market information.
Note: Issue size is assumed to be PRs 200 million.

trustee fees, advisers' fees, and rating fees, amounts to 7.4 percent of an issue of PRs 200 million (table 5.11). A cost perceived as particularly high, the stamp duty levied on an issue of term finance certificates (0.15 percent of the face value), was abolished in 2007.

Bond issuers may not incur all expenses listed in the table or may not incur them at the level shown. Most of the expenses are negotiable. Moreover, as more market intermediaries enter the bond market, competition will drive down the fees. Even so, concerted efforts are needed at all levels to bring down the cost of bond issuance. The Debt Market Committee formed by the Securities and Exchange Commission has recommended that the cost be brought down.

Procedural hassles add to the transaction costs. Administrative and regulatory compliance and disclosure requirements for issuing term finance certificates are complicated, and the turnaround time for applications excessive. For these reasons corporate clients used to meeting their funding needs, including long-term finance, through bank loans prefer to avoid the bond route.

Lack of liquidity also hampers development of the bond market. Although term finance certificates are listed on the stock exchange in Pakistan, trading is limited. Without a well-functioning secondary market the investors are likely to demand a higher liquidity premium and interest rate risk premium. Low liquidity in the secondary market also stems from the small scale of issues, the variety of characteristics among instruments, and the aptitude of the investor base. The small scale of many of the local issues means that even limited trading can affect the price.

Demand Side: The Investor Base

Pakistan's investor base remains small by all standards. Commercial banks and other financial institutions, with short-term liabilities, do not provide a stable source of demand for long-term instruments. By contrast, pension funds and insurance companies, with long-term liabilities, are the ideal institutional investors for a sophisticated corporate debt securities market. But in Pakistan pension funds (with assets at 1.6 percent of GDP in 2004) and the life insurance industry (2.1 percent) lag far behind their counterparts in economies at similar stages of development, subtracting a potentially important source of long-term funds from the country's capital market.

Some positive developments have taken place in the pension sector, however. In January 2007 the Securities and Exchange Commission introduced the Voluntary Pension System, which will be open to participation by nationals over 18 years of age. A regulatory framework for developing the private pension industry was also spelled out, and four asset management companies registered to operate as pension fund managers.

The most favorable recent development in strengthening the Pakistani investor base has been the remarkable growth of the mutual fund industry, which has benefited from a booming stock market, excess liquidity in the market, and a consequent rise in the demand for investment channels.

Contractual Savings Institutions

By far the largest institutional investors in Pakistan are the state-owned State Life Insurance Company and Employees' Old-Age Benefit Institution. The State Life Insurance Company manages PRs 110 billion in assets, 70 percent of which is apparently invested in Pakistan Investment Bonds. Other important investors are the Workers Welfare Fund (a national provident fund with assets of about PRs 10 billion) and local government provident funds such as the Punjab Benevolent Fund (with assets estimated at about PRs 6 billion) and the Sindh Government Servants Benevolent Fund. Fauji Foundation (a holding company for army investments), the National Insurance Corporation, Karachi Port Trust, and the provident funds of major state-owned and private companies are also major investors.

Public sector retirement schemes (other than the Employees' Old-Age Benefit Institution) have assets totaling an estimated PRs 25 billion. These assets are believed to be invested almost entirely in government debt, mainly national savings instruments (especially Defense Savings Certificates). The assets of private schemes are not known because of a lack of regulation, but they are understood to total less than PRs 50 billion.

The investment regulations for life insurance, pension, and provident funds are relatively liberal and do not restrict investments to government debt Such funds are allowed to invest up to 50 percent of their assets in equities, up to 50 percent in secured debt, and up to 20 percent in real estate. But investments in unsecured loans are restricted to 2.5 percent of assets, somewhat constraining development of the corporate bond market.

The importance of the role of contractual savings institutions in developing the long-term bond market cannot be overstated. According to data from the U.K. Office for National Statistics, U.K. pension funds and insurance companies held up to 64 percent of all U.K. gilts (treasury bonds) at the end of September 2004 and an even larger share of index-linked and long-maturity gilts.

In Pakistan lack of suitable assets, including corporate equity and bonds, has clearly hampered the development of institutional investors. But the relative underdevelopment of contractual savings has in turn inhibited the development of equity and bond markets.

Mutual Funds

Mutual funds had an early start in Pakistan. The first were operated by the state: the National Investment Trust was set up in 1962, followed later by ICP Mutual Funds. But progress was slow for the next four decades. The industry suffered from both poor management and government intervention.

Since 2002, however, the industry has seen major improvements and growth prompted by positive changes in government policy and regulation, including privatization and measures to allow new entrants. Beyond the favorable investment environment, the mutual fund industry also benefited from liberalization, which has facilitated entry of the private sector and increased competition, enhancing the quality of fund management.

At the end of June 2006 mutual funds accounted for 38.34 percent of the assets of the nonbank financial sector in Pakistan, having seen more than fivefold growth in their net assets, to PRs 160 billion, in the previous four years. The sector's total market capitalization was PRs 162 billion. The country had 27 open-end funds and 17 closed-end funds, with broad product offerings. Equity funds accounted for the largest share of mutual fund assets (63 percent), followed by income funds (10.6 percent), asset allocation funds (8.16 percent), money market funds (7.3 percent), balanced funds (7.23 percent), and Islamic funds (5.62 percent).

In 2006 the Securities and Exchange Commission helped lower barriers to entry by new fund managers by lifting the requirement that asset management companies seek foreign collaboration in managing open-end funds. However, the agency requires asset managers and investment advisers to obtain, from credit rating agencies in Pakistan, both ratings specific to their fund management quality and ratings specific to the performance of the mutual funds they manage. Now that the Voluntary Pension System rules are in place, asset managers are exploring the opportunity to manage private pension schemes in the country.

Funds mobilized by mutual funds come mostly from institutions, not retail investors. Thus, restoring permission for institutional investors to invest in national savings instruments has posed a major competitive threat to mutual funds. Several measures could help the mutual fund industry scale up its operations, including encouraging a level playing field for different investment instruments, allowing the establishment of dedicated mutual funds to cater to the needs of specific investor categories, and permitting mutual funds operational flexibility in such areas as security lending, hedging through derivatives, short selling of securities, and buyback of own certificates from the open market. There is also a need to build the capacity of fund managers and improve governance standards and accountability.

Market Infrastructure

Pakistan's bond market infrastructure has some essential elements in place—such as a primary dealer network for government debt securities and credit rating agencies—but lacks others.

Primary Dealers

Government debt securities are distributed through a network of 11 primary dealers. Only primary dealers are allowed to participate in the auctions for government debt securities, while all scheduled (commercial) banks are allowed to participate in open market operations conducted by the State Bank. Each primary dealer is required to underwrite at least 3.5 percent of an issue of Pakistan Investment Bonds and maintain a bid-ask spread of 50 basis points when acting as a market maker. Market conditions, however, often lead to much greater quoted spreads. In addition, primary dealers can submit up to PRs 10 million in noncompetitive bids for distribution through the retail account.

Both Pakistan Investment Bonds and treasury bills are fully dematerialized (paperless) and are purchased and traded in book-entry format.

Secondary Market

The secondary market for government debt securities remains thin and illiquid. The market is dominated by repo trades in treasury bills, which account for as much as 92 percent of the daily trading volume; outright trades account for only 8 percent.

Government debt securities are held primarily by banks, to meet the statutory reserve requirements, and when held to maturity they are not required to be marked to market. In a scenario of rising interest rates banks prefer to hold the bonds to maturity, rather than trade them, to avoid booking losses. A central bank policy directive in July 2004 permitted banks to shift a substantial share of the Pakistan Investment Bonds already issued to the held-to-maturity category. This directive, aimed at helping banks immunize their bond portfolio from mark-to-market losses, represents a setback in the development of a secondary market for government bonds.

For corporate bonds the dearth of supply hampers secondary market development because investors have few options to choose from. Another impediment is the lack of an electronic trading, clearing, and settlement system.

Clearing and Settlement

The Pakistani market has yet to implement a fully electronic means of trading, settlement, and clearing. The payment and settlement process is expedited at the expense of a shorter trading day, which ends at 1:00 p.m. Settlement documents must be submitted in person to the State Bank by the cutoff time of 1:30 p.m. A two-tier depository system is in place: financial institutions have two subsidiary general ledger accounts for bank-owned government securities and another account for customer-owned government securities. A manual book-entry system is used for recording.

The lack of a real-time gross settlement system undermines the efficiency of the Pakistani bond market, and the planned implementation of such a system later in 2008 is a welcome development.

Credit Rating Agencies

Two credit rating agencies operate in Pakistan: Pakistan Credit Rating Agency (PACRA) and JCR-VIS Credit Rating.

PACRA was set up in 1994 as a joint venture among IBCA Limited (an international credit rating agency), the International Finance Corporation of the World Bank Group (no longer a shareholder), and the Lahore Stock Exchange. The first credit rating agency in Pakistan, PACRA has completed well over a hundred ratings, including major industrial corporations, financial institutions, and debt instruments. In addition to local ratings, PACRA has completed two international ratings in collaboration with Fitch Ratings.

JCR-VIS Credit Rating, established in 2001, is a joint venture among four entities: Japan Credit Rating Agency (JCR), Japan's major rating agency; Vital Information Services Limited (VIS), Pakistan's only data bank and financial research organization; the Karachi Stock Exchange; and the Islamabad Stock Exchange.

Securitization

Detailed guidelines issued by the government have led to a growing trend of asset-backed securitization in Pakistan in recent years. In 1999 the Securities and Exchange Commission issued the Companies (Asset-Backed Securitization) Rules to support the establishment of special-purpose vehicles to carry out asset-backed securitization. Before these guidelines were in place, the country's only significant securitization transaction had been the securitization of net settlement receivables by Pakistan Telecom in 1997.

In 2002, in response to requests from many financial institutions, the State Bank issued guidelines permitting banks and development finance institutions to participate in asset securitization through special-purpose vehicles (State Bank of Pakistan 2002). These guidelines limit the total exposure of a bank or development finance institution to securities issued by a special-purpose vehicle to 5 percent of its own paid-up capital or 15 percent of the total value of the asset-backed securitization issued by the special-purpose vehicle, whichever is less. In addition, the aggregate exposure on account of asset-backed securitization is limited to 20 percent of the total paid-up capital of the bank or development finance institution.

Legal and Regulatory Framework

The State Bank of Pakistan has overall responsibility for supervising financial markets and issuing government debt securities. The governing law is the Public Debt Act, 1944 and the Public Debt Rules, 1946. In an effort to increase the State Bank's independence and improve public debt management, the Fiscal Responsibility and Debt Limitation Act was passed in 2005, restricting government borrowing to the annual stipulated limit. The Exchange and Debt Management Department of the State Bank is responsible for managing the issuance and administration of government debt.

The Securities and Exchange Commission of Pakistan, set up in 1997 as the successor to the Corporate Law Authority, is responsible for the regulation of securities, the insurance business, and companies in Pakistan. The Policy Board advises the government on matters relating to the securities industry and the regulation of companies and is responsible for approving the budget and regulations of the Securities and Exchange Commission.

Regulatory Issues

The Securities and Exchange Commission has clear responsibilities as a regulator, and it appears to be able to operate free of external influences. The commission can bring to bear an array of powers in governing the registration, inspection, and investigation of market intermediaries. But concerns remain on a number of issues.

The Securities and Exchange Commission appears to lack adequate resources to attract and retain skilled professionals to the extent required by its wide-ranging powers. A new compensation scheme was recently introduced to bring employees' salaries into line with market rates; however, the salary increase entails a tradeoff in the duration of the contract, which would be converted from permanent to temporary, reducing pension benefits. As a result, the commission is still unable to present itself as an attractive employer. Staff shortages lead to delays: although self-registration procedures for debt securities are in place, the lack of sufficient staff leads to long processing times, placing an additional burden on corporate debt issuance.

Moreover, the commission lacks the power to summon and investigate those who do not fall under its explicit authority. This issue has recently been of particular concern in relation to insider trading: the commission does not have the power to take action against people who are not insiders as defined by law, but who nevertheless have received information from insiders and used it to their advantage.

There are also deficiencies in granting equal treatment to players in different segments of the securities market. While the law requires full, accurate, and timely disclosure of financial information to shareholders of companies and those holding interests in collective investment schemes, there is no requirement for such disclosure to holders of debt securities.

Finally, there are concerns relating to the three stock exchanges (Karachi, Islamabad, and Lahore), which operate as self-regulatory organizations under the general oversight of the Securities and Exchange Commission. The exchanges lack formal plans for their monitoring, surveillance, and investigation work. In addition, they appear to have no understanding in place with the commission about priorities for regulation and the allocation of resources.

Reform Initiatives

The Securities and Exchange Commission has in recent years launched a plethora of reforms and regulatory initiatives. These measures, aimed at developing a fair, efficient, and transparent regulatory framework, are designed to foster the growth of a robust corporate sector and a broad-based capital market (see annex 5.3). The reforms have focused in particular on strengthening risk management and improving governance and transparency.

In addition, the Securities and Exchange Commission has recently taken a lead role in developing the corporate bond market in Pakistan by establishing the Debt Capital Market Committee. The committee, made up some of the most qualified professionals in the Pakistani bond market, has identified the main impediments to developing the market and proposed measures to address them (Debt Capital Market Committee 2007).

Tax Regime

According to the Finance Act, 2006, Pakistani residents are subject to a 10 percent withholding tax on national savings instruments and term finance certificates, but face no additional tax or income deductions relating to interest on these instruments. Earnings from other debt instruments are taxed at the normal income tax rates, making these a less attractive investment option. Nonresidents are subject to a 30 percent withholding tax on all income on debt instruments. Companies are subject to a 10 percent withholding tax on interest income. Capital gains are not taxed, however.

Recommended Actions

At 26 percent of GDP, Pakistan's debt securities market remains too small to meet the growing investment needs of an expanding economy. It remains dominated by government securities and subject to the distortions generated by the national savings schemes. The corporate bond market, while it picked up in the second half of fiscal 2007, accounts for a mere 0.8 percent of GDP, pointing to the corporate sector's continuing reliance on bank financing. Outlined below are recommended actions for developing the domestic bond market.

Supply Side

Improving Cash Management and Creating a Credible Sovereign Benchmark. Introducing sound cash management practices by the government, including an issuance calendar specifying volumes, is critical for the development of the bond market. To be viewed as a credible borrower and support development of a sovereign interest rate benchmark, the government needs to regularize Pakistan Investment Bond issues and assume the role of a price taker during auctions.

Reviewing the National Savings Schemes. The national savings schemes, as an on-tap source of financing, continue to hamper the government's debt management. To address this issue, consideration should be given to integrating national savings instruments into the mainstream capital market by converting them into long-term, marketable paper. As part of this, the implicit cost-free put option should be removed or offset by imposing a fee for early redemption. This subsidized program could continue to serve a safety net function by targeting specific sectors of the population through the distribution network. By contrast, the ban on institutional investment should be reinstituted.

Supporting the Issuance of Term Finance Certificates. The corporate debt securities market can be developed only with the support of the government. Such support could include regulatory and tax incentives for corporations to publicly issue debt rather than resorting to bank financing. In addition, collective savings schemes could be encouraged to approach corporations directly for debt issuance.

Demand Side

Fostering the Development of an Investor Base. While the mutual fund industry has been booming recently, adequately developing the insurance and pension fund industries will require government efforts. A comprehensive review of these two industries is needed to identify impediments to their development and ways to address them.

Legal and Regulatory Framework

Improving Regulatory Resources. Lack of adequate human resources imposes a severe constraint on the ability of the Securities and Exchange Commission to carry out its extensive regulatory functions. Consideration should be given to bringing its employees' compensation into line with current market practices, increasing its ability to attract and retain skilled professionals.

Annex 5.1 Banking Sector Reforms

Bank Restructuring and Privatization Program (1990s)

- Amendment to Banks (Nationalization) Act, 1974 empowering the government to sell all or part of the share capital of nationalized commercial banks and to allow entry of new banks
- Establishment of the Privatization Commission
- Merger of weaker banks with bigger ones (11 banks regrouped into 5 large ones)
- Recapitalization of banks through an equity injection in public sector banks and writeoffs; employee layoffs in two phases; and the closing of more than 2,000 unviable branches and divestiture of strategic shareholdings in two large banks, now with foreign investors
- Privatization of four banks
- Divestiture of a 26 percent equity stake in the largest bank, the National Bank of Pakistan, through the stock market

Entry of New Banks

- Twenty-eight new banks licensed in the past 16 years, of which six are microfinance banks and five Islamic banks
- Introduction of a comprehensive branch licensing policy allowing banks to make independent decisions on branch housing within broad parameters

Consolidation of Banks, Leasing Companies, and Investment Banks

- Statutory amendment to allow the merger of nonbank financial companies with banks under provisions of the Banking Companies Ordinance
- Amendment to Income Tax Ordinance to allow carryforward of tax losses of both amalgamated (target) and amalgamating (surviving) institutions

Reforms to Hasten Loan Recovery and Company Restructuring

- Establishment of the Committee for Revival of Sick Industrial Units and the Corporate and Industrial Restructuring Corporation to acquire the nonperforming loans of public sector banks and creation of a National Accountability Bureau cell at the State Bank of Pakistan to expeditiously process the cases of willful defaulters
- Enactment of Financial Institutions (Recovery of Finances) Ordinance, 2001 to facilitate speedy recovery of loans

Grant of Enhanced Autonomy to the State Bank of Pakistan

- Empowerment of the State Bank of Pakistan to deal independently on monetary management and banking sector policies
- Switch to market-based indirect monetary instruments and market-based pricing of central bank borrowing
- Capacity building of central bank staff to equip them to deal with numerous transition challenges

Dismantling of Credit Ceiling at Sector and Bank Levels

- Removal of floor and caps on interest rate structure by fiscal 1998
- Abolishment of concessional lending schemes (except for locally manufactured machinery and export finance schemes)
- Lifting of the cap for project financing
- Flotation of global depository receipts of a few large banks

Setting of Corporate Governance Standards

- Introduction of "fit and proper" criteria for boards of directors, chief executive officers or presidents, and key executives

Prescription of Prudential Regulatory and Supervisory Framework to Achieve International Standards

- Increase in the minimum capital requirements to PRs 6 billion by the end of December 2009
- Prescription of capital requirements under the Basel II Capital Accord to include capital charge for operational risk alongside credit and market risks

Annex 5.2   Size and Composition of Government Debt

In fiscal 2006, for the fifth consecutive year, the ratio of total government debt to GDP recorded a significant reduction. The ratio hit 56 percent, down sharply from the 79.7 percent in fiscal 2002 and far exceeding the target of 60 percent set for fiscal 2013 under the Fiscal Responsibility and Limitation Act, 2005.

The stock of public debt increased by about 6.75 percent in fiscal 2006, to PRs 4,321 billion (table A5.1). But this modest growth was more than offset by positive trends in the economy—robust economic growth, sustained increase in export earnings and workers' remittances, and higher capital inflows, particularly in foreign direct investment due to privatization programs.

Domestic currency debt accounted for 53 percent of the total (PRs 2,299 billion), and foreign currency debt for 47 percent (PRs 2,022 billion). The ratio of domestic public debt to GDP fell from 39 percent in fiscal 2002 to 29.8 percent in fiscal 2006, while the ratio of external public debt to GDP fell from 40.8 percent to

Table A5.1   Government Debt, Pakistan, Fiscal 2002–07

Indicator	2002	2003	2004	2005	2006	2007 (Q1)
Outstanding debt (PRs billions)						
Domestic currency debt	1,718	1,854	1,979	2,133	2,299	2,346
Foreign currency debt	1,795	1,769	1,810	1,912	2,022	2,065
Total	3,513	3,623	3,789	4,045	4,321	4,411
Percentage of total debt						
Domestic currency debt	48.9	51.2	52.3	52.7	53.2	53.2
Foreign currency debt	51.1	48.8	47.7	47.3	46.8	46.8
Percentage of GDP						
Domestic currency debt	39.0	38.4	35.1	32.4	29.8	26.6
Foreign currency debt	40.8	36.7	32.0	29.1	26.2	23.4
Total	79.7	75.1	67.1	61.5	56.0	50.1
Percentage of revenue						
Domestic currency debt	275	257	246	237	210	189
Foreign currency debt	288	245	224	212	185	167
Total	562	503	470	449	394	356
Foreign currency debt *(US$ billions)*	29.9	30.6	31.2	32.1	33.6	34.1
Exchange rate *(PRs to US$)*	60.1	57.7	57.9	59.7	60.2	60.5
GDP *(PRs billions)*	4,402	4,823	5,641	6,581	7,713	8,808
Total revenue *(PRs billions)*	624	721	806	900	1,095	1,239

Sources: State Bank of Pakistan; Pakistan, Ministry of Finance, Budget Wing; calculations by Pakistan Debt Policy Coordination Office staff.
Note: Data are for the end of the fiscal year, June 30, except for fiscal 2007.

Figure A5.1   Government Debt, Pakistan, Selected Fiscal Years, 2002–07

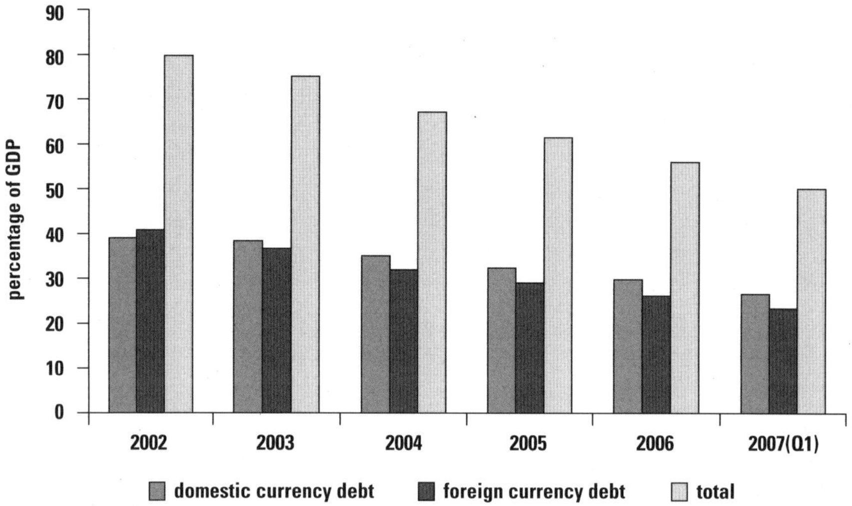

Source: Pakistan, Ministry of Finance 2007.
Note: Data are for the end of the fiscal year, June 30, except for fiscal 2007.

26.2 percent (figure A5.1). External debt is predominantly long and medium term, and more than 99 percent is public or publicly guaranteed. Multilateral development banks are the largest creditors for Pakistan's external public debt.

In fiscal 2002–06 the burden of interest payments on the domestic budget declined sharply, from 4.2 percent of GDP to 2.5 percent. Total debt service on domestic debt was PRs 191.4 billion in fiscal 2006, equivalent to 2.5 percent of GDP and 17.5 percent of total revenue. Interest payments on Defense Savings Certificates accounted for the largest share of the total, 23.6 percent, while those on Pakistan Investment Bonds accounted for 14.6 percent.

In fiscal 2007, for the fourth consecutive year, the share of bank debt increased considerably. This rise was due to net government borrowing of PRs 160 billion from commercial banks in that year. Commercial bank debt rose from 53.4 percent of total bank debt in fiscal 2006 to 64.6 percent in fiscal 2007, while State Bank debt declined from 46.4 percent to 35.4 percent.

Annex 5.3   Capital Market and Regulatory Reforms Taken or Proposed by the Securities and Exchange Commission of Pakistan

Market Development Reforms
- Introducing trading in futures contracts
- Developing an over-the-counter (OTC) market
- Setting up the Central Depository Company
- Establishing the National Clearing Company as a central clearinghouse
- Establishing the National Commodity Exchange for trading in derivatives
- Introducing the Continuous Financing System (CFS) to enhance liquidity

Risk Management Reforms
- Redefining net capital balance in line with international standards
- Converting carry-over trade transactions into CFS
- Introducing capital adequacy standards for brokers
- Strengthening margin deposits
- Defining position limits for brokers in the ready, futures, and CFS markets
- Eliminating group accounts
- Prohibiting brokers from trading through the accounts of other brokers
- Launching a universal identification number for stockbrokers to strengthen the disclosure regime and deter wrongdoing
- Implementing a T+3 settlement system in place of weekly settlement
- Introducing appropriate control measures ("circuit breakers") to avoid excessive volatility

Investor Protection Reforms
- Streamlining arbitration procedures
- Facilitating redress of investors' complaints
- Funding investor protection funds
- Standardizing account opening procedures
- Arranging road shows to educate small investors

Corporate Governance Reforms
- Introducing a corporate governance code
- Establishing the Pakistan Institute of Corporate Governance to provide training and education for directors of listed companies
- Restructuring the boards of directors of stock exchanges

Transparency Reforms

- Banning in-house badla (a carryforward system invented on the Bombay Stock Exchange as a solution to the lack of liquidity in the secondary market)
- Introducing undisclosed trading to check front running
- Replacing blank selling with regulated short selling
- Introducing a requirement for publicly held companies to provide quarterly accounts to shareholders

Proposed Reforms

- Introducing a new margin system based on value at risk (VAR)
- Introducing a restriction on netting across markets, across clients, and across settlement periods
- Implementing a mark-to-market loss collection and profit distribution system
- Implementing a VAR-based mechanism for valuation of eligible securities to be held as security
- Introducing a new capital adequacy regime and early warning reserve
- Implementing a stock lending and borrowing mechanism
- Introducing an exchange-traded derivatives market
- Operationalizing the National Commodity Exchange for futures contracts in commodities
- Introducing index futures and options
- Demutualizing and integrating the three stock exchanges to enhance transparency
- Developing a single, well-capitalized clearinghouse
- Creating a licensing regime for market intermediaries
- Finalizing a new Securities Act and Futures Trading Act to strengthen the legal and regulatory framework

Source: Securities and Exchange Commission of Pakistan.

Endnote

1. Designed to comply with Shari'ah, term finance certificates differ slightly from traditional corporate bonds. The key difference is that term finance certificates substitute the words *expected profit rate* for *interest rate.*

References

ADB (Asian Development Bank). 2007. "Pakistan's Public Debt: A Brief Overview." Pakistan Resident Mission, Islamabad.

Arif, Muhammad. 2007. "Developing Bond Market in Pakistan." *SBP Research Bulletin* 3 (1).

BIS (Bank for International Settlements). 2007. *Quarterly Review.* June. Basel.

Debt Capital Market Committee. 2007. "Proposed Reforms to Pakistan's Debt Capital Market." Report prepared for the Securities and Exchange Commission of Pakistan, Islamabad.

Hameed, Farhan. 2006. "Fostering the Corporate Bond Market in Pakistan." State Bank of Pakistan, Karachi.

IMF (International Monetary Fund). 2006. "Pakistan: 2006 Article IV Consultation and Special Statistical Supplement." Washington, DC.

Karachi Stock Exchange. 2007. *Annual Report 2006.* Karachi.

Pakistan, Ministry of Finance. 2007. *Debt Policy Statement 2006–07.* Debt Policy Coordination Office, Islamabad.

SECP (Securities and Exchange Commission of Pakistan). 2007. *Annual Report 2005–2006.* Islamabad.

State Bank of Pakistan. 2002. BPD Circular 31. November 14. Karachi.

———. 2007. *The State of Pakistan's Economy (Money & Banking).* Karachi.

———. 2008. "Credit Ratings of Banks & DFIs Updated as of January 4, 2008." http://www.sbp.org.pk/publications/c_rating/ratings.pdf.

———. Various years. *Annual Report.* Karachi.

———. Various years. *Financial Stability Review.* Karachi.

World Federation of Exchanges. 2006. *Annual Report and Statistics 2005.* Paris.

6

Sri Lanka

Sri Lanka's bond market, like others in South Asia, is dominated by government debt securities. Indeed, government debt virtually crowds out private sector investment. The corporate bond market, lacking both issuers and investors, lags far behind. The corporate sector, like others in the region, relies on bank credit.

The investor base is narrow, overwhelmingly dominated by the country's largest social security system. Secondary market activity remains negligible. The country has made remarkable progress in establishing a modern, efficient clearing and settlement system, however, and much progress in improving the legal and regulatory framework for the capital market.

Introduction

Sri Lanka's economy has proved to be resilient, growing by more than 7 percent in 2006 and by 6 percent in the previous year despite recent shocks, including the 2004 tsunami and the continuing ethnic strife. The country's financial system is relatively well developed and benefits from a modern market infrastructure. Financial system assets amounted to SL Rs 3.3 trillion (127 percent of GDP) at the end of 2006, up 18 percent from 2005 (table 6.1).

Banks dominate the country's financial system. With assets of more than SL Rs 2.2 trillion (79 percent of GDP) at the end of 2006, banks accounted for 67 percent of financial system assets. Commercial banks alone hold about 56 percent of financial system assets and are the main source of funds for both corporations and individuals. The contractual savings industry, dominated by the Employees' Provident Fund, accounts for about 24 percent of financial system assets. Other nonbank financial institutions, with 9 percent of assets, represent the smallest segment of the financial system.

Table 6.1   Structure of Financial System, Sri Lanka, 2005–06

Segment	2005			2006		
	SL Rs billions	Percentage of total	Percentage of GDP	SL Rs billions	Percentage of total	Percentage of GDP
Financial system assets						
Banking system	1,850.9	66.1	78.2	2,216.6	67.2	79.1
Contractual savings	695.7	24.9	29.4	784.2	23.8	28.0
Other nonbank financial institutions	252.5	9.0	10.7	296.2	9.0	10.6
Total	2,799.1	100.0		3,297.0	100.0	
Securities market capitalization						
Domestic debt securities	1,265.7		53.5	1,475.5		50.8
Equity	584.0		24.7	834.8		29.8
Total	1,849.7		78.2	2,310.3		80.6

Sources: Country authorities; World Bank staff estimates and calculations.

The Central Bank of Sri Lanka, the main financial regulator, has to its credit taken a series of well-designed measures, and proposed others, to further strengthen and improve the efficiency of the financial system in recent years (see annex 6.1). With a view to strengthening the legal and regulatory framework supporting financial system stability, policy makers have also proposed amendments to legislation relating to banking.

The stock market has recorded an impressive performance in recent years. The Colombo Stock Exchange has 236 listed companies, and market capitalization more than quadrupled between 2002 and the end of September 2007, increasing from $1.7 billion to $7.3 billion.

The bond market plays a crucial part in the economy. Outstanding debt amounts to 51 percent of GDP, the largest share among South Asian countries (see table 1.3 in chapter 1). Government debt securities account for the lion's share, however. Bonds and debentures remain a marginal source of funds for the corporate sector.

Development of the domestic bond market has been a significant focus of attention since the 1997 East Asian financial crisis (box 6.1). The domestic bond market's role in avoiding the currency and maturity mismatch in investment and funding experienced in East Asia was well appreciated by Sri Lanka policy makers. Moreover, the government's growing funding needs made building an efficient domestic government bond market a pressing policy priority.

The concerted measures by policy makers and financial regulators have yielded positive results overall, contributing to the country's strong economic performance. Yet concerns remain. State banks still play a major role in the financial system, rais-

---

*Box 6.1   Chronology of Bond Market Development
in Sri Lanka*

- 1937: Registered Stock and Securities Ordinance is adopted.
- 1953: Local Treasury Bills Ordinance of 1923 is amended (as it is again in 1992, 1995, and 2004).
- 1981: First six-month treasury bill is issued; secondary market trading in treasury bills is introduced.
- 1989: Treasury bills with multiple maturities are issued.
- 1992: Accredited primary dealer system is introduced.
- 1993: System of sales and repurchase agreements for treasury bills is introduced.
- 1994: Primary dealer system is reformed.
- 1995: Noncompetitive bidding by public sector institutional investors is phased out; repo system for treasury bills is introduced; government debt securities laws are amended.
- 1997: First treasury bond issue takes place.
- 1998: Electronic bidding system is introduced.
- 2000: Dedicated primary dealer system is introduced; callable bonds are issued.

- 2001: Sri Lanka Development Bonds are issued.
- 2003: Twenty-year treasury bonds are issued.
- 2003: Fiscal Management Responsibility Act is implemented; code of conduct for primary dealers is introduced.
- 2004: Scripless securities settlement and central depository systems are established.
- 2005: Index-linked bonds are introduced; sovereign rating is obtained.
- 2006: Risk-weighted capital adequacy system for primary dealers is introduced; domestic bond market is partially opened to foreign investors.
- 2007: International capital market is accessed in October; licensed specialized banks are allowed to operate as dealer direct participants in the real-time gross settlement and scripless securities settlement systems; public debt management strategy is published.

Source: Central Bank of Sri Lanka.

---

ing questions about systemic vulnerability. Public debt, at 99 percent of the domestic bond market, crowds out private sector investment, constricts growth, and poses risks to macroeconomic stability. The fiscal deficit reached 8.44 percent of GDP in 2006. Inflation soared to 21.7 percent in August 2007 and remains high, though it came down in mid-2007. High public debt, accelerating inflation, and pressures on the current account and exchange rate all pose challenges for macroeconomic management.

Supply Side: Debt Instruments and Issuers

The government debt securities market dominates the Sri Lanka capital market, accounting for more than 60 percent of securities market capitalization at the end of 2006. By contrast, the corporate bond market remains largely underdeveloped, suffering simultaneously from lack of issuers and investors. According to the most recent data, at the end of 2006 the corporate bond market accounted for a mere 1 percent of securities market capitalization.

Money Market

The Sri Lanka money market, especially that in repurchase agreements (repos), is well developed even without a master repurchase agreement and netting arrangements. The main participants are commercial banks, primary dealers, finance companies, and institutional investors. The Central Bank uses repo and reverse repo transactions to manage short-term liquidity in the financial system, selling government debt securities to remove liquidity and purchasing them to inject liquidity.

In recent years an important focus for the Central Bank has been to contain inflationary pressures. In 2006 the Central Bank further firmed up the tight monetary policy stance it had adopted in 2004. It raised its policy interest rates four times in 2006 and again in February 2007. In early 2007 the Central Bank also imposed restrictions on commercial banks' use of the reverse repo facility, concerned about the inflationary impact of frequent use by some to fund their assets. In August 2007, however, it withdrew this restriction to avoid high volatility in money market rates. But the Central Bank, because of concerns about systemic risk, has cautioned banks not to continually rely on the interbank call money market. Banks have been urged to instead revamp their asset-liability management strategies and strengthen their balance sheets.

Corporate entities are permitted to raise short-term funds through commercial paper. The commercial paper market is very small, however. In the first six months of 2007 only SL Rs 12 billion was raised in that market.

Performance in the interbank foreign exchange market improved during the first nine months of 2007 as a result of stronger export growth, larger inflows of workers' remittances, portfolio investments by foreign entities in the equity market, foreign loan inflows to the government, and the sale of treasury bonds to foreigners.

Government Debt Issuance

Sri Lanka's domestic government bond market has grown steadily in recent years, increasing from SL Rs 948 billion in 2002 to SL Rs 1.5 trillion in December 2006.[1] The key debt instruments are treasury bills and treasury bonds (table 6.2).

Dissemination of information on public debt issuance has improved. The government announces an annual borrowing calendar and publishes fiscal data and information on auctions of treasury bills and bonds. Issues are fragmented, however, reflecting the lack of a cash management strategy with conscious decisions made about issue size and maturity across the fiscal year. Moreover, while the annual borrowing calendar is followed, volumes are not specified with sufficient advance notice. Issue size is mainly driven by immediate funding needs.

Table 6.2   Features of Government Debt Instruments, Sri Lanka

Feature	Treasury bills	Treasury bonds	Rupee Loans	Sri Lanka Development Bonds
Method of issue	Auction	Auction	Tap system	Auction
Bidding	Electronic	Electronic	By application	By application
Interest rate determination	By market	By market	By government	By market
Method of interest payment	At maturity	Biannually	Biannually	Biannually
Maturity period	91, 182, or 364 days	2 years or more	2 years or more	2 years or more
Transferability	By electronic book entry	By electronic book entry	By registration	By registration
Primary market	Primary dealers; Employees' Provident Fund	Primary dealers; Employees' Provident Fund	Any individual or fund	Foreign citizens and entities; nonresident Sri Lankans

Source: CBSL 2007b.

Debt Instruments. Domestic short-term public debt is raised by issuing treasury bills or by borrowing (through overdrafts) from the two state-owned banks. Medium- to long-term public debt is raised by issuing treasury bonds.

The primary auctions for treasury bills have reflected a marked preference for short maturities, and as a result 78 percent of the treasury bills issued in the first nine months of 2007 were of 91-day tenor. The yield rates in the primary market increased by 390–463 basis points during that same period. The trend was reversed toward the end of October 2007, however, thanks to the success of a five-year international bond issue of $500 million.

The government has also issued nontradable instruments, Rupee Loans, on the basis of administratively determined interest rates. But it is now phasing out these instruments by replacing them upon maturity with treasury bonds, substantially reducing the share of nonmarketable government debt instruments. Rupee Loans now constitute only 8 percent of domestic government debt (table 6.3).

Market-oriented debt instruments—such as treasury bills, treasury bonds, and Sri Lanka Development Bonds—now make up more than 80 percent of domestic government debt. There has been a perceptible shift in the composition of the government's debt portfolio, with the share of treasury bonds doubling from 30 percent in 2000 to 60 percent in 2006.

Maturity Structure. Medium- and long-term debt instruments such as treasury bonds and Rupee Loans are issued with an original maturity of 2–20 years. Despite efforts by the government to lengthen the maturity of its debt instruments,

Table 6.3 Composition of Domestic Government Debt, Sri Lanka, 2000–06
(SL Rs millions)

	2000	2001	2002	2003	2004	2005	2006
Treasury bills	134,996	170,995	210,995	219,295	243,886	234,174	257,732
Rupee Loans	263,888	292,813	287,701	248,414	164,758	140,563	116,713
Treasury bonds	204,124	229,174	347,128	483,107	643,349	751,569	885,972
Other	73,652	122,983	102,562	69,153	91,396	139,416	218,813
Total	676,660	815,965	948,386	1,019,969	1,143,389	1,265,722	1,479,230

Source: Central Bank of Sri Lanka.
Note: Data are for the end of the fiscal year, December 31.

investor preferences have continued to move toward the shorter end of the market as a result of inflationary expectations, rising interest rates, and high government budget deficits. More than 45 percent of the treasury bonds and Rupee Loans are set to mature in 2007–08, while 40 percent of total domestic government debt must be rolled over in 2009 (figure 6.1). The average duration of the debt stood at 1.8 years in 2007.

Private Placement of Public Debt. In today's inflationary environment the government understandably finds it difficult to act as a price taker. Bids at auctions are rejected when the rates offered are substantially higher than those that the government is willing to accept. The practice of primary dealers pricing themselves out of the market reflects the mismatch in interest rate expectations between the Central Bank and market participants.

The government's reopening of the existing bond series, with a concentration of maturities, has added to its dilemma. A large stock of bonds, nearly SL Rs 30–40 billion, is due to mature on a single day. If auctions were held for reissuance, interest rates would soar—by as much as 400–500 basis points in a single auction. The government thus faces a situation of adverse market perceptions, a large stock of bonds coming up for bid at auctions, and limited appetite from primary dealers, which are in no position to absorb more than SL Rs 3–4 billion in fresh bond issues at a time.

In response, the government has relied on private placement for a large share of its debt. It places about 80 percent of its medium- and long-term debt privately with the Employees' Provident Fund and the state-owned National Savings Bank. The CBSL claims that the debt is priced at the latest average auction price or the prevailing market rate.

New Products. The introduction of new debt instruments has contributed to the already substantial fragmentation of long-term issues due to the excessive number of treasury bond series. In 2005 the government introduced the first inflation-index-linked bonds, with a maturity of three years. The coupon rate for the first year was fixed at 11.2 percent, while those for the second and third years were

Figure 6.1 Maturity Structure of Treasury Bonds and Rupee Loans, Sri Lanka

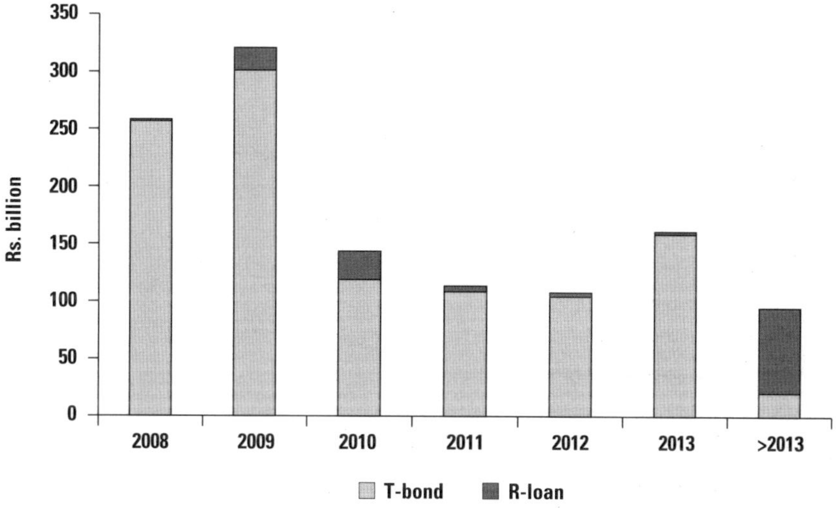

Source: Public Debt Department Central Bank of Sri Lanka 2007.

based on the annual moving average of the Colombo consumer price index during the previous six months plus a margin of 1 percent.

Sovereign Yield Curve

The government's difficulty in acting as a price taker in the face of differing market expectations and the fragmentation of the treasury bond market pose obstacles to efforts to develop a market-based sovereign yield curve. Another obstacle is that primary dealers are not in a position to offer the two-way quotes that would facilitate the development of benchmark securities.

The large fiscal deficits and inflationary pressures, understandable given such external factors as the ongoing ethnic strife, have placed pressure on the short end of the market and adversely affected demand for long-term debt securities. Even so, from January 2006 through April 2006 the rising trend in yield rates was reversed by such positive factors as a resumption of peace negotiations, lower uncertainty in the domestic market, and a downward trend in inflation as well as in investors' inflationary expectations. After May 2006, however, a reversal of these positive factors along with the four increases in policy interest rates in 2006 brought a gradual increase in the yield rates (figure 6.2).

Public Debt Management

The government's total (domestic and external) debt portfolio, at SL Rs 2.6 trillion at the end of 2006, is equivalent to about 90 percent of GDP. Managing this

Figure 6.2   Yield-to-Maturity Curves for Government Debt Securities, Sri Lanka, Selected Dates, December 2005–June 2007

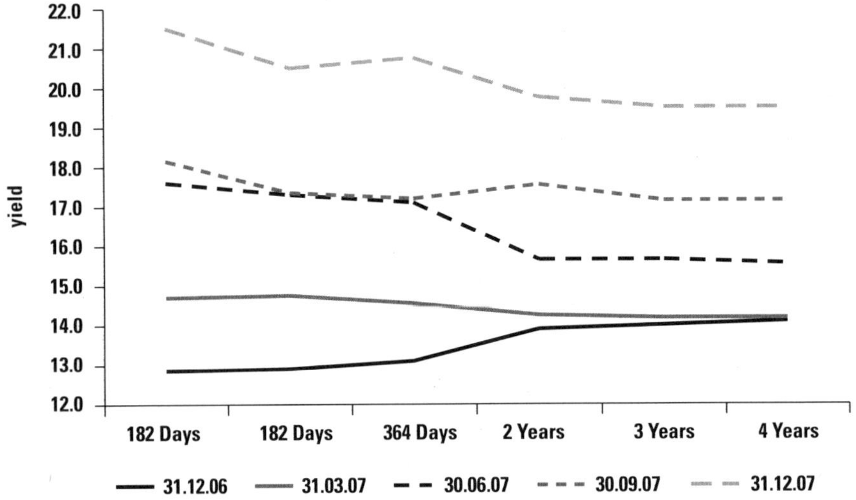

Source: CBSL 2007b.

debt portfolio effectively is critical to maintaining the stability of the economy. Recognizing this, the Central Bank, as debt manager for the government, recently published a comprehensive medium-term strategy for strengthening public debt management practices (CBSL 2007b). The document sets out four strategic objectives: minimize borrowing costs, prevent excessive concentration of redemptions to facilitate timely servicing of debt obligations, maintain the risk of the portfolio at an acceptable level, and promote efficient functioning of the debt securities market, including by developing and improving the infrastructure of public debt management.

The strategy identifies critical issues for the medium term and proposes policy initiatives to address those issues in the five-year period ending 2010:

• *Reduce debt financing.* The government plans to curtail borrowings, through fiscal consolidation and targets, to reduce the budget deficit from the past decade's average of 8.5 percent of GDP to less than 5 percent. It also plans to gradually reduce the ratio of debt to GDP, which stood at 89 percent in 2006, to 73 percent by 2010. Other steps proposed include encouraging public-private partnership and transferring mega infrastructure projects to the private sector under build-operate-own and build-operate-transfer structures.

• *Improve bond duration.* The strategy calls for reducing the share of short-term domestic rupee debt from 20 percent in 2006 to 10 percent by 2010 while increasing the duration of domestic debt to 2.5 years. To do so, several diversified

Table 6.4   Targets Identified by Sri Lanka's Medium-Term Strategy for Debt Management

(percent except where otherwise specified)

Indicator	Starting value 2006	Target value 2010
Refinancing risk		
Average time to maturity of domestic debt (years)	2–4	3–5
Short-term domestic rupee debt/total domestic rupee debt	20	10
Interest risk		
Duration of domestic debt (years)	1–8	2–5
Floating debt/total debt	6	20
Average time taken to refixing of domestic debt (years)	2–3	3
Foreign exchange risk		
Foreign investment in treasury bonds/total bond stock	—	15
Foreign currency commercial debt/official reserves	68	<50
External debt/total debt	43	35
Debt sustainability		
Debt/GDP	89	73
Foreign debt service payments/official reserves	23	15

Source: Central Bank of Sri Lanka.
— = Not available.

debt instruments with longer tenor, such as floating-rate bonds, inflation-linked securities, or zero-coupon bonds, would be introduced. These instruments would cater to the needs of a variety of investors and thus help broaden the investor base.

- *Manage exchange risk.* The government intends to reduce external debt from 43 percent of the total in 2006 to 35 percent by 2010. It also plans to reduce the share of foreign currency commercial borrowings in the country's foreign exchange reserves from the currently high level of 68 percent to less than 50 percent.

- *Consolidate fragmented debt stocks.* To tackle the problem of fragmentation, the Central Bank proposes to introduce buyback or conversion techniques, reduce the number of bond series, introduce a benchmark bond series, and develop a benchmark yield curve. It has already cut the number of bond series from 92 in 2003 to 42 in 2007 and is working to further reduce that number. A buyback program, proposed for implementation in 2008, has undergone test runs with primary dealers.

The strategy also sets targets for risk indicators and debt sustainability (table 6.4). Beyond these issues, the strategy document also addresses the governance framework, acknowledging the government's awareness of the potential benefits to the Central Bank's credibility of separating debt management from monetary policy implementation.

The Central Bank's publication of the strategy marks a significant and commendable step in formalizing public debt management in Sri Lanka. With external debt making up 43 percent of total public debt, similarly detailed coverage of foreign currency borrowings would also be useful. Producing a joint document with the Treasury, which has a significant role in the management of public debt, particularly external debt, would be helpful in compiling a comprehensive strategy. A joint strategy would aid in decision making that spans both portfolios, such as the ratio of domestic to foreign currency debt, which involves tradeoffs between cost and currency, rollover, and interest rate risks.

In addition, rather than setting targets at a single point for 2010, a range could be considered to allow for unforeseen changes in the market environment or for microeconomic outcomes that necessitate changes in the annual financing plan. Including additional targets for exposure to interest rates and currency composition in foreign debt might also be useful.

Corporate Bond Market

The corporate bond market in Sri Lanka remains in its infancy, lagging substantially behind the equity market. In 2005 the market capitalization of the eight listed and outstanding corporate bonds amounted to SL Rs 13.6 billion, 2 percent of the market capitalization of the Colombo Stock Exchange. No new listings were made in 2006 or 2007, and the number of issues remained minimal (table 6.5).

The Colombo Stock Exchange has a main and a second board for listing. Listing on the first requires that the listing entity have a guarantee from a bank or qualified multilateral institution or that the securities be investment grade or secured by collateral. The second board is equivalent to a "junk" board, for which the only listing requirement is that the company must have been in business for at least three years.

Despite this modern infrastructure, trading volumes remain low: in 2006 there were 321 transactions for a turnover of SL Rs 405 million, and numbers showed a decreasing trend in 2007 (table 6.6). As a result, corporate debt instruments are significantly illiquid compared with their government counterparts and with equities.

Table 6.5   Corporate Debt Securities Listed on the Colombo Stock Exchange, 2002–06

Indicator	2002	2003	2004	2005	2006
Issues	12	2	14	8	7
Issuers	5	1	4	2	2
Amount raised (SL Rs millions)	2,979	2,244	2,163	350	1,257
New listings	2	0	0	1	0

Source: Colombo Stock Exchange.

Table 6.6   Secondary Market Activity in Corporate Bonds and Equity, Sri Lanka, 2002–06

Indicator	2002	2003	2004	2005	2006
Corporate bonds					
Annual turnover (SL Rs millions)	341	180	200	207	405
Trades	2,445	1,685	1,362	625	321
Market capitalization (SL Rs billions)[a]	10	10	12	—	—
Equity	`				
Annual turnover (SL Rs millions)	30,183	73,837	59,052	114,599	105,153
Trades	280,681	482,954	645,083	1,100,451	952,382
Debentures traded (thousands)	13,597	2,708	2,193	2,211	—
Market capitalization (SL Rs billions)[a]	162.6	262.8	382.1	584.0	834.7

Sources: Colombo Stock Exchange; Securities and Exchange Commission of Sri Lanka.
a. Data are for the end of the fiscal year, December 31.
— = Not available.

Activity in the corporate bond market continues to be subdued for a number of reasons but mainly because of the lack of both qualified issuers and investors. The limited size of the issuer base for corporate securities can be traced to industry structures in the country. State-owned institutions, which dominate the economy, rely on banks' attractive negotiated rates for their funding needs, depriving the capital market of significant players. Non-state-owned enterprises of significant size are mostly family owned and thus reluctant to go public and to face the large transaction costs typical of small markets.

Another factor is the cost of bond issuance in Sri Lanka. At 2.744 percent of the issue size, this cost allows room for reduction (table 6.7).

Table 6.7   Cost of Bond Issuance, Sri Lanka, 2007

Item	Share of issue (%)	SL Rs
Securities and exchange commission registration	0.211	422,000
Printing of prospectus and applications	0.145	290,000
Printing of certificates; postissue expenses; postage	0.728	1,455,000
Listing fee	0.025	50,000
Issue manager or underwriter	0.750	1,500,000
Trustee fee	0.100	200,000
Credit rating; bankers; legal and audit	0.550	1,100,000
Broker commission	0.250	500,000
Total cost	2.744	5,517,000

Source: Country authorities and market information.
Note: The size of the bond issue is assumed to be SL Rs 200 million.

Demand Side: The Investor Base

The investor base for government debt securities is largely institutional and over-whelmingly dominated by the Employees' Provident Fund, the country's largest social security system. Recent initiatives have been undertaken to broaden the investor base.

For corporate bonds the investor base consists mostly of institutional investors and individuals of high net worth. But the Employees' Provident Fund, by far the biggest institutional investor, gears its asset allocation almost exclusively to government debt securities, though its investment policy allows up to 10 percent exposure to corporate debt. In addition, investors in corporate debt generally intend to hold the securities until maturity, contributing to the illiquidity in the secondary market.

Institutional Investors

The Employees' Provident Fund accounts for 13 percent of financial assets and 63 percent of the SL Rs 784 billion in assets held by institutional investors in 2006. As further evidence of its importance to the country's financial sector, the fund accounts for 32 percent of the gilt stocks (table 6.8). Commercial banks follow with 19 percent, and savings institutions with 11 percent.

Provident Funds. The Employees' Provident Fund, which caters primarily to private sector employees, invests 97 percent of its portfolio in government debt securities, mostly long-term bonds (table 6.9). The fund absorbs about 30 percent of domestic government debt issuance, mostly through private placement but also in primary auctions.

The dominance of government debt securities in the fund's portfolio reflects the investment environment. The fund needs to fetch the best possible returns for members at reasonable levels of risk. But suitable investment opportunities, such as investment-grade corporate bonds and profitable projects, are lacking. As in other South Asian countries, domestic corporate and other business entities look to commercial banks, licensed specialized banks, and leasing companies to fund their business needs.

In 2007, however, the Employees' Provident Fund took a step toward diversifying its portfolio by investing in corporate bonds and a long-term power project. Whether or not the fund intends to hold its investments until maturity, unfavorable market conditions have prevented it from actively participating in the secondary market. Even so, the fund has prepared to do so by dividing its portfolio into trading and investment accounts in the first quarter of 2007.

Other provident funds also invest in government debt securities. The largest of these, the Universities Fund, invests in government debt securities through one of the two state-owned banks.

**Table 6.8   Total Government Debt and Domestic Government Debt
by Investor Category, Sri Lanka, 2002–06**

(SL Rs millions except where otherwise specified)

	2002	2003	2004	2005	2006	Share of total, 2006 (%)
Domestic debt by investor category						
Banking sector	248,243	228,411	272,982	298,412	395,470	27
Central Bank	76,342	44,587	113,017	78,364	117,624	8
Commercial banks	171,901	183,824	159,965	220,048	277,846	19
Nonbank sector	700,143	791,558	870,407	967,310	1,083,760	73
Market borrowings	692,520	784,104	858,321	951,547	1,069,577	72
Savings institutions	116,632	138,939	151,158	169,590	166,456	11
Sinking funds	100	100	100	100	100	0
Insurance funds	26,853	24,828	27,398	20,704	21,170	1
Provident and pension funds	292,081	333,289	369,205	423,283	480,193	32
Official funds	32,612	40,739	46,341	65,825	95,981	6
Private business and individuals	224,242	246,209	264,119	272,045	305,677	21
Nonmarket borrowings	7,623	7,453	12,088	15,764	14,183	1
Total domestic debt	948,386	1,019,969	1,143,389	1,265,722	1,479,230	100
Foreign debt	721,956	843,882	996,138	956,621	1,128,493	
Total government debt	1,670,342	1,863,851	2,139,526	2,222,343	2,607,723	

Sources: Central Bank of Sri Lanka; World Bank staff calculations.
Note: Data are for the end of the fiscal year, December 31.

**Table 6.9   Composition of Employees' Provident Fund Investment
Portfolio, Sri Lanka, December 2005**

Investment category	At cost (SL Rs millions)	Present value (SL Rs millions)	Share of total (%)
Rupee Loans	56,068	55,924	13.9
Treasury bonds	335,504	332,868	82.7
Treasury bills	4,422	4,550	1.1
Corporate debt securities	4,439	4,439	1.1
Equity investments	3,110	3,147	0.7
Other investments	1,199	1,199	0.2
Total	404,742	402,127	100

Source: Employees' Provident Fund.

Contractual savings schemes other than the Employees' Provident Fund are minimal in size. This can be traced to the need for reform in the pension sector, to pave the way for more of the nation's savings—virtually all of which are absorbed by major institutional funds—to be pooled into investment schemes and used to foster the development of Sri Lanka's capital market. A comprehensive review of the pension sector has long been due—and is essential if institutional investors are to play a more active role in developing the domestic bond market.

Insurance Sector. The insurance sector accounts for a mere 14 percent of the assets held by institutional investors. The sector had relatively strong growth in 2002–07. But its development has been hampered by the public's limited awareness of and trust in insurance products. As a result, the insurance sector plays only a small role in the bond market.

In addition, current market conditions, with most debt issuance taking place at the short end of the market, are a poor match for the asset-liability management needs of insurance companies. While most market participants operate at the shorter end of the yield curve, insurance companies always access the long-term bond auctions through primary dealers. They face no constraints in the availability of long-term bonds: adequate stocks are held by some primary dealers and commercial banks.

Most insurance companies maintain a certain percentage of government debt securities in their portfolio because the securities are risk free and fairly liquid. A restriction on their investing in certain types of corporate debt has been lifted by the Insurance Board.

Mutual Funds. Mutual funds, also known as unit trusts, were first introduced in Sri Lanka in 1991. The Securities and Exchange Commission of Sri Lanka has licensed five companies to operate mutual funds, and these companies have launched 13 open-end funds: 3 growth funds, 3 income funds, 4 balanced funds, 1 gilt-edged fund, 1 money market fund, and 1 index fund. The funds have both institutional investors and retail (mostly individual) investors.

The performance of the mutual fund industry cannot be considered impressive. At its peak the industry was able to attract only 25,000 unit holders, and the number has been declining (table 6.10). The Securities and Exchange Commission and the mutual fund industry in 2007 signed a memorandum of understanding to develop the industry.

Retail Investors

The retail investor base remains small because of a lack of awareness of government debt securities among the general public, particularly outside the Western Province. Primary dealers are undertaking investor awareness campaigns to popularize government debt securities—though there is an inherent conflict of interest for primary dealers' sponsor banks, which also aim to market their own products.

Table 6.10   Performance of Mutual Fund Industry, Sri Lanka, 2002–06

Indicator	2002	2003	2004	2005	2006
Unit holders	25,252	24,066	23,650	23,654	23,661
Units issued (thousands)	458,623	317,441	339,872	345,528	356,467
Net asset value (SL Rs millions)	4,415	3,560	4,158	4,495	4,856

Source: SEC 2007.
Note: Data are for the end of the fiscal year, December 31.

The Central Bank has also started a vigorous program to educate investors and broaden access to the retail market. As part of this program it has opened 13 retail outlets in 10 districts of the country.

The Securities and Exchange Commission has identified the mutual fund industry as the best conduit for broadening the retail savings base and is supporting development and marketing initiatives by the industry. In addition, new listing rules will enable these funds to list their units on the Colombo Stock Exchange, increasing their accessibility to retail investors.

Foreign Investors

The rupee-denominated treasury bond market was partially opened to foreign investors on November 1, 2006, with a view to broadening the investor base and increasing market competition for government debt securities. New rules allowed foreign investors to invest in up to 5 percent of the total value of outstanding treasury bonds of all maturities. In December 2007 this limit was raised to 10 percent.

In addition, foreign contractual savings institutions approved by the Securities and Exchange Commission, businesses incorporated abroad, and foreign citizens are allowed to buy approved government debt securities in the primary or secondary market from primary dealers and licensed commercial banks. They are also free to sell these securities in the secondary market with no restrictions.

The interest income from treasury bonds, as well as all proceeds from the sale of treasury bonds or upon maturity, can be fully repatriated. The 10 percent withholding tax applicable to all participants in the government debt securities market is imposed upon issuance. All documents used in the issue, transfer, or redemption of treasury bonds are free from stamp duty.

The corporate bond market has not yet been opened to foreign investors.

Market Infrastructure

Sri Lanka has in place a primary dealer network for government debt securities, a modern and efficient clearing and settlement system, and a credit rating industry. Activity in the secondary market for government debt securities remains light, however.

Primary Dealers

Primary issues of marketable domestic government debt instruments are open only to a group of dedicated primary dealers and the Employees' Provident Fund. There are 11 primary dealers. Seven are subsidiaries or separate units of commercial banks, and the other four are dedicated primary dealer companies established under the Company Law.

Those operated by a commercial bank must ensure organizational, financial, and operational separation from the bank, acting as a separate business entity and maintaining separate capital and accounts. The minimum capital adequacy ratio prescribed for primary dealers is 8 percent, and the minimum capital SL Rs 300 million (up from SL Rs 250 million in 2006).

To promote transparency, primary dealers must have their annual financial statements audited by an external auditor approved by the Central Bank. In addition, they must publish semiannual and annual financial statements in newspapers within two months after the half year and six months after the end of the financial year.

Primary dealers have both privileges and obligations. Their main privilege is the exclusive right, shared with the Employees' Provident Fund, to participate in auctions of government debt securities. Their obligations are to subscribe to 10 percent of the amount offered at each auction and to act as market makers in the secondary market by providing two-way quotes on selected benchmark series. But these privileges and obligations appear to be incompatible with current market conditions, resulting in lower activity in the primary and secondary market in treasury bonds. Several incompatibilities are evident:

- Primary dealers' practice of deliberately pricing themselves out of the auctions by bidding higher rates than the authorities will pay—motivated by their different expectations about return on debt securities—makes the 10 percent subscription requirement irrelevant.
- The minimal liquidity in the secondary market makes the obligation for primary dealers to provide two-way quotes unrealistic.
- Government debt securities acquired on a regular basis for trading must be held in the trading account and marked to market using the weighted average yields in the secondary market as compiled by the Central Bank. The rising trend in interest rates creates an incentive for primary dealers to limit their trading portfolio so as to reduce mark-to-market losses.
- With interest rates following a rising trend, the current business model of primary dealers, being focused on a single product, exposes them to market losses.
- Short selling of securities is prohibited. Thus when primary dealers obtain securities as collateral on reverse repo transactions (which do not confer ownership rights), they cannot trade those securities.

Recognizing the problems facing primary dealers, the Central Bank has proposed allowing them to diversify their business to improve its viability. Accordingly, the Central Bank is drafting legal amendments that would permit primary dealers to expand their operations into the following areas:

- Forming or investing in a mutual fund or unit trust invested entirely in government debt securities
- Investing in ordinary shares or debentures of related companies
- Investing in other quoted shares or debentures or in bonds and commercial paper
- Trading (acting as a broker) in corporate bonds or debentures, quoted and unquoted
- Engaging in such services as brokering, portfolio management, project appraisal, consultancy services, loan syndication services, and merger and acquisition advisory services

Secondary Market for Government Debt Securities

Secondary market activity in government debt securities remains negligible, mainly because of investors' tendency to hold debt instruments to maturity.

In the secondary market for treasury bonds, activity dropped significantly in 2005 and 2006 compared with 2004. Secondary market trading picked up during the first nine months of 2007, however. This, together with the decreasing demand for treasury bonds in primary auctions, may suggest that the government deficit, high inflation, and market uncertainty have depressed the public demand for treasury bonds, in which trading dropped by 62 percent between 2003 and 2006 (table 6.11).

But there was a significant development in the repo market for government debt securities in 2007, when most investors attempted to mitigate their risks by engaging in repo transactions. Nevertheless, these transactions continue to suffer from the lack of a master repurchase agreement (in Sri Lanka a master agreement is used only for Central Bank repos). The repo market between banks and primary dealers lacks activity. The Primary Dealers Association has been asked by the Central Bank to prepare a suitable master agreement for repo transactions.

To help increase liquidity in the market and lower trading costs, consideration should be given to creating a securities borrowing and lending facility. Securities lending would enable market participants, especially primary dealers, to sell securities they do not own knowing that they could borrow before settlement; this prevents settlement failures and increases arbitrage opportunities. Securities lending would also enable institutional investors to earn additional income from their fixed-income portfolio. And it would enable primary dealers and other securities dealers to act as market makers, helping to create a healthy secondary market. In

Table 6.11   Secondary Market Trading of Treasury Bills and Bonds, Sri Lanka, 2001–October 2007

(SL Rs millions)

Type of transaction and instrument	2002	2003	2004	2005	2006	Jan.–Oct. 2006	Jan.–Oct. 2007
Outright transactions							
Treasury bill							
Purchased	27,092	37,408	71,048	66,591	72,636	61,832	194,129
Sold	214,917	265,757	311,537	367,635	414,549	340,586	437,920
Total	242,009	303,166	382,585	434,226	487,185	402,418	632,049
Treasury bonds							
Purchased	107,987	346,801	171,282	135,859	130,176	126,827	181,878
Sold	185,814	426,865	220,266	172,376	170,311	165,356	178,993
Total	293,801	773,665	391,548	308,235	300,487	292,183	360,870
Repurchase transactions							
Treasury bills							
Repos	396,523	1,058,459	264,909	488,518	575,982	445,974	649,742
Reverse repos	201,931	240,911	557,742	324,338	328,961	229,507	698,660
Total	598,454	1,299,371	822,651	812,856	904,943	675,481	1,348,401
Treasury bonds							
Repos	1,006,379	1,938,581	2,176,654	1,257,020	1,194,443	1,069,040	740,955
Reverse repos	225,896	304,995	859,897	1,074,628	783,516	637,519	768,746
Total	1,232,275	2,243,576	3,036,551	2,331,648	1,977,959	1,706,559	1,509,701
Total for all transactions	2,366,539	4,619,778	4,633,335	3,886,965	3,670,574	3,076,640	3,851,023

Source: Central Bank of Sri Lanka.
Note: Volumes traded are as reported by primary dealers.

this connection, short sales for fixed-income securities should be permitted with proper safeguards.

Clearing and Settlement

The infrastructure for securities settlement in Sri Lanka has seen great advances in recent years. In September 2003 the Central Bank introduced a real-time gross settlement system—an interbank electronic fund transfer and settlement system for large-value, time-critical rupee payments. A scripless securities settlement system known as LankaSecure followed in February 2004 for government debt securities. LankaSecure is an electronic, centralized system in which scripless securities are traded, settled, and instantaneously recorded on a delivery-versus-payment basis. In the initial years of operation the two systems, collectively called LankaSettle and operated by the Central Bank, have functioned well and proved to be reliable.

In addition, an order-driven, screen-based automated debt securities trading system (DEX) paved the way for the Colombo Stock Exchange to begin trading the beneficial interest in government debt securities along with its secondary market trading of listed corporate debt. Transactions in both government and corporate debt securities are settled through the Central Depository System (Private) Ltd., a fully owned subsidiary of the stock exchange. Fund settlement takes place through only one bank, and each participant is therefore required to maintain an account with the settlement bank. Facilitating fund settlement through the Central Bank's real-time gross settlement system would both increase the efficiency of transactions and reduce the vulnerability of the settlement system. Another way to reduce vulnerability would be to introduce a centralized depository, clearing, and settlement system for unlisted corporate debt, which now requires physical delivery of bond certificates.

To record trade information for scripless government debt securities, the Central Bank established a central depository system in its Public Debt Department. This depository maintains all information on trades and ownership of scripless government debt securities, with details recorded to the level of individual investors.

Participants in the central depository system include all licensed commercial banks, primary dealers, the Central Bank's Domestic Operations Department, and selected institutional investors. Licensed banks and primary dealers, known as "dealer direct participants," are allowed to maintain and operate accounts in the system on behalf of themselves and their customers. Institutional investors such as the Employees' Provident Fund, known as "direct participants," are permitted to maintain accounts only in their own name.

Securitization

Securitization remains at a very early stage of development in Sri Lanka. In 2004–05 three issuers attempted securitization as an alternative form of funding. The lack of a proper regulatory framework made these instruments costly, however, discouraging other issuers from following suit.

The transaction that comes closest to securitization is the state-sponsored Housing Development Finance Corporation's SL Rs 722.2 million securitized paper. Cash collateral of 12.5 percent on the pool balance and subordinated papers of SL Rs 99.8 million resulted in a cushioning of 51.95 percent (excluding interest spread). Despite this high level of cushioning, the instrument achieved a rating of only AA–. The high cost of this transaction discouraged others from following suit.

Even so, securitization of vehicle leases, by transfer through mortgage or assignment with recourse where no true sale takes place, has been quite widespread among leasing companies.

To provide impetus to the development of asset-backed securities, the Securities and Exchange Commission issued a draft securitization act for public comment in May 2007. Among the issues addressed is the securitization of vehicle leases.

Credit Rating Industry

Two credit rating agencies, both international, operate in Sri Lanka. Fitch Ratings was the first to enter the market. Lanka Ratings, owned by a Malaysian agency and now renamed RAM Ratings (Lanka), followed in 2005. Pursuant to a proposal in the 2004 budget, the Central Bank advised all banking institutions to obtain credit ratings from independent rating agencies and publish them to further improve investor confidence in the financial system. By the end of December 2005, 20 financial institutions, including 10 banks, had obtained and published a credit rating.

Legal and Regulatory Framework

Sri Lanka has made significant progress in developing a comprehensive regulatory framework for the capital market, though governance arrangements for the Securities and Exchange Commission remain a concern. Corporate governance arrangements, which remain voluntary, also raise concerns.

Regulatory Framework

The Monetary Law Act gives the Central Bank responsibility for managing public debt through its Public Debt Department. This department issues and services public debt through the network of primary dealers. It also services foreign loans, which are negotiated by the External Resources Department of the Ministry of Finance. In addition, the department regulates the primary dealers, regulates market development activities, maintains a database on public debt, and promotes investor awareness of government debt securities.

The Securities and Exchange Commission is responsible for regulating all aspects of the listed securities market outside government debt, while the Registrar of Companies regulates the issuing process and information disclosure for corporate bonds that are publicly offered. The commission was created under the Securities and Exchange Commission Act of 1987, which gives it primary responsibility for developing the capital market. Specific mandates include protecting the interests of investors, promoting the development and maintenance of a sound capital market, regulating the securities market, and ensuring that market participants comply with the law.

Noteworthy progress has been made in implementing the 2003 amendments to the Securities and Exchange Commission Act, which extend the commission's jurisdiction to more market intermediaries: underwriters, clearinghouses, margin providers, investment managers, and credit rating agencies. The amendments also give the commission powers to summon and investigate, enhancing its effectiveness as a regulator.

The Securities and Exchange Commission is leading the way in implementing the Capital Market Master Plan, a 10-year road map for developing the capital market prepared in August 2006 with the assistance of Ernst & Young Malaysia (SEC 2006). The commission has recruited new staff with a view to implementing the most pressing recommendations as early as possible.

Despite these positive developments, several factors constrain the effectiveness of the Securities and Exchange Commission as a regulator. The amendments do not address the regulation of unlisted companies that publicly offer debt securities; these companies, while covered by the Companies Act of 2007, escape the disclosure requirements for listed companies. Moreover, there are several agencies with overlapping responsibility, including in the regulation of secondary market trading in unlisted corporate debt. New amendments to the Securities and Exchange Commission Act are expected to address this concern.

In addition, there is room for improvement in the governance arrangements for the Securities and Exchange Commission, which are critical to establishing its credibility as an independent and neutral body. The subordination of its operations to the oversight of the Ministry of Finance, which appoints the director general and has final say on recruiting policy and salary structure, raises questions about the commission's ability to operate free of external influences. Moreover, the makeup of the commission's board creates a potential for conflicts of interest: the board consists entirely of part-time, nonexecutive directors who also hold key positions in industries regulated by the commission.

Corporate Governance

Corporate governance arrangements also allow room for improvement. The Securities and Exchange Commission and the Institute of Chartered Accountants of Sri Lanka jointly issued a voluntary code of corporate governance in 2002. In addition, the Colombo Stock Exchange introduced corporate governance standards for listed companies on April 1, 2007. These standards relate to the minimum number of nonexecutive and independent directors, the criteria for determining independence, disclosure requirements, remuneration, and audit committees. Because the standards are voluntary, however, only a handful of companies have adopted them. Moreover, the unclear division of labor between the Colombo Stock Exchange and the Securities and Exchange Commission, which carry out separate and redundant inspections of brokerage firms, has created an unnecessary strain on resources.

The Colombo Stock Exchange itself operates as a self-regulatory organization, supervised by the Securities and Exchange Commission. If the exchange should decide to demutualize, a question pending since 1997, its regulatory framework would need to be reviewed. Demutualization might lead to greater responsibilities for the new self-regulatory organization, such as the supervision of broker-dealer associations.

Tax Regime

Sri Lanka has taken some positive steps to ensure equal tax treatment for investors across different instruments and asset classes. For individuals a 10 percent tax is applied to interest, whether on fixed deposits and savings accounts or on government and corporate debt securities. Tax is withheld at source at the time of issuance for government debt securities, and upon realization for corporate debt securities.

Corporations benefit from a 10 percent tax credit on interest. Investors in corporate debt securities cannot obtain the tax credit, however, which discourages the purchase of these securities in the secondary market.

Capital gains are tax free except in the case of institutions that deal with bonds as part of their business; these incur the normal income tax levy, which ranges from 5 percent to 30 percent. Stamp duties have been eliminated.

Recommended Actions

Sri Lanka has made clear progress in developing its bond market. Even so, a number of issues remain to be addressed if the market is to become an efficient engine of capital allocation: The government dominates the local debt securities market. The corporate bond market, lacking qualified issuers as well as investors, remains in its infancy. And the financial system is characterized by excessive dependence on banks as a funding source, raising concerns about the systemic vulnerability of the economy.

Some of the actions needed relate to broad macroeconomic issues: fiscal consolidation and reduction of high and volatile inflation are prerequisites for lowering the risks in the domestic debt portfolio and providing a conducive climate for bond market development. Others are closer to the bond market and its participants.

Supply Side

Consolidating Fragmented Debt Stocks. The excessive fragmentation of treasury bond issues and the government's cash management practices impede development of a benchmark yield curve. Even with the sizable reduction in the number of treasury bond series since 2003, there are still too many series, all of them too small to support active trading of any issue. In addition, the bunching of maturities increases rollover risk.

The steps proposed by the Central Bank in its debt management strategy—introducing buyback or conversion techniques, reducing the number of bond series, introducing a benchmark bond series, developing a benchmark yield curve—will all be important in tackling this issue (CBSL 2007b).

Building a Credible Sovereign Benchmark. The issuance of benchmark debt is constrained by the government's cash management practices, in which cash flows match maturing debt and no concerted plan is devised on the distribution of maturities and the size of issues. Strengthening cash management will require improvements in the accuracy of cash forecasting by line ministries and agencies. Implementing such improvements goes beyond the usual responsibilities of a debt and cash management body, falling more into the realm of budget implementation and public expenditure management. Combining numerous treasury accounts into a single account could help improve cash forecasting.

Building a sovereign benchmark also calls for concerted efforts to reduce the heavy reliance on private placement of treasury bonds. Moving to a market-determined process would help build the credibility of the treasury bond market and boost investor confidence.

Developing the money market is key to building a short-term benchmark yield curve. Today only overnight call and repos are actively traded in the money market. Creating a reliable short-term benchmark could encourage trading in derivatives and in corporate bonds with floating-rate coupons by providing a reference rate for these instruments.

Exploring Potential Suppliers of New Qualified Private Securities. State-owned enterprises, though the major players in Sri Lanka's economy, remain conspicuously absent from the capital market, meeting their funding needs through banks instead. Their participation could help boost market development. While government policy does not contemplate full privatization, selling 5–10 percent blocks of these companies' shares to the public through the Colombo Stock Exchange would be one way to increase their participation. Another possible way to draw state-owned enterprises, as well as large family-owned ones, into the capital market is to provide incentives for publicly issuing debt securities. Further exploring securitization of common products such as housing loans could also help broaden the issuer base.

Demand Side

Broadening the Investor Base. Institutional investors could play a greater role in the development of the domestic capital market. Toward that end, the investment policies of the Employees' Provident Fund, which already allow investment of up to 10 percent of assets in corporate bonds, should be revised to raise the limit on investment in equities above the current 2 percent. Continuing to limit the fund's corporate debt exposure to investment-grade securities would keep the added risk to its portfolio low and maintain the guaranteed stable returns to its participants.

The concentration of government debt securities in the Employees' Provident Fund could be addressed by giving its members the choice of investing their funds through collective savings schemes (Outsourcing part of the investment funds to private fund managers is likely to encounter strong opposition from both the management of the Employees' Provident Fund and the public, given a failed attempt in 1993 and the requirement of guaranteed returns. But once the market has become reasonably developed and the right expertise is available, this option could be tried on a pilot basis with appropriate oversight.)

Private provident funds, while major players in corporate bond markets in other countries, have invested mainly in government debt securities in Sri Lanka. They have minimal exposure to the corporate bond market as a result of their conservative investment policies and their limited knowledge of corporate bonds and bond fund management. These funds too should be encouraged to revise their investment policies to allow greater exposure to equity and corporate bonds.

More active participation by private mutual funds also would help further the development of the capital market in Sri Lanka. Thus the Securities and Exchange Commission should continue its initiative to develop the country's mutual fund industry.

Market Infrastructure

Strengthening the Primary Dealer System. The primary dealer system needs diversification, both in its makeup and in its business. The system is dominated by commercial banks that have little incentive to market government debt securities to their clients. And the business model for primary dealers, focused only on treasury bonds, appears to be unsustainable in the face of the rising trend in interest rates.

As noted, the Central Bank has recognized the constraints facing primary dealers and has proposed permitting them to diversify their operations into new activities. This step should improve the viability of their business. Another step that would improve viability is to relax the requirement for primary dealers to act as market makers by providing two-way quotes. Given the illiquidity of the market and the inability of primary dealers to sell securities short, this requirement is hardly supportable.

Legal and Regulatory Framework

Strengthening Regulatory Independence and Governance. While the Securities and Exchange Commission has made commendable progress in advancing its role as a regulator, questions remain about its independence from the Ministry of Finance and thus its freedom from external influences. Constraints on its independence appear not to have been a major issue in the recent past. Still, a review of the commission's independence, through a transparent process, is recommended. Also recommended are a review of the composition of the commission's board, with a view to including full-time directors, and public disclosure of the procedures for avoiding conflicts of interest for other members of the board.

To reduce redundancy in regulatory responsibilities, a clearer division of labor between the Securities and Exchange Commission and the Colombo Stock Exchange should be determined for inspections. Finally, the Securities and Exchange

Commission Act should be reviewed with a view to expanding the commission's jurisdiction to unlisted companies that publicly offer debt securities and secondary market trading of unlisted corporate debt securities.

Eliminating Differential Tax Treatment. Removing the differential tax treatment of government debt securities and corporate bonds would help encourage investors to purchase corporate bonds and thus infuse some liquidity into the secondary market.

Annex 6.1   Recent or Proposed Measures by the Central Bank to Strengthen the Financial System

Measures Implemented or Under Way

- Implementing a real-time gross settlement system (2003) and a scripless securities settlement system (2004)
- Introducing an enhanced capital requirement for banks to maintain financial system stability (2005)
- Forming the Working Group of Regulators for Financial Conglomerates to develop a mechanism for monitoring the systemic risk of conglomerates (2005)
- Enacting the Payment and Settlement Systems Act, 2005; and formulating the Payment and Settlement Policy to Mitigate Risks and Increase Efficiency (2006)
- Enacting the Prevention of Money Laundering Act, 2006; and the Financial Transactions Reporting Act, 2006
- Introducing online data reporting of trading in government debt securities (2006)
- Introducing a market risk factor in the computation of capital adequacy (2006)
- Strengthening prudential norms for classification, valuation, and operation of banks' investment portfolios (2006)
- Introducing risk-based supervision to strengthen the primary dealer system (2006)
- Introducing a phased increase in the core capital requirement for existing finance companies (2006)
- Prescribing general loan loss provisions on performing advances and greater risk weights on residential mortgage and "other" loans to cover potential credit risk (2006)
- Revising norms for single-borrower exposure in line with improved risk management of banks (2007)
- Requiring broad-based ownership of banks, restricting share ownership by a single investor generally to 15 percent, and addressing conflicts of interest that arise due to large shareholdings (2007)
- Improving access to finance and expanding outreach under microfinance programs (2007)
- Implementing the Basel II Capital Accord under the standard approach (2008)
- Strengthening the regulatory framework for registered leasing businesses, including by introducing comprehensive on-site inspections of selected leasing businesses (2008)

- Adopting internationally accepted accounting and reporting standards in the financial sector (2008–11)

Measures Proposed

- Introducing "stress testing" by banks to assess their resilience to internal and external shocks
- Changing the supervisory approach for banking institutions from compliance based to risk focused
- Replacing voluntary codes of corporate governance with mandatory rules
- Introducing a uniform format for banks' financial statements to improve disclosure
- Setting up a SWIFT service bureau
- Allowing primary dealers to diversify their activities while ensuring appropriate regulatory and prudential safeguards
- Introducing prudential guidelines on credit card issuance and minimum credit card payment requirements

Proposed Amendments to Legislation Relating to Banking

- Debt Recovery Law: to expedite the recovery of debt and create a creditor-friendly environment
- Asset Management Company Law: to allow speedier resolution of the nonperforming loans of failed banks
- Credit Information Bureau Act: to widen the scope of the credit information bureau and provide more credit information (including positive information)
- Computer Crimes Law: to reduce potential risks arising from computer fraud
- Finance Leasing Act: to permit well-capitalized leasing companies to mobilize funds from the public through the issuance of debt instruments, enabling them to broaden their funding sources and prudently expand their operations
- Finance Companies Act: to introduce more stringent provisions for dealing with unregistered businesses and individuals conducting finance business in contravention of the laws
- Business Recovery Law: to provide a procedure for resuscitating sick industries
- Microfinance Institutions Act: to bring all microfinance institutions under the regulatory framework (with licensing and supervision authority assigned to the Monetary Board and supervisory functions delegated to agents)

Source: CBSL 2007c (with updates by authors).

Endnote

1. The government bond market comprises treasury bonds, treasury bills, Rupee Loans, and other government borrowings.

References

BIS (Bank for International Settlements). 2007. *Quarterly Review.* June. Paris.

CBSL (Central Bank of Sri Lanka). 2006. *Financial System Stability Review 2006.* Colombo.

———. 2007a. *Annual Report 2006.* Colombo.

———. 2007b. *Public Debt Management in Sri Lanka: Performance in 2006 and First Half 2007; Strategies for 2007 and Beyond.* Colombo.

———. 2007c. "Roadmap: Monetary and Financial Sector Policies." Colombo.

Lanka Rating Agency. 2006. "Debt Market Review." Colombo.

SEC (Securities and Exchange Commission of Sri Lanka). 2006. "Capital Markets Master Plan, Sri Lanka 2006." Colombo.

———. 2007. *Annual Report 2006.* Colombo.

Index

Boxes, figures, notes, and tables are indicated by *b*, *f*, *n*, and *t*, respectively.

Nepal's lack of, 118, 123
Pakistan, 18, 141
Sri Lanka, 18, 170–71, 178
provident funds. *See* pension and
    provident funds
public cash management, xxiii, 13
    Bangladesh, 51
    India, 92
    Nepal, 113, 122
    Pakistan, 134, 145
    Sri Lanka, 158, 176–77
public debt management, 13. *See also*
    budget deficit
    Bangladesh, 13, 38–39, 51
    Nepal, 13, 113–14
    Pakistan, 13, 133–35, 133*t*, 134*f*, 149–50,
        149*t*, 150*f*
    Sri Lanka, 13, 161–64, 163*t*
public sector undertaking (PSU) bonds in
    India, 65

recommendations and reforms. *See* action
    plans and reform programs
regional integration of bond markets,
    xxi, 3–4
regulatory framework. *See* legal and
    regulatory framework
remittances
    Bangladesh, 41–42
    Nepal, 110
    Sri Lanka, 158
repo and reverse repo markets
    Bangladesh, 30–31, 32*t*, 33*f*, 44, 45
    India, 70, 72, 73*b*, 99–199*t*
    Malaysia, 19*b*
    Nepal, 110, 111*t*
    Pakistan, 128, 129*t*, 142
    Sri Lanka, 157*b*, 158, 170, 171, 172*t*, 177
Republic of Korea. *See* Korea, Republic of
retail investors
    Bangladesh, 16, 39, 45, 52
    India, 68, 69, 74, 75, 99–100*t*
    Nepal, 112, 119, 122, 132
    Pakistan, 136, 137, 141
    in South Asia generally, xxii, xxiv, 10, 11,
        16, 21, 23
    Sri Lanka, 16, 168–69

retirement funds. *See* pension and
    provident funds
risk transfer mechanisms, 20. *See also*
    securitization

savings schemes, national
    Bangladesh, 34–37, 36*t*, 51
    Nepal, 112*t*
    Pakistan, 132–33, 133*t*, 145
secondary markets, 18–19
    Bangladesh, 19, 45, 52
    India, 18, 70–72, 71*t*, 82–83
    Malaysia, 18, 19*b*
    Nepal, 19, 119
    Pakistan, 18–19, 142
    Sri Lanka, 18, 165*t*, 171–72, 172*t*
securitization, 20
    Bangladesh, 45–47, 46*b–t*, 52
    India, 83–86, 84*f*
    Pakistan, 143
    Sri Lanka, 173–74
settlement. *See* clearing and settlement
    systems
Shari'ah-compliant instruments, 37*b*, 153*n*1
short sales in government debt securities
    India, 72
    Sri Lanka, 172
Singapore, 4, 5*t*, 7*t*, 24*n*4
size of bond markets, 8, 9*t*
small investors in Bangladesh, 51–52
South Asian bond markets, xxi–xxvi, 1–26.
        See also specific countries, e.g.
        Bangladesh, India, Nepal, Pakistan,
        Sri Lanka
    action plans for. *See* action plans and
        reform programs
    budget deficits, 4, 5, 8–9
    comparison of, xxii, 4
    constraints on, xxii–xxvi, 10–23. *See also*
        demand side; legal and regulatory
        framework; market infrastructure;
        supply side
    corporate bonds. *See* corporate bond
        market
    data sources and methodologies, xx
    diversification, importance of, xxi, 1, 2
    East Asian markets compared, xxii